At its core, Buddhism is a uniquely practical faith,
with a small body of basic principles.
ESSENTIAL BUDDHISM focuses on this core and discusses:

- Living as a buddha: moral and ethical conduct
- Cultivating wisdom and compassion
- Exploring questions of life, death, and rebirth
- Engaging in Buddhist liturgy
- Buddhism and the new millennium
- And much more

OTHER BOOKS BY JACK MAGUIRE

Waking Up: A Week Inside a Zen Monastery

The Power of Personal Storytelling

Creative Storytelling

Care and Feeding of the Brain

Night and Day: Using Dreams to Transform Your Life

East-West Medicine: Combining Chinese and Western Health Care
  (with Dr. May Loo)

Essential Buddhism

A Complete Guide to Beliefs and Practices

JACK MAGUIRE

POCKET BOOKS
New York London Toronto Sydney

An *Original* Publication of POCKET BOOKS

 POCKET BOOKS, a division of Simon & Schuster, Inc.
1230 Avenue of the Americas, New York, NY 10020

ISBN: 0-671-04188-6

First Pocket Books trade paperback printing June 2001

10   9   8

POCKET and colophon are registered trademarks of
Simon & Schuster, Inc.

Cover design by Brigid Pearson
Front cover photo by Grant V. Faint/The Image Bank

Printed in the U.S.A.

This book is dedicated to
LAURA (LULU) TORBET
my good friend who pointed the way

Contents

Acknowledgments

While putting together *Essential Buddhism,* I drew on the works and teachings of many different authorities, past and present, to provide multiple perspectives on key aspects of the religion, its history, and its applications. Expressing in Buddhist terms my indebtedness to these individuals, I can only say that myriad labors went into this book besides my own.

I credit the source of each quotation as it occurs in the text, so that readers can know its exact origin as they encounter it. For a full list of the books that I consulted, all of which I recommend for further reading, see the bibliography.

I am especially grateful for the words and deeds of three prominent Buddhists in the contemporary American Buddhist scene who have had a significant, positive impact on my life as well as this book. They are John Daido Loori Roshi, abbot of Zen Mountain Monastery and my Dharma teacher; Robert Thurman, professor of Indo-Tibetan Buddhist studies at Columbia University; and Jack Kornfield, founding teacher of the Insight Meditation Society and the Spirit Rock Center, representing the vipassana tradition of Theravada Buddhism.

I also thank Daido Roshi for allowing me to reprint his "Invocation of a New Millennium," and Dharma Communications for permitting me to use its formulations of several Buddhist chants and scriptures, including the "Heart Sutra."

Quotations from other Buddhist scriptures in the book represent my own adaptations based on numerous different English, Sanskrit, Pali, Japanese, and Tibetan versions. Researching with dictionaries, I chose the English words that were closest in meaning to the original ones or, if I was unable to make such a determination, the English words most commonly used in widely available scholarly translations. In certain cases I quoted directly from a particular source, as indicated in the text.

Marsha Melnick of Roundtable Press and Nancy Miller and Kimberly Kanner of Simon & Schuster were the midwives of this book and enriched it with their excellent counsel. I very much appreciate their sensitivity to the subject matter as well as their consistently patient and reliable guidance.

Throughout this project, as in countless others I've undertaken, I was blessed to have the support, encouragement, inspiration, and magically practical advice of Tom Cowan. Tá grá agam duit, Tom.

Introduction

Like the moon,
Come out from behind the clouds!
Shine.

— the Buddha

Today approximately 400 million people on the planet call themselves, in one way or another, Buddhists. At least, that's the average estimate. Experts disagree heartily about what constitutes a Buddhist and which population statistics to trust. Some say there are as many as 600 million; others, no more than 200 million. No one questions, however, that Buddhism is among the five most populous religions in the world (along with Christianity, Judaism, Islam, and Hinduism) and has been for most of its 2,500-year history.

Many authorities even maintain that Buddhism is the oldest world religion. Hinduism and Judaism may have begun earlier, the argument goes, but they haven't spread as far beyond their homelands or assimilated as easily or thoroughly into other cultures.

Now Buddhism is spreading throughout the West. Yet as cosmopolitan as we westerners like to imagine ourselves, most of us know little about this powerful, Eastern-spawned faith taking root all around us.

How did it begin?

How did it turn into such a dynamic force in the world?

What do its adherents believe?

How do they express their faith?

Why are so many westerners drawn to it?

How can we go about investigating its relevance to our individual lives? To our society as a whole?

Essential Buddhism responds to these questions and others by offering a global perspective on the religion's past, present, and future. It identifies how Buddhism's principal concepts and practices originated and evolved through diverse cultural adaptations into three basic formats: Theravada (most familiar to Americans as the school of vipassana, or insight, meditation); Mahayana (including Zen); and Vajrayana (commonly known as Tibetan Buddhism). It also examines major ways these concepts and practices functioned in the past—and manifest themselves now—in the everyday lives of Buddhists. Finally, it explores the growing popularity of Buddhism among westerners and the promise it holds for the future of humanity.

Many of the formal conventions and expressions of Buddhism can bewilder the unfamiliar observer, but at the core of it is a uniquely practical religion with a small body of basic tenets and a sensible approach to daily living. I encourage you to use this book as a map for charting your own journeys through the vast complex of highways, roads, and trails crisscrossing the Buddhist terrain. Ideally, it will also serve as a lens to help you see through the outer trappings of Buddhism, dazzling or opaque as they may be, to the inner simplicity that makes this religion beneficial and adaptable to so many different lives and cultures.

Essential Buddhism is not meant to teach you how to be a Buddhist. That learning process requires you to build a committed relationship with a teacher who has received formal transmission in a specific teaching lineage. Actually, what qualifies me the most to write the book are my continuing years as a student, rather than a teacher, of Buddhism. Those years exposed me to each of Buddhism's three major schools—Theravada, Mahayana, and Vajrayana—before leading me to the teacher with whom I felt, and still feel, the strongest personal connection: Abbot John Daido Loori Roshi of Zen Mountain Monastery in Mount Tremper, New York.

I'm confident that my experience and perspective as a student enable me to function in these pages as an effective mediator between people who don't know much about Buddhism or certain aspects of it and people who teach particular forms of it. I trust that the wide variety of Buddhist teachers, students, and commentators I quote throughout the text offers you a broadly representative, multidimensional perspective on each of the topics covered. And I believe that my lengthy career as a writer equips me to put together a comprehensive reference source for Buddhist subjects and issues that can be useful to you, regardless of how far along you are on the Buddhist path.

Still, it can be daunting to assume *any* kind of educational mission relating to Buddhism, a faith that has profoundly transformed billions of lives in its history. I've been comforted in that task by reminding myself that Buddhism's ultimate authority rests entirely in the life of the individual practitioner.

Buddhism is not a religion of the book or the revealed word, as are Christianity, Judaism, and Islam. Instead, it is a religion that makes itself known through personal realization. As the well-known Vietnamese Zen teacher Thich Nhat Hanh points out, "Our own life is the instrument with which we experiment with Truth." This means that whatever information may be provided here or in any other written work—even in one of the official Buddhist sutras (scriptures)—the reality of Buddhism lies inextricably, indefinably, and inviolably in how it is lived.

My personal introduction to Buddhism occurred during the 1960s, when I took what were then called "Oriental Studies" courses as an undergraduate at Columbia University. It remained what I thought of as an academic interest for many years afterward, but in hindsight, I now realize that I was covertly drawing spiritual strength from it as well. Time and time again, my mind would turn to incidents in the Buddha's life, to passages from Buddhist writings, to images of Buddhists I'd seen in the media (fairly common during the Vietnam War years), and most especially, to Buddhist teaching tales, personal narratives, and folklore.

Eventually I turned to Buddhism as a religion. The final catalyst, I admit, was reaching what I could no longer deny was middle age, with all its accompanying intimations of mortality. I realized I had many pressing questions about life and death to answer, and Buddhism offered me the way.

I share this personal experience with you because that's the essence of Buddhism: personal experience. Also, it's important to bear in mind that the material in this book is being presented by a particular individual. If someone else took up the same charter that I have here—to be as objective, accurate, and inclusive as possible, within the constraints of this book's necessarily limited size and scope—he or she would assuredly express or organize certain things differently. There are as many ways to describe Buddhism's structures, beliefs, and practices as there are Buddhists.

To enhance your appreciation of the vital, personal dimension of Buddhism, I've added many life stories to the text, both factual ones based on significant past and present Buddhists and fictional ones drawn from the wealth of time-honored teaching tales that continue to figure prominently in each of the three main vehicles. As much as Buddhism may deserve to be called a rational religion because of its intellectual appeal, it is also a very intuitive one. By incorporating numerous and diverse narratives into the book, I've sought to engage the intuitive, experiential part of your brain in grasping and appreciating this point.

To activate the other, more logical dimension of your brain, I've relied on several Buddhist-appropriate devices. One of them is the same instructional method famously employed by the Buddha himself, as well as by his near contemporaries Confucius and Socrates: question and answer. Each chapter features a section that expresses, and responds to, the most commonly asked questions relating to its subject matter. Hopefully they will inspire and assist you to form your own questions about Buddhism, which you can pursue not only in these pages but also elsewhere. At the back of the book is an extensive glossary that provides a quick reference source for common Buddhist words, names, expressions, and concepts.

So far in this introduction I have referred to Buddhism as a religion. Perhaps because Buddhism doesn't posit the existence of a creator god or a soul independent of the body, some westerners—and quite a few Western bookstores—alternatively classify it as a philosophy. It's true that one can extract philosophy from Buddhism, just as one can from Christianity, Judaism, or any other religion. Many Buddhist concepts and practices in particular can be adopted relatively easily by people who don't consider themselves religious or who profess another faith. Even a devout believer in God, gods, or soul can justify simultaneously embracing basic Buddhist principles, since Buddhism doesn't really preclude such convictions.

Nevertheless, Buddhism is first and foremost a religion—a vision of fundamental truths that offers a much more profound and all-encompassing approach to living than a philosophy does. Our Judeo-Christian culture predisposes us to assume, erroneously, that a religion by definition must include belief in a creator god and a soul. In fact, the basis of a religion can be *any* organized system of beliefs based on faith rather than reason, on the heart (or, if you prefer, the intuition) rather than the intellect alone.

The great religions of the world have evolved their own distinctive liturgies, traditions, and institutions to express their different—and in some cases oppositional—belief systems. However, each of them, from the very beginning, has derived its core strength from the same kind of power: an ability to provide both individuals and groups with a vital means of addressing the fundamental questions of life, death, and the universe.

Like Christianity, Judaism, Islam, and Hinduism, Buddhism developed and exists today primarily as a spiritual practice with its own special capacity to inspire devotion, transform lives, and ennoble humanity. This fact alone justifies knowing more about it, however much we may personally be committed to another religion.

Prior to the current, more globally interconnected era, in times when people lived more exclusively within their own communities or even their own households, each person's religious activity could be more strictly confined to the codes and behaviors of a particular faith. Now such activity is compelled to include at least an understanding of, and hopefully an empathy for, other people's faiths, whether or not anything specific is adopted from them.

Investigating other faiths helps us to see our own spiritual selves more clearly, regardless of any particular religious affiliation we have now or once had. Indeed, it may be a crucially important step in that direction. Rodger Kamenetz, a poet and professor of English at Louisiana State University, was moved to rediscover his Jewish identity precisely through his exploration of Buddhism, an ecumenical odyssey he recounts in *The Jew in the Lotus*. In that book, he states,

> Our ancient sources of wisdom call on human beings to rise to their highest capacity and behave in extraordinarily open and generous ways to one another, under difficult circumstances to transcend differences and create understanding across barriers of convention and fear. This wisdom is fragile, threatened by an overwhelming material culture. I believe in a spiritual ecology. In today's world, Judaism and . . . Buddhism and other wisdom traditions are endangered species. (288)

Learning about other religions helps teach us that all people of faith share a common goal: the betterment of humankind. At the 1994 John Main Seminar sponsored by the World Community for Christian Meditation, the Dalai Lama, the spiritual leader of Tibetan Buddhists, reinforced this message:

I believe the purpose of all the major religious traditions is not to construct big temples on the outside, but to create temples of goodness and compassion inside, in our hearts. Every major religion has the potential to create this. The greater our awareness is regarding the value and effectiveness of other religious traditions, then the deeper will be our respect and reverence toward our own religion, other religions, and religion in general. (Tenzin Gyatso, *The Good Heart*, 39–40)

Emphasizing that this special awareness inevitably opens up new vistas of thought and feeling in our lives, he concludes, "My appeal to all of you is this. Please ensure that you make the precious human life you have as meaningful as possible."

May this book, and your further inquiries into Buddhist beliefs and practices, help you make your own life more meaningful!

Notes on the Text

Throughout the text, unless otherwise noted, Sanskrit words are used for Buddhist names and terms. I chose not to include diacritical marks on these words in order to make them easier for westerners to read.

Sanskrit is the liturgical language of the Mahayana and Vajrayana vehicles of Buddhism, while Pali, a closely related dialect, is the liturgical language of the Theravada vehicle. The decision to use Sanskrit words here is based on the fact that Americans are more familiar with them, having been exposed more to Mahayana and Vajrayana (especially in the forms of Zen and Tibetan Buddhism) than to Theravada.

For the sake of consistency and smooth reading, I put Buddhist terms in the lower case whenever practical, although they may often be capitalized in other texts, especially religious ones. However, I do consistently capitalize certain select Buddhist terms in order to distinguish major doctrines: for example, the Four Noble Truths.

Also, when alluding to the founder of Buddhism, whose proper name is Siddhartha Guatama and whose byname is Shakyamuni or "Sage of the Shakya Clan," I always say "the Buddha." I capitalize *Buddha* (a word meaning "awakened one") and add "the" to make it clear that I'm quoting his title. When referring to a buddha as *any* enlightened being—not Shakyamuni in particular—I always use lower case.

I take a similar approach to the word *dharma*. It is capitalized ("Dharma") when it refers specifically to the teachings of Shakyamuni. It is put into lower case ("dharma") when it refers to the truth in general or to all things in the phenomenal world—each of which, according to certain Buddhist schools, has it own teachings to offer.

Out of respect for religious neutrality, I identify dates when appropriate as C.E. (Common Era) rather than A.D. (Anno Domini), and B.C.E. (Before the Common Era) rather than B.C. (Before the Christ). For the names of countries, I've generally used current political designations: for example, Myanmar instead of Burma.

Essential
Buddhism

I The Great Awakening: The Buddha and His Legacy

> You are your only master.
> Who else?
> Subdue yourself,
> And discover your master.
> —the Buddha

One evening, soon after the Buddha's enlightenment, a man named Dona was walking down a rural road in northern India when he saw the Buddha walking toward him. Dona knew nothing about the Buddha but was nevertheless struck by the radiance surrounding this individual. I've never seen a mortal being look so joyful and serene, he thought, so when the Buddha came close enough to converse, Dona couldn't resist asking, "Are you, by chance, a spirit?"

"No," said the Buddha.

"Then are you an angel?" asked Dona.

"No," said the Buddha.

"Are you, perhaps, a god?" asked Dona

"No," said the Buddha.

"Well, what *are* you?" asked Dona.

The Buddha replied, "I am awake."

A fundamental part of Buddhism's appeal to billions of people over the past two and half millennia is the fact that its central figure, commonly referred to by the title "Buddha," was not a god, or a special kind of spiritual being, or even a prophet or an emissary of one. On the contrary, he was a human being like the rest of us who quite simply woke up to full aliveness.

The Sanskrit word *buddha* means "the awakened one" and derives etymologically from the same Indo-European root that gives us the English word *bud*. In a sense, the Buddha was a sentient being who managed to bud and then bloom into total consciousness of his nature, or, to use a more traditional expression, into enlightenment. The amazing truth of the matter is that we are all potential buddhas, perfect and complete right at this moment, but very few of us realize it.

The historical Buddha's awakening may have been a *simple* accomplishment, but it wasn't an *easy* one. It took him many years—and, according to strict Buddhist belief, countless lifetimes—of single-minded endeavor before he finally achieved it. Nevertheless, once he did, he claimed that any individual could do the same thing: that is, realize his or her own "buddha nature," as it came to be called in the Mahayana tradition. He devoted the rest of his life to teaching the way.

Buddhism is therefore a religion centered around a teacher instead of a divine being. As such, it can be said to feature lessons rather than creeds, precepts rather than commandments, and reverence rather than worship. These distinctions are examined and clarified later in the book. First, let's take a closer look at the historical Buddha's existence, for it continues to explain many features of the Buddhist religion and to serve as an inspiring prototype for the Buddhist way of life.

Throughout the twenty-four centuries since the Buddha's death, the basic design of his biography has been embroidered over and over again to suit different purposes. As a result, we now have many versions to consider, and woven into any one of them are likely to be various ideological biases, liturgical details, cultural references, mythical touches, and psychological shadings—all embellished with a certain amount of plain old yarn-spinning.

The following account of the Buddha's eighty-four years on Earth synthesizes the most prevalent versions into three separate sections describing his early years, enlightenment, and teaching career. The commentary in each section discusses major points relating to Buddhism in general and alludes to especially significant or intriguing story variations.

THE EARLY YEARS OF THE BUDDHA

In 566 B.C.E., the Buddha was born into the childless royal family of the Shakya kingdom, located in the Himalayan foothills of what we now call southern Nepal. His clan name was Guatama. Prior to his conception, his mother, Queen Maya, wife of King Suddhodhana, had taken a spiritual vow of celibacy. However, one night, as she slept in her chaste bed in the rose marble palace in Kapilavastu, she had a wondrous dream: Into her bedroom strode a magnificent white elephant with six dazzling white tusks. His trunk arched gracefully above his head, holding aloft a perfect golden lotus flower. He knelt beside her bed and caressed her right side with the flower. At that very moment, she felt charged with new life and woke up.

Queen Maya roused her husband and told him about the dream, and he immediately summoned his chief counselor to interpret it. "You will give birth to a son destined for greatness," the counselor told them. "If he remains at the palace and follows a secular path, he will enjoy many triumphs and become a mighty ruler, emperor of the world. But if he leaves the palace, seeking something more spiritual, he will endure many hardships and eventually become a buddha, a great teacher to gods, beasts, and humankind."

Months later, on a fine spring day around the time of year we now call April, Queen Maya and her attendants set out for her parents' home, the customary place for a mother-to-be to give birth. On the way, they came to a beautiful park near the town of Lumbini. They lin-

gered there in a grove of *sala* trees. Queen Maya was standing beneath
the most ancient and luxurious tree, gazing upward into its crown,
when a transcendent sensation all over her body told her the birth was
beginning. The tree bent down a branch to her, and she grasped it and
smiled.

Suddenly, a host of wonders occurred all at once. From the sky fell
white and golden lotus petals. From the now-trembling earth rose the
fragrant scents of jasmine and sandalwood. From the air resounded the
lilting music of bells, lutes, and ethereal voices. And from the right side
of Queen Maya, without causing any pain, emerged the baby.

Gods appeared and bathed the infant in heavenly dew, then set him
down on his feet. Fully conscious, he took seven steps forward. In advance of each step, a lotus blossom sprang up to support his foot. Then,
pointing one hand up toward the sky and the other down toward the
ground, he announced in a loud, clear voice: "Behold, I am all between
heaven and Earth! In this lifetime I shall awaken!"

The miraculous baby then assumed the normal state of a newborn
and was named Siddhartha, which means "every wish fulfilled." The
phrase referred to his parents' long-standing desire for a child, but his
daily existence as a young prince seemed to reflect it as well. His father
Suddhodhana, himself a monarch, was determined that his only son
would pursue a grand career as an emperor rather than a grueling one
as a buddha, so he treated him accordingly. Confining Siddhartha to
the palace, he lavished every worldly luxury upon him, made sure he
was surrounded only with beautiful, happy people, and prevented him
from witnessing or even hearing about any of life's adversities.

Although Siddhartha's mother died shortly after he was born, he
was lovingly raised by her sister, Prajapati. Under her astute care, he
grew up to be remarkably wise, kind, good-looking, and strong. At age
sixteen, he won the hand in marriage of the loveliest woman at court,
his cousin Yasodhara, by piercing seven trees with one arrow, and his
subsequent displays of charm, intelligence, and athleticism earned him
popularity and respect throughout the kingdom. His future as a valiant,
uniquely successful military leader seemed assured.

Then, at age twenty-nine, came a crucial turning point in Siddhartha's life. His wife, pregnant with their first child, was indisposed and urged him to seek some diversion on his own. As it happens, he had overheard someone talking earlier in the day about the splendors of spring just unfolding in the forest beyond the palace. Eager to see them, he pleaded with his father so ardently and persuasively for permission to travel there that he couldn't refuse. Instead, the king secretly commanded servants to remove or conceal all disturbing sights along the route from the village adjoining the palace walls to the forest some miles away. The gods, however, decided to intervene and send the pampered prince a sign that would spur him on to his greater, spiritual destiny.

As Siddhartha rode on horseback through the village streets, that sign suddenly appeared in front of him—a man with white hair, wrinkled skin, and frail limbs. The mystified prince asked his driver, "What is this creature?"

The driver, his tongue loosened by the gods, explained, "He is an old man. He, too, was once young like you. And you, too, will age as he did, losing your strength and beauty. It is the lot of every human being."

Siddhartha was shocked and then deeply saddened. Later, as he sat in the palace gardens thinking about the encounter, he asked himself, "Knowing what I do about old age, what pleasures can these gardens now afford me?"

Future excursions to learn more about the outside world brought him two other signs of mortal afflictions: a sick person and a corpse. Finally he confronted the fourth sign sent by the gods, a bald man wearing a ragged robe and carrying a begging bowl but nevertheless projecting uncommon tranquillity. When he asked his driver to explain this man, the driver replied, "He is a monk. He has put worldly matters behind him and is seeking a higher good."

That very night, as Siddhartha rode back into the palace grounds, he heard everyone celebrating the birth of his son. Instead of welcoming the news, he despaired, thinking of the cycle of birth and death beginning yet again; the generational dynasty that bound him to his present, now frivolous-seeming lifestyle; and the restrictive, authoritarian role he'd need to assume as a father.

Despite Siddhartha's great personal love for his family, he decided that it was best for him and for others if he renounced the life of a materialistic warrior-prince to lead the life of a spiritually questing monk. Perhaps then he could find out for himself and all humankind how to escape life's grave troubles, or at least how to understand and tolerate them better.

Siddhartha wasted no time. That same night, he secretly rode away from Kapilavastu, the gods themselves silencing the hooves of his horse. At sunrise, after crossing a distant riverbank in the kingdom of Magadha, he changed from his aristocratic garments into a humble robe, shaved his head, and sent his chariot and driver back to the palace.

So began six years of homeless wandering in search of the truth about life and death. Siddhartha studied with the most renowned meditation masters of his time and, in keeping with one of that era's primary spiritual disciplines, starved himself until his body turned skeletal. Gaining more and more fame as the Great Ascetic, he gradually acquired five disciples—called the Band of Five—who followed him everywhere.

Still, Siddhartha believed that his quest so far had accomplished nothing. He later described this period as being "like time spent trying to tie the air into knots."

One day, walking along the Nairanjana River, a tributary of the Ganges River, near the village of Uruvela, Siddhartha chanced to hear a boatman tuning a three-stringed instrument. When the boatman plucked the first string, it made a gratingly high-pitched *ping!* because it was wound too tight. The second string, wound too loose, emitted an unpleasantly twangy sound. Only the third string, not wound either too tight or too loose, produced a beautiful, perfectly pitched tone. Extrapolating from this incident, Siddhartha suddenly realized that the "middle way" of life was the best: neither so austere that existence itself was threatened, nor so sybaritic that one lived selfishly just for pleasure and power.

Meanwhile, a farmer's daughter was passing by on her way to make an offering of curds to a sacred fig (or pipal) tree nearby. Moved by the sight of the emaciated Siddhartha, she offered him the curds instead. He accepted them as a first gesture in taking the Middle Way, thus breaking his austere dietary habits and causing the Band of Five to desert him in disgust. He then bathed in the river and, just before sunset, sat beneath that same sacred fig tree with his eyes facing east. Vowing not to rise again until he achieved enlightenment, he crossed his legs, lowered his eyes, and began to meditate.

Commentary. Unlike other major religions, Buddhism has no world creation story. Instead, the Buddha's life functions as a kind of substitute: the creation of a fully enlightened being. As Buddhism evolved, borrowing heavily from its parent religion Hinduism, the Buddha's personal history was given more cosmic and mythological resonance by being linked more significantly with his prior existences, each succeeding life representing another step up the spiritual ladder. For more on his rebirths, see "The Jataka Tales" on page 8. For more on the relationship between Buddhism and Hinduism, see pages 25–30.

The Buddha's previous lifetimes originated in the beginningless past and occurred intermittently over *kalpas* (huge periods of time) extending up to the birth of Siddhartha. Buddhist literature is replete with mind-boggling metaphors that attempt to convey how indescribably long a kalpa is and, therefore, how inconceivably impressive the Buddha's journey was—part of a consistent message in Buddhism that many things cannot be grasped by the rational mind. For example, suppose an eagle's wing brushes against the top of a high mountain once a century. A kalpa is how long it would take for that action to wear the mountain entirely away. Imagine a wooden yoke with one hole, thrown into the ocean to float. If a one-eyed turtle rises to the surface of the ocean once a century, a kalpa is how long it would take before the turtle just happened to rise through the hole of the yoke.

The individual we know as the Buddha—also called Siddhartha Guatama or, alternatively, Shakyamuni (in Sanskrit, "Sage of the Shakya

THE JATAKA TALES

The Buddhist canon consists of about 550 *jatakas* (birth stories) that recount the previous lives of the Buddha. Resembling folktales in structure and moral content, they collectively depict the Buddha's progression through various stages of being—plant, animal, and eventually human—before he finally earns his birth as Shakyamuni. Some tales filtered into the West as "Aesop's Fables" during and after Alexander the Great's occupation of Asian territory in the fourth century B.C.E.

One of the most famous jataka tales concerns the Buddha's life as the Banyan deer, leader of his tribe. There came a time when the tribe was driven into a park for the local king's hunting convenience. Grieving over the large number of deer wounded or killed on a daily basis, the Banyan deer proposed to the king that only one deer be killed each day, selected by lot to come to the palace. The king consented, but he was so impressed by the speaker's magnificence that he insisted this deer be excluded from the lottery. Eventually a pregnant doe drew the sacrificial lot. After she begged the Banyan deer to let her first have her child, he showed up at the palace in her place. The king was so moved by the Banyan deer's story of the doe and his selfless response that he spared them both. "But what about the others in my tribe?" asked the Banyan deer. The king realized that they too deserved to live, and as the Banyan deer kept pressing his argument, the king wound up saving all sentient beings in his kingdom from the danger of being hunted.

Clan")—is not even the first or the last buddha. Depending on which particular tradition you consult, anywhere from seven to countless numbers of buddhas lived, one after the other, each many kalpas apart, before Shakyamuni was born. Many kalpas from now, the next buddha, called Maitreya (in Sanskrit, "friend"), is destined to appear and revive the spiritual teachings long after they've been forgotten. Thus, Shakyamuni is the buddha of our age, and our age is fortunate to have one, because many do not.

Some Buddhist traditions pay more attention than others to the previous lives of the Buddha—and, indeed, to the entire concept of rebirth, as other sections of this book make clear. One of the virtues of Shakyamuni Buddha's life story all by itself is that it symbolizes so beautifully the core spiritual struggle that human beings in general go through.

In our childhood, we begin life with a pervasive joy, innocence, and security that give us a sense of royal entitlement, of belonging to the universe. Then, sooner or later, comes a personal knowledge of life's adversities that forever separates us from that childhood realm. We leave the land of our birth and wander out into the cold, cruel world, seeking greater meaning and purpose in life.

The same paradigm appears in Genesis. Adam and Eve live in the Garden of Eden, where everything is provided for them. Only one thing is prohibited: the knowledge of good and evil. When they feel driven to gain this knowledge nevertheless, they are expelled from the garden. For Shakyamuni, that expulsion took the overt form of a renunciation, but deep inside, he truly felt he had no choice. Indeed, the gods of his universe worked to make his renunciation inevitable, as it was destined to be, despite the overwhelming incentives to linger.

To many non-Buddhists, Siddhartha's renunciation of his family can seem stunningly irresponsible. To others, including Buddhist believers, its shock value operates differently, as a startling and humbling example of a supreme act of compassion, of putting the salvation of humanity far above the most compelling personal interests. In essence, his renunciation is similar to the one Buddhist or Christian monastics make in giving up their worldly ties to devote themselves to the spiritual welfare of everyone.

Shakyamuni's immediately preceding lifetime can be viewed as a test to discover if he would be capable of this kind of sacrifice. Living as Prince Visvantara, a wealthy, spiritually driven young man, he gained so much fame for his generosity that he attracted challenges to it from the most learned spiritual leaders of his time. Step by step, he gave up all that he had. With great anguish, he even turned over his two children and his wife to brahmins (members of the Hindu priestly caste) who solicited them as slaves. Thereby convinced of his sincerity, these brahmins revealed themselves to be gods in disguise, and his loved ones were restored to him.

Shakyamuni visited his family not long after his enlightenment. By that time he felt he was better prepared to enter and help transform the life of his son Rahula (meaning "fetter," a word Siddhartha was overheard to utter in referring to his son's birth before departing). Eventually Rahula became a monk in the Buddha's sangha.

The above account of the Buddha's early years touches on two important Buddhist doctrines that are discussed more thoroughly elsewhere in the book: interdependence and the Middle Way. Siddhartha's first pronouncement immediately after his birth, "I am all between heaven and Earth" (phrased different ways in various texts, including "I am the only one") is not an egotistical statement but just the opposite: It expresses the concept that all things are connected or interdependent, that there is no such entity as a separate self, except as a functional—or dysfunctional—illusion. The doctrine of the Middle Way, which is not always illustrated by the anecdote of the boatman cited here, lies open to many interpretations, but one of the most prevalent is the notion of avoiding dualistic extremes.

THE BUDDHA'S ENLIGHTENMENT

The evening that Siddhartha sat beneath the fig tree was full moon night in the month we call May, 531 B.C.E. It's a soft, warm, dreamy time of the year known in India—then and now—as Cowdust, when the air is lambent and flecked with golden sand stirred from the roads. Once he sank into utter silence and stillness, however, he was overwhelmed with tormenting visions sent by Mara, the evil one, who sought to divert Siddhartha from his path toward enlightenment.

First Mara bade his own three daughters to dance lasciviously in front of Siddhartha. As they did, Mara shot him with flower-tipped arrows to inflame his sensuality. When Siddhartha managed to resist this temptation, Mara appealed to his pride. "It is shameful for a prince to live like a beggar!" he cried. "Take command of your people, and be the true warrior you are!"

Siddhartha remained unmoved. Furious, Mara then waged fierce battle against him. Legions of grotesque demons hurled huge spears, fiery trees, and whole mountains at him, but his sheer composure either deflected them or turned them into sun motes or lotus petals.

At a loss for any other strategy, Mara finally rose to his full, awesome splendor and commanded Siddhartha, "Rise from your seat! It rightfully belongs to me, not you!" Pointing to his demons, he added, "All these beings are witnesses to my right! Who bears witness to yours?"

Siddhartha, still sitting motionless, touched the ground with a finger of his right hand, and Earth thundered back, "I bear witness!" Mara instantly disappeared in defeat.

With Mara gone, Siddhartha's meditation deepened and went through three periods, or watches. During the first watch, he recalled each one of his past lives with full clarity. During the second watch, he became aware that all those lives and the lives of others were governed by the law of *karma* (in Sanskrit, "action"): For every cause, there is an effect, which in turn becomes a cause, and so on. During the third watch, he perceived the links by which birth is connected to death and rebirth—the Wheel of Life—and this realization awakened him to the Dharma (Great Law). He later formulated it into the following basic teachings:

THE FOUR NOBLE TRUTHS

1. All life is suffering.

2. The cause of suffering is desire.

3. Suffering can be ended.

4. The way to end suffering is the Noble Eightfold Path.

THE NOBLE EIGHTFOLD PATH

1. right understanding

2. right thought

3. right speech

4. right action

5. right livelihood

6. right effort

7. right mindfulness

8. right meditation

As dawn broke, Siddhartha looked up for the first time since he began sitting and saw the morning star (Venus) in the eastern sky. At that exact moment, he attained a state of all-knowingness or enlightenment and spoke these words:

> Many houses of life have held me. Long have I sought to find him who made these prisons of the senses. But now, you builder, I have seen you at last. Never again will you construct such houses of pain! The walls are broken and the ridgepole shattered! Now that the bonds of ignorance and craving are sundered, deliverance is obtained for all! Wonder of wonders! Intrinsically all living beings are buddhas, endowed with wisdom and virtue!

The earth trembled, and the gods sang in the heavens. Siddhartha had at last become the Buddha.

Commentary. The concepts of enlightenment, the Four Noble Truths, and the Noble Eightfold Path as they apply to the religion of Buddhism are discussed in chapter 3. Focusing on Shakyamuni's enlightenment in particular, we are struck right away by the dramatic contrast between his stillness under the tree and the universally vast, turbulent, and revolution-ary nature of the visions that came to him in this state. We are also doubly impressed by the overnight time span: so brief considering the magnitude of his discovery, and yet so lengthy considering the sheer number of hours he kept his mind, body, emotions, and spirit absolutely quiet.

To understand each of these phenomena a little better, it's necessary to appreciate that Shakyamuni's night of enlightenment was the culmi-nation of a long, anguished seeking for the truth—six years of intensive asceticism and study in his present lifetime and countless previous life-times of suffering, single-minded effort, enormous sacrifice, and hard-won wisdom. The Buddhist scholar Clive Erricker, in his 1995 book *Buddhism,* offers a useful analogy for grasping how that single night's meditation functioned to resolve such an extensive period of searching:

> We might think of times when, in trying to understand apparently complex, insoluble problems, we have hit on an instant when an-swers revealed themselves so obviously that it was as though we had previously missed what was right before our eyes. Moments when we have said, "Of course, how could I have been so blind!" . . . It is as though the truth has been there all the time, but we have not had the capacity to realize it. It was this capacity that Siddhartha devel-oped and finally fulfilled. (26)

Although the teaching content of the Buddha's enlightenment re-mains basically the same from account to account and school to school, certain other details vary. For example, disagreement exists over the chronological nature of the meditation itself. Most versions concur that the three watches and final enlightenment took place on one spe-cial night. Some insist the battle with Mara took place during a previ-ous night or a series of days and nights. A few imply that weeks of meditation occurred before and/or after the night of enlightenment that helped induce, support, or amplify it.

Virtually every account says that Shakyamuni pointed to the ground, and Earth bore witness for him. This mudra (in Sanskrit, "hand gesture") often appears in artistic renderings of him. The overt reference is to all the previous lives on Earth that he endured on his way to enlightenment. Additionally, the earth can be taken to symbolize what Buddhists call the "ground of being," the fundamental nature of things, which, according to Mahayana Buddhism, manifests itself in living creatures as their "buddha nature."

Every account also includes Shakyamuni's statement of liberation, although the precise wording varies. It's important to understand that the "builder" or "you" here refers to the self (in the Buddha's case, himself). Liberation depends upon transcending the notion of a separate, isolated self, one that appears to live only within the "house" of an individual life or, as the Zen expression goes, within a specific "skin bag."

Instead of remaining trapped in this very limited, conditioned existence, we can become one with the universe, immense and unconditioned. In rediscovering this truth, the Buddha liberated all sentient beings, not just himself, because he cleared the way for every person to realize that he or she, too, is intrinsically a buddha (or, as some schools prefer to express it, capable of being enlightened). When the awakening came to him, it reentered human consciousness after untold ages of being entirely forgotten.

Just as accounts of Shakyamuni's life differ regarding certain story details, they also vary in literary style, from the spare, realistic, barebones reports one finds in many Zen sources to the elaborate, highly symbolic, visionary sagas more typical of Theravada or especially Tibetan (Vajrayana) sources. As an example of the latter, consider the following deliberately mesmerizing sentence composed by Tse Chokling Yongdzin Yeshe Gyaltsen, a famous eighteenth-century Tibetan teacher, describing the celestial response when Shakyamuni first sat down beneath the tree:

> Innumerable Bodhisattvas gathered from the buddhaverses of the ten
> directions and manifested various magical displays; creating flower
> palaces, radiating thousands of colors from their bodies, radiating
> sunlike rays, shaking the earth, carrying four oceans on their heads

and sprinkling the ground with fragrant waters, offering jewel-offering trees, flying in the sky, dissolving their bodies and turning into garlands filling the universe, pronouncing millions of discourses from the pores of their bodies, making their bodies huge, bringing trees with Bodhisattva bodies emerging halfway from each leaf, bringing axial mountains, stimulating masses of water with their feet, making great sounds like great drum rolls filling a billion universes. (Thurman, *Essential Tibetan Buddhism,* 72)

The above sentence uses the word *bodhisattva,* which has various meanings depending on its specific context as well as the school of Buddhism involved. In its most orthodox usage—and in the Theravada tradition—it refers to someone seriously on his or her way to being awakened. Thus Shakyamuni Buddha, for example, could be labeled a bodhisattva up until his enlightenment, and so could all of the sentient beings he was in his previous lives—plant, animal, or human.

In Mahayana Buddhism, which in its broadest definition incorporates the Tibetan or Vajrayana tradition as well as Pure Land, Zen, and other schools, *bodhisattva* can have the same meaning. However, it more pointedly refers to an enlightened being who postpones his or her own liberation from the Wheel of Life (into a state sometimes called nirvana or the extinction of craving) to help others achieve enlightenment. Furthermore, there are enlightened bodhisattvas such as Avalokiteshvara or Manjushri that can be said to exist on a different plane altogether, one where idealized, universal forces dwell—part of the Trikaya (or Three Body) concept discussed in chapter 2. The bodhisattvas in the passage quoted above belong to the latter category.

As for Shakyamuni and his enlightenment, Buddhists and other individuals continue to honor it today by making pilgrimages to Bodh Gaya, India, which occupies the site of ancient Uruvela. For over two thousand years, monasteries, shrines, and stupas (memorials) have been built there, but the hub of veneration has always been the *bodhi* (or *bo*) tree, claimed to be a direct descendent of the sacred fig tree under which the Buddha sat and had his great awakening.

THE NAMES OF THE BUDDHA

The historical figure best known as the Buddha actually has many different names. Here are the most common ones in Sanskrit and Pali (in parentheses, if different), the two major, closely related liturgical languages of Buddhism:

- *Buddha.* Literally, "the awakened one," the title given to him after his enlightenment.
- *Bodhisattva* (Bodhisatta). Literally, "a being of enlightenment;" in Theravada, the Buddha on his way to enlightenment, through previous lifetimes and the earlier part of his final one; in Mahayana, the same, but also the Buddha after enlightenment, because he chooses to postpone entering nirvana until all sentient beings are saved; also in Mahayana, any enlightened being who does the same.
- *Siddhartha* (Siddatta). Literally, "every wish fulfilled," the first name given to him at birth.
- *Gautama* (Gotama). His family or last name.
- *Shakyamuni* (Sakyamuni). Literally, "Sage of the Shakya Clan," a name given to him after his enlightenment, referring to the clan (and region) of his birth
- *Tathagata.* Literally, "the thus-perfected one," a title given to him after his enlightenment.
- *Sugata.* Literally, "the happy one," a title given to him after his enlightenment.

THE BUDDHA'S TEACHING CAREER

After his enlightenment, Shakyamuni debated with himself about whether or not to teach what he had learned. As blissful as his awakening had been, it was obviously something one had to do for oneself.

Unfortunately, the people he observed around him gave no indication in their behavior that they would listen to his message and take on that responsibility. They appeared to be too caught up in their personal identities, interests, and ambitions to believe that they were not, in fact, separate beings, or to aspire to a self-liberating form of awareness.

Seeing Shakyamuni's hesitation, the gods Indra and Brahma descended from heaven to plead with him to teach. "Now that you have crossed the ocean of the world of becoming, have pity on others!" they cried. "Rescue those that have sunk so low in suffering they may not even see it!" Stirred by their words, Shakyamuni told himself that some people with "only a little dust in their eyes" might be liberated if he would just point the way.

Shakyamuni's first step was to reconvene with the Band of Five, now settled in Deer Park at Sarnath, near Varanasi. When he approached his former associates, his beaming figure impressed them in the same manner it would later affect the traveler Dona, as recounted at the beginning of this chapter. Although they began by scorning him anew for not practicing self-mortifying austerities—the most obvious explanation for his glowing health—they couldn't sustain their attack. The power of his presence soon mollified them and persuaded them to ask, "What is this truth you say you have seen?"

In response, Shakyamuni delivered the Sermon at Deer Park, his initial act of teaching, or as it came to be phrased, "the first turning of the wheel of the Dharma." His sermon articulated the doctrine of the Middle Way, the Four Noble Truths, and the Noble Eightfold Path. Upon hearing it, the Band of Five vowed to rejoin their former leader and help him spread the Dharma.

Thus Shakyamuni launched a thirty-five-year teaching career that followed the same pattern each year. During the nine months of favorable weather in northeast India, he and his disciples wandered from place to place to teach, begging in silence for food and lodging as they traveled. During the three-month monsoon season, they retreated to a shelter (at first a cave, but later a monastery built for them) and engaged in more intensive group practice.

As the Buddha's entourage grew in size, each follower forsaking any other home, job, or personal entanglement, rules and regulations became necessary to ensure harmonious living conditions. These early codes led to the formation of two monastic orders: first, *bhikshus* (male beggars) and later, after repeated petitions from his stepmother Prajapati, *bhikshunis* (female beggars). Thus evolved the concept of a community of seekers, rather than the solitary wanderer. This community is referred to as a *sangha*. For more on Prajapati and her often-cited role as mother of Buddhism, see page 19.

The Buddha frequently conveyed the Dharma through stories, parables, and experiential learning assignments given to individual seekers (see, for example, "The Story of Kisa Guatama" on page 21). His converts included the rich and the poor; the high caste and the low; the intellectual and the uneducated; family members, friends, and strangers. Among the more prominent ones were:

- Ananda, the Buddha's cousin, who became his personal attendant and is generally recognized as the monk closest to his heart

- Devadatta, also the Buddha's cousin, who, seeking to institute a more austere discipline in the sangha, unsuccessfully tried to control it and even to kill Shakyamuni

- Kashyapa (also Mahakashyapa), who in some traditions is regarded as the only individual to whom the Buddha formally transmitted the Dharma (that is, qualified to be a teacher) through a specific gesture acknowledging Kashyapa's enlightened state

- Shariputra, directly addressed as the listener in several of the Buddha's surviving sutras (sermons), including the most quoted one in the Mahayana tradition, the Heart Sutra

- Rahula, the Buddha's son, who was fully ordained as a monk at the minimum age of twenty

- Vimalakirti, who in the Mahayana tradition achieved enlightenment and continued to practice and teach as a layperson or "householder" rather than a monk

THE MOTHER OF BUDDHISM

Maya is honored as the mother of the Buddha. However, her sister Prajapati is frequently dubbed the mother of Buddhism, not because she raised young Siddhartha (although she did), but because of her pivotal role in bringing women into the Buddha's sangha.

Like the other major world religions—Christianity, Judaism, Islam, and Hinduism—Buddhism evolved in a patriarchal society and inevitably took on some of the same bias. Even the Buddha was compelled to a certain degree to be a man of his time in this regard, if only to ensure that his teachings would be taken seriously and his disciples wouldn't rebel. He therefore originally restricted membership in his sangha to men. It was Prajapati, encouraged by his teachings that all sentient beings are equally valuable, who persuaded him to defy custom and make his spiritual teachings available to both genders.

Prajapati became Siddhartha's stepmother when her sister died, just seven days after his birth. According to some accounts, Prajapati was already a second wife in the harem of Siddhartha's father, Suddhodhana, having married him at the same time that Maya did. Other versions say that Prajapati married Suddhodhana after the death of her sister. In either case, she is described as someone who was destined from the beginning to be very influential, her name meaning "leader of a great assembly."

When Shakyamuni first returned to Kapilavastu after his enlightenment, Prajapati, then in her late fifties or early sixties, was highly respected as a queen, an elder, and a powerful individual in her own right. Indeed, she was the head of a group of displaced women known as the Five Hundred, including Yasodhara, Siddhartha's abandoned wife, and others who were widowed one way or another, most of them as a result of the numerous local wars during this period.

Prajapati asked her illustrious stepson three times to allow women to renounce their homes and "enter into a homeless state under the Dharma of the Buddha." On each occasion he told her, somewhat ambiguously, "Do not set your heart on this." Finally she appealed to his closest disciple Ananda for help, and Ananda pleaded with his teacher on her behalf. The Buddha had to agree that a woman was capable of being enlightened, just as a man was, and so he granted Prajapati the right to start an order of nuns, albeit with special rules of deference toward men. Most authorities interpret the creation of these extra requirements as a gesture of respect for Indian tradition.

It is said that Yasodhara herself joined her mother-in-law's order, along with many other women in the Five Hundred, and that it continued to attract vigorous followers throughout the Buddha's lifetime and beyond. In acknowledgement of Prajapati's work and stature, she has since also been called Mahaprajapati, "Great Prajapati." For more on women in Buddhism, see page 221.

At the age of eighty, in 486 B.C.E., the Buddha, now feeling weary in body, prepared for his death—an event traditionally called *parinirvana,* "completed extinction," indicating that the spiritual nirvana he attained during his enlightenment was now being complemented by a physical release. Discussing this eventuality with a grieving Ananda, he promised, "As long as monks like you gather in a group, follow the rules, and train themselves, the Dharma will thrive. Be lamps unto yourselves. Holding fast to the Dharma, be your own refuge. Do not seek refuge beyond yourselves. In this way, you will overcome darkness."

The specific mechanism leading to Shakyamuni's fatal illness (and in many traditions engineered by him) was a piece of spoiled boar's meat innocently placed into his begging bowl by a blacksmith named

Cunda. Out of gratitude, Shakyamuni was obliged to eat it. Later, weak with dysentery, he entered the small village of Kusinagara and reclined on the ground between two trees.

There Shakyamuni lay peacefully for hours, free of any pain, fear, or doubt. To make sure that Cunda would not feel bad about what had happened, he summoned him and told him that the two meals he was most thankful for receiving in his lifetime were the curds before his enlightenment and the meat Cunda gave him.

THE STORY OF KISA GUATAMA

In the time of the Buddha there lived a poor widow, a distant kinswoman of the Buddha, whose only joy was her baby son. Then he got sick and died. Wailing inconsolably, she refused to admit he was gone. Instead, she carried his body everywhere with her, clutched tightly against her chest. One morning she went to see the Buddha, who was teaching in a nearby woods. "O Great Healer," she cried, "please give me something to restore my child's life!"

The Buddha answered, "I can help you, but first you must bring me three grains of mustard seed from a home where no one has died."

Kisa Guatama ran from door to door in her village, but in every house she heard another heartbreaking tale of bereavement—a mother's death two years before, a grandfather's death that spring, an aunt's death only a week ago. By evening she realized that death was a part of being human, and the sorrow of death was shared by all. She carried the body of her son back to the Buddha, who assisted in burying it. Then she herself took refuge in the Buddha's teachings.

As night descended, crowds of people gathered around Shakyamuni to pay homage and hear his final words, which were, "All created things are impermanent. Strive on with diligence." Death brought a smile to his face, and for the third time in his life, the earth trembled. At dawn, his disciples cremated his body and collected the remaining relics—bone fragments and teeth—to place under stupas.

Commentary. In the above account of the Buddha's teaching career, we see the crystallization of the Three Jewels (or Treasures) of Buddhism: Buddha, Dharma, and Sangha. Specifically they refer, in order, to Shakyamuni, the Great Law revealed to him during his enlightenment (later codified into official sutras), and the monastic community committed to realizing that law.

However, each jewel has also come to be understood in a more general, cosmic way. The Buddha component of the Three Jewels is often interpreted to mean any qualified teacher of the Dharma or, in the Mahayana tradition, the buddha nature that exists within every sentient being. The word *sangha* (lower case) can be applied to any group of people forming a Buddhist community, or even to all sentient beings, who are interdependently linked. *Dharma* can refer not only to the official body of Buddhist teachings, but also (usually in lower case) to the entire phenomenal universe, which continually provides teachings to those aware enough to see them.

Throughout the rest of the book, we'll examine the Three Jewels and their paramount significance, as well as other Buddhist doctrines, practices, and institutions relating to Shakyamuni's teaching career and death. Special mention will also be made, when appropriate, of common Buddhist images or objects that derive from Shakyamuni's lifetime.

For example, both the Wheel of Life, symbolizing the cycle of birth-death-rebirth that Shakyamuni saw during his enlightenment, and the Wheel of the Dharma, representing the teachings that he first "turned" in Deer Park, are major Buddhist icons. They appear frequently as artworks in their own right (for example, Tibetan mandalas) or as design

THE BLIND MEN AND THE ELEPHANT

Once the Buddha's monks, out begging in town, overheard a mixed group of wandering ascetics and brahmins arguing with each other over which one's doctrine represented the truth. Some insisted the world was finite; some, infinite; others, part finite and part infinite; still others, neither finite nor infinite; and so on.

When the monks returned to their master, they told him about the quarrelsome scene, and he replied, "Those who stake their truth against the truths of everyone else are blind. They do not see into the supreme truth that binds them all together."

Then the Buddha told them a parable. "Long ago," he said, "a king ordered all the blind men in his capital who had never heard of an elephant to assemble in a field near the royal palace. His servants arranged them in a circle in the middle of the field, surrounding an elephant they could not see. The king announced to the blind men, 'Straight ahead of you stands an elephant. Advance, feel the elephant for yourself, and tell me what it is.'

"Each blind man walked forward and wound up feeling a different part of the elephant. One man ran his hand over the head and trunk and declared, 'The elephant is like a pot.' Another felt an ear and cried, 'No, it is more like a winnowing basket.' A third touched a tusk and yelled, 'You are both wrong! It is like a plow.' A fourth patted the body and one leg and shouted, 'Nonsense! It is a granary mounted on a pillar!' A fifth handled the tail and screamed, 'Fools, all of you! It is a broom!' And on and on it went.

"Well, the king just laughed and laughed, my monks," the Buddha concluded. "And so should you laugh over the beggars you saw today, each one ignorantly pleading his own narrow view."

elements in larger works. Only the contextual details of a given wheel clarify which theme it is portraying.

The wheel itself, in fact, was a symbol of kingship throughout Indian culture well before the Buddha's lifetime. According to many accounts, one of the primary indicators of the infant Buddha's great destiny was alleged to be a wheel pattern on the soles of his feet—a recurring motif in Buddhist art. Footprint images with or without markings were often used in this era to represent important or "weighty" individuals, including the Buddha after his death. For several centuries, representations of his body or face were considered inappropriate, partly because he wasn't a god.

QUESTIONS AND ANSWERS

What are the sources for the Buddha's life story? How historically accurate are they?
Although the known facts of Shakyamuni's time on Earth are few and sketchy, historians agree that he did exist and led an eighty-year life following the same basic pattern as the one described above. No written records date from his lifetime, but the oral transmission from that period to the time of the first written accounts is strong and credible.

After all, the Buddha was the son of a prominent warrior-caste man (more likely a tribal chieftain than a king) and led a very public and peripatetic life for forty-five years. At the time of his death he was known and respected throughout northeast India, and his disciples immediately began spreading word of his life and teachings even farther afield, a process that has continued ever since.

Authorities do disagree over the exact years of the Buddha's life and death. Most accept the dates generally adopted within the Buddhist world: 566 to 486 B.C.E. Some Buddhists and non-Buddhists, however, claim it was more recent: 488 to 368 B.C.E. Each span is calculated by working backward, using a different equation, from Ashoka's consecration in 268 B.C.E., Ashoka being the first major, historically datable ruler to embrace Buddhism (see page 40). The former, more commonly acknowledged time frame is called the long version; the latter, the short version.

The earliest document describing the Buddha's entire life is the Buddhacarita ("the Buddha's acts"), a classic Sanskrit poem written by the Buddhist scholar Ashvaghosha in the first century, before Buddhism split into distinctly different schools. The short biography offered above is drawn primarily from this work.

Another, later Sanskrit source is the Lalitavistara, an anthology of legends about different events in the Buddha's life. Some tales in this anthology first appeared elsewhere in written form as early as the first century B.C.E.

Hundreds of other stories depicting specific biographical episodes or details, including many that are not featured in Ashvaghosha's poem or that differ from his rendition, are incorporated into Sanskrit, Pali, or native-language works dating from the second century onward. Shakyamuni himself is presumed to have spoken only Magadhi, a northeast Indian dialect. No writings in Magadhi of any kind survive from his era.

If the Buddha himself isn't a god, what are we to make of all the references to gods in his life story and elsewhere in Buddhism?
Based on all the available evidence, including the manner in which Buddhism developed during its first few centuries of growth, Shakyamuni did not worship any god, did not advocate such worship, did not claim to be a god himself, and was not deified after his death. More to the point, he achieved enlightenment through his own endeavor, not through the grace of a god.

However, the Buddha never denied the existence of gods. Throughout ancient Indian society, virtually everyone believed in supernatural beings of some sort. In many cases, these deities weren't especially powerful, except perhaps in terms of the magical feats they performed every now and then. They also weren't very involved in human affairs, at least on a steady basis. Among all these deities, the many gods in the Hindu pantheon were certainly the most prominent and widely worshiped, but they too tended to be regarded as remote forces who might grant favors, work miracles, or wreak mischief as they saw fit, rather than ever-present, omnipotent, judicious regulators of human existence.

The Buddha's spiritual vision rose out of a predominantly Hindu culture, and his career as a teacher was geared toward refining common religious beliefs rather than overthrowing them. As a result, Buddhism wound up with numerous references to Hindu gods in its sacred writings and liturgy. In this sense, it was an *evolutionary* spiritual movement instead of a *revolutionary* one. If nothing else, these allusions simultaneously helped to legitimize the new religion, to make it more familiar to the populace, and to lend it a compelling aura of grandeur.

The fact that the Buddha enjoyed a long, popular, and relatively untroubled teaching career during a religiously volatile era testifies to his skill in avoiding controversy on the topic of gods or other core aspects of Hinduism. Thus the story of his life came to feature, for example, Indra and Brahma—two of the principal Hindu gods—urging the Buddha to become a teacher despite his own initial reluctance.

Nevertheless, the Buddha as a mortal being, symbolizing the human potential to become fully awakened to the truth and at one with the universe, remains "superior" in Buddhism to any deity. This perspective is dramatically illustrated in a passage of the Buddhacarita that recounts a day when the child Siddhartha, accompanied by his father and aunt, visited a temple of the Hindu gods:

> As the child stepped across the threshold, the statues came to life, and all the Gods, Siva, Skanda, Vishnu, Kuvera, Indra, Brahma, descended from their pedestals and fell at his feet. And they sang: "Meru, king of the mountains, does not bow before a grain of wheat; the Ocean does not bow before a pool of rainwater; the Sun does not bow before a glowworm; he who will have the true knowledge does not bow before the Gods." (Herold, *The Life of the Buddha,* 23)

Buddhism also has gods of its own, but they are relatively inactive denizens of the highest, most comfortable realm of existence in the

Buddhist cosmology. According to most Theravada schools of Buddhism, the other four realms (in descending order) are made up of humans, animals, hungry ghosts, and demons. In many Mahayana schools, there's a sixth realm of demigods between that of humans and that of gods.

HEAVEN AND HELL

The various realms in Buddhist cosmology range from a heavenly one of *devas* (godlike beings) to a hellish one of demons. In addition to symbolizing the different worlds into which beings can be born, they also represent psychological, spiritual, or emotional states. The following Zen story illustrates this truth.

A big, tough samurai once went to see a little monk. In a voice accustomed to meeting with obedience, the samurai said, "Monk, teach me about heaven and hell."

The monk looked up at this mighty warrior and replied in a voice of utter contempt, "Teach *you* about heaven and hell? I couldn't teach you about *anything*. You're filthy. You stink. Your sword is rusty. You're a disgrace to the samurai class! Get out of my sight!"

The samurai was speechless with rage. His muscles bulged. His face got red. He swung his sword high above his head, preparing to slay the monk.

"That is hell," the monk said softly.

The samurai froze. Suddenly he was overwhelmed by the compassion of this tiny, defenseless man who had just risked death to give this teaching. As he slowly lowered his sword, he was filled with gratitude and wonder.

"That is heaven," the monk said softly.

This scheme of different worlds relates to the cycle of rebirths, a concept Buddhism also carried over from Hinduism. In the next life, a being advances upward or downward into one world or another depending on the particular karmic results of the present life. Gods also go through birth and death, but their life span is much longer than a human one, and their day-by-day existence much more agreeable.

Still, the state of enlightenment, with its promise of liberation, is far preferable to life as an unenlightened god, and the former state can only be attained (or, as some schools express it, can *most easily* be attained) during a human existence. The reason is that human beings occupy a kind of middle ground in the scheme. They possess a consciousness that is capable of being enlightened, and yet they must also go through a great deal of suffering, which spurs their will to seek enlightenment. In most traditions, the realm of the gods consists entirely or partly of beings who were once human and are waiting to be reborn into the human realm, where they will again have an opportunity to become enlightened.

Another dimension of Buddhism's five (or six) realms is strictly symbolic in nature. Every human being has the potential to dwell emotionally, psychologically, or spiritually in any of these worlds at different moments or periods in his or her life. The specific qualities attributed to each realm vary from tradition to tradition, but they correspond logically with the type of inhabitants involved. In Tibetan Buddhism, for example, the six realms of demons, hungry ghosts, animals, humans, demigods, and gods are associated respectively with (among other things) the poisonous emotions of anger, greed, ignorance, desire, jealousy, and pride. For further discussion of this cosmology, see "Heaven and Hell" on page 27.

What is the historical context from which Buddhism grew? Why did it appeal so strongly to so many people at the time?
The middle of the first millennium B.C.E. was a time of uniquely vigorous spiritual, philosophical, and political development in world history, so much so that it's often referred to as the Axial Age. Breakthroughs in Iron Age technology and, as a result, agriculture and

human health gave rise to strong, socially more stratified city-states. These mini-civilizations competed with each other for leadership in all areas of life, from athletics and aesthetics to mercantile trade, military power, and territorial rights.

The beginning of this era saw the Trojan Wars in the eastern Mediterranean, the rebellions in China that toppled the Chou dynasty, and, in India, the conflicts that form the background of the national epic, the Mahabharata. In response to these upheavals and others, all sorts of novel questions and belief systems arose regarding a human being's proper or ideal place in the universe.

Shakyamuni articulated one such system, and so did a host of well-known historical figures whose lifetimes are roughly contemporaneous. The Jain religious leader Mahivira (who may have studied with Shakyamuni) taught that the individual soul must be kept pure through nonviolence. The Chinese sages Confucius and Lao Tse each formulated codes for living ethically and harmoniously with others. The prophets Jeremiah and Ezekiel exhorted their fellow Jews to take more personal responsibility for their destiny. Zoroaster (or Zarathustra) preached among the Persians that people must continuously choose between good and evil. In Greece, Heraclitus philosophized that everything was transitory, and Socrates promoted a morality based on conscience rather than social demand.

As the answer to the preceding question indicates, the Buddha's teachings were in part a reformational response to the nature of Hinduism at that time. Many merchants, artists, and political leaders chafed at the Hindu-based caste system, which ranked them on a lower level than priests (brahmins). Furthermore, the Hindu religion as supervised by the brahmins was then perceived by increasing numbers of people as being too heavily ritualized (hence, static instead of dynamic) and too tightly oriented around gods rather than humans.

As a result, the roadways and villages of northeast India, somewhat removed from the stronghold of Hinduism farther west, were full of solitary persons and groups who sought or promoted new spiritual points of view. Robert Thurman, professor of Indo-Tibetan studies at

Columbia University, captures this scene in his 1998 book *Inner Revolution*:

> Wandering ascetics, holy men, and philosophers traveled from town to town, questioning the old myths and traditions. They championed the power of reason and the importance of the individual quest. They challenged the violent honor codes of the kings, the elitism of religious ideas and practices, and the validity of social hierarchy. The world was ripe for a new, critically deepened understanding of causation, of evolution, of the purpose of life. It was a time for a new possibility for human happiness and evolutionary fulfillment, and many people hoped for the appearance of a fully awakened being, a buddha, to lead them. (46)

SAINT BUDDHA

Sometime early in the second millennium C.E., the Roman Catholic Church unwittingly made the Buddha a saint. It happened when a centuries-old hero named Jospahat was canonized. Church authorities knew him only by popular legend, but that's all it took back then, as long as the story was engrossing, inspiring, and doctrinally sound.

Josaphat's story qualified on all three counts. He was born to a royal couple in India, at which time it was prophesied that he would become a religious leader rather than succeeding his father as king. Determined to thwart this fate, the king wouldn't allow his son to leave the palace grounds for many years. Finally Josaphat did, and what he saw horrified him: the old, the sick, and the dead. Fortunately, he also encountered Barlaam, a Christian monk from Sennar (or Sri Lanka), whose wise counsel impressed him so much that he too became a monk.

Desperate to win Josaphat back, the king gave him half the kingdom to rule. Josaphat quickly turned this land into a model Christian state. His father was so moved by the results that he himself converted to Christianity. When he died shortly afterward, Josaphat refused to take the throne. Instead, he joined Barlaam as a wandering ascetic and performed many miracles before his peaceful and widely mourned death.

In Josaphat's legend, modern scholars recognize the story of the Buddha, which apparently shape-shifted as it traveled west from region to region. They attribute the name Josaphat to a linguistic contortion of the Buddha's title, Bodhisattva (in an earlier, Arabic version of Josaphat's story, his name is Yudasaf). Even the name Barlaam probably derives from the term *Bhagavan* (Blessed One), which is often bestowed on the Buddha. Thus Josaphat's story can be interpreted symbolically to describe Josaphat saving himself—a truly Buddhist concept!

Although Josaphat is no longer liturgically celebrated by the Catholic Church, his name remains in the Roman Martyrology, the official catalog of saints, and his day of worship is still listed as November 27. Because he was made a saint before the canonization process was reformed (1588), and perhaps also because a pope bestowed the honor rather than a lesser authority, Josaphat, like the Buddha, survived the test of time.

2 The Three Vehicles of Buddhism: Theravada, Mahayana, and Vajrayana

Whoever honors his own sect and condemns other sects . . . injures his own more gravely. So concord is good: Let all listen and be willing to listen to the doctrines professed by others.

—Ashoka, Mauryan emperor

As soon as Shakyamuni passed from being a living teacher to being the legendary founder of a new religion, all sorts of Hindu-style miracles began to be attributed to his career. One of the most impressive is said to have occurred during his approach to a menacing gang of hecklers near his monastery in Sravasti. To confound them, he instantly transformed himself into a hundred buddhas, each sitting on his own lotus throne.

This dazzling multiple-buddha image became especially popular among Mahayana practitioners, who still often employ it in paintings and sculptures to represent, among other things, a celestial pantheon of enlightened beings celebrating the Dharma throughout space and time. To the student of religious history, it

33

can also symbolize the numerous similar but slightly divergent expressions of Buddhism that appear among its past and present schools.

Many sacred Buddhist texts have been developed by monks and scholars over the centuries since Shakyamuni walked the roads of northern India, including an abundance of sutras assumed to be literal transcriptions of his sermons, either preserved orally from the time he was alive or somehow revealed later to especially worthy teachers. Indeed, the number of works now claimed to be sacred in one Buddhist tradition or another is arguably greater than the number of holy texts generated by any other major religion.

Despite this fact—or because of it, depending on your perspective—Buddhism lacks a single written source of doctrine equivalent to the Torah in Judaism, the Bible in Christianity, the Koran in Islam, or the Vedas in Hinduism. Furthermore, it is by nature a religion of internal realization rather than external code. As a result, there are very few core beliefs, but a multitude of different guidelines and systems designed to help people, groups, and even whole societies put such beliefs into practice.

Chapter 3 examines the basic teachings that inform all varieties of Buddhism. First, however, it's important to account for what is most apparent on the surface of the Buddhist world when we initially regard it: the very different-looking contexts within which the teachings are manifested. A preliminary, developmental overview of the three major contexts in this chapter will make it easier to understand later how they vary among each other in the interpretation of a given teaching.

Virtually all sects of Buddhism belong to one of these three schools, or as they are more commonly called, vehicles (from the Sanskrit *vada* or ferryboat, alluding to the "other shore" of enlightenment):

Theravada (pronounced "TAIR-ah-VAH-dah" and meaning "teaching of the elders"). Theravada Buddhism traces its origins to the period immediately after Shakyamuni's death in 486 B.C.E. Over the following few centuries, it remained the largest among a group of schools that considered themselves conservative keepers of the tradition.

When a more liberal school calling itself Mahayana ("great vehicle") arose in the first and second centuries C.E., its advocates pejoratively referred to the older, more orthodox group as Hinayana ("little vehicle"). The nickname stuck to Theravada, the eventual lone survivor of the conservative schools. Outsiders still sometimes employ the term as an alternative to Theravada, although usually without meaning to cast aspersions. It's never used by Theravada practitioners themselves.

Placing an especially strong emphasis on moral discipline, renunciation, monasticism, and sutra study, Theravada's ideal figure is the *arhat* ("worthy one"), a person who achieves enlightenment and, after the present lifetime, becomes blissfully liberated from the sorrowful cycle of birth and death. Theravada Buddhism prevails today in Cambodia, Myanmar, Sri Lanka, and Thailand. It's also the most well known form of Buddhism among Europeans, due to Europe's long history as a colonizing force in that part of the world. Theravada monks typically wear orange robes.

Mahayana (pronounced "MAH-hah-YAH-nah" and meaning "great vehicle"). Mahayana formally emerged in the first and second centuries as a kind of reformed Buddhism intended to make liberation possible for a wider number and range of individuals, including laypeople (hence, the name). In keeping with this objective, its ideal figure is the bodhisattva, a concept that early Mahayana teachers broadened to indicate, among other things, an enlightened being who compassionately postpones his or her own postenlightenment liberation in order to help free others.

Today, Mahayana Buddhism predominates in China, Japan, Korea, Vietnam, and Tibet (in Tibet, it is often classified as a separate vehicle called Vajrayana; see page 36). The United States' closer proximity to these countries and its wartime involvements with Japan, Korea, and Vietnam have made Americans more familiar with Mahayana than Theravada. Different monastic schools of Mahayana wear different colors of robes. In Japanese Zen, for example, the robes tend to be black; in Tibetan Vajrayana, yellow.

*　　*　　*

Vajrayana (pronounced "VAHJ-rah-YAH-nah" and meaning "diamond vehicle"). Named for the indestructibility of its message and based on esoteric tantras (literally, "texts"), Vajrayana unfolded gradually from Mahayana during the third through eighth centuries, as Buddhism spread from northern India into the neighboring Himalayan kingdoms and, eventually, Tibet. Its roots lie in a widespread movement after Shakyamuni's death to invest Buddhism with the same kind of magical elements that had long permeated Indian spiritual life, first in various nature religions and later in Hinduism. As this form of Mahayana Buddhism penetrated Tibet, it quickly absorbed many of the ritualistic, visionary, and charismatic features of the native, shamanistic Bon (pronounced "bern") religion that it ultimately supplanted there.

Vajrayana is true to the Mahayana tradition in revering the bodhisattva as the ideal figure. It is currently the dominant form of Buddhism in Tibet, Bhutan, Mongolia, Sikkim, and parts of Nepal. Since the Tibetan diaspora caused by the Chinese invasion and occupation of that country in the early 1950s, Vajrayana and its preeminent representative, the Dalai Lama, have become increasingly well known throughout the world.

Now that we have a working definition of the three major vehicles of Buddhism, let's explore in more detail how they evolved up to the modern era.

EARLY DEVELOPMENT OF BUDDHISM IN INDIA

Throughout Shakyamuni's forty-five-year teaching career, his disciples debated with him and among themselves about the manner in which the Dharma should be communicated. Out of this ongoing discussion emerged several key questions:

- What particular lifestyles and practices should be endorsed as the most conducive to enlightenment?

- How much, if at all, should laypeople be included in the sangha?

- Who besides the Buddha might have the authority to teach, or to manage a sangha?

- How could this power be detected, earned, granted, or controlled?

After Shakyamuni's death (486 B.C.E.), the need to address these issues grew much more urgent. The very next year, the First Council was called by Kashyapa (also Mahakashyapa), then considered the Buddha's most learned disciple and later regarded by Mahayana as the only one to whom the Buddha actually transmitted the Dharma. Kashyapa invited 499 other, carefully chosen Buddhists, who were thereby deemed to be *arhats* (enlightened beings).

Understandably, the First Council established the authority of the arhat in all matters and, to bolster the cause of monasticism, devised a strict, detailed, and highly comprehensive code of rules for monastic life (the Vinaya). Because Ananda, the Buddha's closest companion, was not yet acknowledged as an arhat, he was not invited to be part of the council. However, he was asked to recite Shakyamuni's sermons to the other members—the beginning of an oral tradition that preceded by centuries the actual writing of scriptures (see "Sacred Texts of Buddhism," below).

SACRED TEXTS OF BUDDHISM

In the Theravada vehicle, the major body of scriptures is the Pali Canon, named for the language in which it was written. Most of the text dates from the first century B.C.E. but reputedly contains material transmitted orally ever since the death of Shakyamuni Buddha three hundred years earlier. The canon consists of three parts known as the Tripitaka ("Three Baskets"):

Vinaya-pitaka ("Basket of Order"). Monastic codes, accounts of the Buddha's life and early sangha development, and inspirational sayings of the Buddha (the most famous anthology being the Dhammapada).

Sutra-pitaka ("Basket of Teachings"). Various discourses of the Buddha and his disciples and over five hundred jataka tales (see page 8).

Abhidharma-pitaka ("Basket of Special Learning"). Advanced teachings for monastics.

The Mahayana scriptures (also sacred within the later-evolving Vajrayana vehicle) were written in Sanskrit between the first century B.C.E. and the sixth century C.E., but the oldest surviving texts are in Tibetan or Chinese translations. They consist of a variety of materials that can be classified as follows:

- *Sutras* (scriptures), which claim to be the words of the Buddha himself. These include:
  - Prajnaparamita (or Mahaprajnaparamita)-sutra ("Sutra of the Wisdom That Reaches the Other Shore"). A collection of smaller sutras exploring in particular the doctrine of emptiness, the most well known being the Heart Sutra (the shortest and most widely used one for chanting and meditation: see page 79) and the Diamond Sutra.
  - Saddharmapundarika-sutra ("Lotus [or Lotus of the Good Law] Sutra"). Commonly regarded as encapsulating the Buddha's most essential teachings.
- *Shastras* (treatises), which present various points of doctrine, such as elaborations of the Three Body doctrine, as developed by different teachers.
- *Tantras* (texts), which offer esoteric teachings related to mystical beliefs and practices.

The First Council gave early Buddhism a strong structural base for growth, but it also created sharper divisions between those who supported a tightly governed, monks-only model and those who sought looser rules and the broader inclusion of laypeople. Proponents of the latter cause were further split into a host of factions. One of these factions advocated the bodhisattva ideal and, in the spirit of this argument, sought ways to mediate between the mundane world and the transcendent universe of enlightened beings. This group quickly grew to become the strongest among several alternatives to the dominant, arhat-oriented group.

The Second Council in 383 B.C.E., almost a hundred years after Shakyamuni's death, and the Third Council in 250 B.C.E. attempted to resolve the escalating conflicts among the various Buddhist contingents by reaffirming and even strengthening the arhat mandate. Instead, they wound up polarizing Buddhism into the two major camps that eventually came to be known as Theravada and Mahayana.

Meanwhile, regardless of this internal division, Buddhism was rapidly flourishing throughout the Indian peninsula as a spiritual, social, and even political force. Although Buddhist monks formally renounced an ordinary life, they spent a great deal of time wandering among people of all kinds, begging for their food and lodging, performing compassionate acts as they saw the need, and helping to spread the Dharma to others by the power of example and, occasionally, by public teaching.

It was generally assumed that laypeople could not actively seek enlightenment, given the extent of their involvement in worldly matters. Nevertheless, Buddhism did have much to offer them. They could improve the quality of their life by adopting its practices and principles in whatever manner best fit their circumstances. Furthermore, by supporting the monks and performing other good deeds to help advance the Dharma, they could earn merit toward a favorable rebirth. Thus a well-functioning, symbiotic relationship developed between monks and laypeople that helped to stabilize communities and offset many of the inequities and glitches built into the long-entrenched caste system.

Between the Second and Third Councils, Buddhism gained a re-markable patron who helped make it a much more popular, re-spectable, and influential religion throughout most of present-day India and beyond. It was during these years that the Mauryan warrior clan rose to power in Magadha, the kingdom where Shakyamuni spent most of his teaching career. Through sheer military aggressiveness, the first two Mauryan rulers quickly forged an empire that extended over much of the subcontinent as well as westward into Central Asia and southward onto the island of Sri Lanka. Ashoka, the grandson of the dynasty's founder, became emperor in 272 B.C.E. and eight years later fought an extremely gruesome battle to subdue the holdout region of Kalinka on the eastern Indian coast. By his own estimation, over 100,000 people were slaughtered and another 150,000 taken into slav-ery. He was so appalled at the human cost of his victory that soon afterward he publicly foreswore Hinduism and declared himself a Buddhist.

Ashoka continued to reign for another twenty-four years. Although he could only practice as a lay Buddhist, not a monastic, his supreme position in society and his passionate commitment to Buddhist ethics made him a uniquely visible, active, and effective promoter of the faith. Throughout the empire his representatives erected rock pillars topped with his signature four-lion capital and carved with edicts expounding the Dharma. Dozens of these pillars, including the one containing the quote that begins this chapter, still stand today, and the official seal of modern India preserves the same four-lion capital.

In addition to broadcasting the Dharma on pillars, Ashoka virtually set up Buddhism as a major spiritual force in the world by pursuing a policy of Buddhist-related peace, justice, and generosity never before— or since—exercised on such a vast scale. He also dispatched Buddhist missionaries westward through present-day Afghanistan as far as the Mediterranean Sea and southward onto the island of Sri Lanka.

Still, Ashoka's government did not impose Buddhism on its subjects in any formal manner typically associated with the creation of a state religion. Dr. Richard Gombrich, the highly regarded English Buddhologist, discusses this important point in his well-known anthology *The World of Buddhism:* "In the best tradition of Indian kingship, Ashoka supported all religions; though he put it in on public record, his Buddhist piety was a personal matter. . . . We must remember that in Buddhist estimation, the Doctrine is only established where the Sangha is established, and, in turn, that is considered to be the case only when a monastic boundary has been duly established" ("Buddhism in Ancient India," in Bechert and Gombinch, *World of Buddhism,* 83).

Ashoka did, however, spread the Buddha's message of nonviolence far and wide, and as it happens, down through the ages of Indian politics. Jawaharlal Nehru, one of the primary architects of the modern Indian nation, paid tribute to this legacy in a letter he wrote while a prisoner of war to his daughter Indira, later his successor as prime minister of India: "The palace of massive stone is gone, leaving no trace behind, but the memory of Ashoka lives over the whole continent of Asia, and his edicts still speak to us in a language we can understand and appreciate. And we can still learn much from them" (quoted in Schulberg, *Historic India,* 80).

Ashoka's empire did not long survive his death, nor, without royal patronage, did the dominance of arhat-based (later called Theravada) Buddhism in India. Slowly but surely over the succeeding centuries what came to be known as Mahayana Buddhism began making inroads. In 120 C.E., it was embraced and greatly strengthened by King Kanisha of the Kushan dynasty, ruler over much of present-day Pakistan and northern India. He called a Fourth Council that launched the start of the great Mahayana scriptural canon in Sanskrit (see "Sacred Texts of Buddhism" on page 37) and dispatched Mahayana missionaries to China, Tibet, and Myanmar.

Also during Kanisha's forty-year reign, Buddhist sculptors and muralists, inspired by the Hellenic art they saw in the Central Asian territories once governed by Alexander the Great, produced the first images of the Buddha as a man. He had previously been represented only by symbols: primarily footprints (see p. 24), a royal parasol (suggesting both his caste and spiritual rank), or an empty seat beneath the bodhi tree. The new Hellenic-style human depictions helped to popularize the Buddha among laypeople as well as monastics, and therefore to attract all the more individuals to the Mahayana vehicle.

Another king in the second century, Sharaditya of Magadha, founded a Mahayana monastery called Nalanda that metamorphosed over the centuries into a widely renowned university for studying Buddhism and a host of other spiritual and worldly subjects. It continued to attract scholars and monks from all over Asia until the Mongol invasions of the 1200s.

It was these same invasions that brought an end to Buddhism as a significant religion in India. During the entire first millennium C.E., it had slowly but surely been losing ground to Hinduism. Thanks in large degree to the creative stimulus of Buddhism, Hinduism had been flowering into the more devotional and philosophical religion we know today, taking on many of the themes and doctrines of Buddhism that, after all, had been partly derived from Hinduism in the first place. By the eighth century, Shakyamuni himself had been co-opted into the Hindu pantheon as the ninth incarnation of the god Vishnu.

Hinduism's grand renaissance triggered a correspondingly impressive resurgence in its popularity. As the political scene across India degenerated into endless strife among small, upstart powers, masses of Indian people reembraced Hinduism to gain a stronger sense of their common, enduring identity.

When the Islamic Mongols set about conquering India, they found it much more troublesome to combat Hinduism, with its deep, newly revitalized roots in the cultural soil, than Buddhism, with its comparatively shallower, less vigorous ones. Buoyed by early successes in attacking Buddhist communities, Mongol military leaders went so far as to target Buddhists in several decisive massacres. The result was an even greater swing toward Hinduism among the native Indians.

Other factors that contributed to Buddhism's disappearance from the turbulent India of the preinvasion era were more intrinsic to the religion's nature. Being a faith that did not lend itself to supporting worldly affairs, accumulating wealth, waging war, or even proselytizing (except in the context of isolated missionary campaigns), it could not consistently count on the kind of strong patronage it needed in order to maintain a secure power base.

However, while Buddhism was fading away from the Indian sub-continent during the first millennium, it was thriving in other parts of Asia. To the north, Mahayana was working its way into the mainstream of the Chinese, Korean, Japanese, and Tibetan cultures. Simultaneously Theravada was developing into the primary religion across most of southeast Asia.

THERAVADA: THE SOUTHERN TRANSMISSION

In 250 B.C.E., Ashoka sent his own son, the Buddhist monk Mahinda, as a missionary to the king of Sri Lanka. Meeting in a park outside Anuradhapura, the ancient capital of the island kingdom, the two men engaged in a lengthy public discourse. According to legend, the spectacle climaxed in the king's conversion. He announced it in a letter to Ashoka and requested a branch of the bodhi tree itself, which by then had become a living shrine in newly named Bodh Gaya, India. The branch was carried to Sri Lanka by the nun Sangamitta, another child of Ashoka, and planted in that same park. Thus commenced what has since been called the southern transmission, the cultivation of Buddhism beyond the southern borders of India.

Only twenty miles of typically placid water separate Sri Lanka from the Indian mainland, but that slim barrier probably saved orthodox Buddhism, in the form we call Theravada, from extinction. During the decades after 43 B.C.E., when non-Buddhist Tamils from India first began invading the island, Sri Lankan monastics finally committed the huge body of oral Theravada teachings into writing. They used the local official language, Pali, a dialect of Sanskrit and an import from India. Their purpose was to ensure that the Dharma would survive in Sri Lanka even if the sangha members themselves were exterminated.

The feared calamity never occurred, but the precaution against it

gave history a supremely rich and instructive library of sacred literature known as the Pali Canon—the oldest collection of Buddhist
teachings in writing (see "Sacred Texts of Buddhism" on page 37).
For Theravada Buddhists ever since, the works in the Pali Canon have
remained the primary religious texts, and Pali has persisted as the
liturgical language.

Two thousand years ago, however, the Pali Canon's chief value lay in
helping Theravada not only to stay alive on that relatively small island
but also to spread farther across Southeast Asia. Before we track that
movement, let's examine the vehicle itself. What is the particular nature
of Theravada that distinguishes it from the later-arising Mahayana
and its offshoot Vajrayana, both of which are more familiar to Americans? What attributes give this ancient form of spiritual practice its
own special beauty?

Several broad distinctions between Theravada and Mahayana Buddhism have existed ever since the two schools diverged from each
other in the early part of the first millennium:

- As already mentioned, the Theravada student strives to become an
  arhat, or spiritually enlightened person, whose objective is nirvana: the extinction of all desire through personal liberation from
  the cycle of being. Thus the Theravada vehicle places an especially
  strong emphasis on self-perfection through moral conduct, which
  includes strict renunciation of the worldly aspects of life. After all,
  nirvana can only be attained, and fruitless cravings extinguished,
  through one's own efforts.

  In Mahayana, the student seeks to become a bodhisattva, or
  buddha-in-the-making, who, though also spiritually enlightened,
  postpones his or her own entrance into nirvana to assist others in
  becoming enlightened. Thus the Mahayana vehicle posits that enlightenment can be achieved, in part, through the intervention of
  others as well as through one's own efforts, and that certain kinds
  of engagement in the world-as-is provide opportunities for experiencing or facilitating the process.

- The Theravada vehicle teaches a comparatively rational view of the universe, while the Mahayana vehicle tends to present a more metaphysical vision, including (among other concepts) the notion of absolute qualities and bodhisattva powers that exist on a universal rather than a human scale. Speaking of this difference, Dr. Hans Wolfgang Schumann, a German expert on Theravada and author of the book *Buddhism: An Outline of Its Teachings and Schools*, writes: "In relation to the reality of the world [Theravada] holds a psychological realism; Mahayana, an idealism. Consequently [Theravada] regards suffering as real; the Mahayana, as an illusion (which, however, only the sage recognizes as such)" (91).

  During the mid- to late nineteenth century, Theravada was introduced to mainstream westerners as a result of European colonization in southeast Asia. For a while, it was the only form of Buddhism they knew, and because their pragmatic mind-set was immediately attracted to the many rational aspects of Theravada, they developed the impression that Buddhism as a whole was a "scientific religion." Hailed in 1893 at the World's Parliament of Religions in Chicago as "surprisingly progressive," Theravada scriptures were praised for being "logically constructed to explain the nature of life and the need for moral conduct" without requiring belief in a deity or acceptance of a mythology.

- Theravada is associated with a reverence for scholarship, wisdom, and all-knowingness. Its practice, therefore, can include particularly rigorous educational and intellectual training. Mahayana is commonly considered to place more emphasis on intuitive, experiential, and imaginative understanding.

- Theravada has a long, solid tradition of creating strong, tightly knit, well-functioning monasteries. Throughout history, these institutions have been skillful at allying themselves comfortably with the surrounding social and political powers without overly compromising their own integrity. Mahayana has had a more volatile monastic history, befitting its relatively more complex involvement with the population at large and, therefore, its greater vulnerability to social and political crosscurrents.

In Sri Lanka, Theravada Buddhism remained a vibrant presence well into the first millennium C.E. In the fourth century C.E., the Buddha's tooth was brought with great ceremony to the city of Kandy, where it is still preserved, and the monk Buddhaghosa, living in Anuradhapura, wrote extensive commentaries on the scriptures that continue to be the bedrock of Theravada doctrine (see below). Thereafter religious seekers from distant lands began flocking to study at the many monasteries dotting the island.

BUDDHAGHOSA, THE GREAT COMMENTATOR

One of the most influential figures in Theravada Buddhism, Buddhaghosa (in Pali, "Voice of Enlightenment") was born to a non-Buddhist family in northern India around the year 400 C.E. As a child of unusual intelligence and independence, he became attracted to the Dharma when he overheard others discussing it, and he did everything he could to learn more about it.

As soon as Buddhaghosa was old enough, he journeyed to Anuradhapura in Sri Lanka to further his studies at the great Buddhist library there. Legend has it that when he arrived, the monks in charge of the sacred texts first gave him a test to find out if he was educated enough to understand them. He immediately sat down and wrote the Visuddhimagga (in Pali, "Path of Purity"), a uniquely eloquent and detailed examination of the basic Theravada beliefs of his time. Right away, he was put to work translating other extant commentaries from Singhalese (the Sri Lankan dialect) into classical Pali, during which process he recorded his own reflections as well.

Buddhaghosa eventually earned the titles "the Great Commentator" and "the Great Translator," and to this day his interpretation of Theravada Buddhism by way both of translation and of his own original writings continues to be the orthodox one. Dr. John Renard, a professor of theological studies at St. Louis University, compares Buddhaghosa's authoritative role in Theravada Buddhism to Saint Augustine's in Roman Catholic Christianity, claiming, "Buddhaghosa set out to reflect on a wide range of religious issues 'in view of nirvana' as St. Augustine had 'in view of eternity.' "

Among other accomplishments, Buddhaghosa is credited with articulating the full value and potential of the practice known as *vipassana* (in Pali, "insight") meditation, through which one engages in focused contemplation of a certain Buddhist-related quality or issue and, in the process, trains the mind for enlightenment. He is also famous—or infamous—for recommending meditation on the corruption of the physical body to discourage any attachment to impermanent things. One of the best-known passages from his Visuddhimagga conveys the Buddhist belief in the nonexistence of any fixed entity called the self:

> Suffering exists, but not the sufferer.
> The deed is done, but there is no doer.
> Peace exists, but not one who is at peace.
> There is no walker, but there is a way.

By the sixth century, Theravada Buddhists of the Sri Lankan stripe could be found throughout Southeast Asia. Then came a period of decline for Theravada in Sri Lanka that can be attributed to the political, social, and economic hardships in neighboring India before and during the Mongol invasion of the eleventh century.

The postinvasion years, which ushered in a new era of stability and prosperity on the island, saw a great nationalistic revival of interest in Theravada. A dynamic new monastery arose at Plonnaruwa. Monks from this increasingly famous institution traveled to Myanmar and succeeded in converting King Anawrahta, who had only recently unified his nation. The king then sponsored the building of many more Theravada monastic communities throughout Myanmar and transformed his showplace capital, Pagan, into an elaborate complex of imposing Buddhist shrines that still attracts tourists.

In the thirteenth century, Sri Lankan missionaries instigated the conversion of Thailand's king, who also launched a massive, nationwide program of founding monasteries and erecting grand temples and stupas. Cambodia and Laos underwent similar transformations a century later.

European colonization in this region of the world began during the 1500s. Over the succeeding centuries until the mid-1900s, it dampened Theravada vitality wherever it held sway. Only Thailand managed to escape altogether. Its particularly devout Buddhist rulers, many of whom were monks in their youth (including King Mongkut of *The King and I* fame), wisely preferred simply to give up various perimeter territories rather than to risk engaging the whole country in brutal and almost certainly hopeless wars of resistance.

Despite the domineering presence of Christian Europeans in Southeast Asia during this lengthy period of time, Theravada did manage to persist quietly and gently among all classes of native people as a unifying source of equanimity, strength, and pride. Its monasteries remained steadfastly loyal to the codes originally developed in first- through fifth-century Anuradhapura, Sri Lanka, then and now dubbed the "Rome of Theravada" by westerners. Every so often, thanks to zealous patrons or the spirit of the times, it even pulsed with new life, resulting, for example, in the erection of many of the beautiful temples with distinctive gold-leafed spires that can be seen in Myanmar today, especially in the major cities of Mandalay (site of the Fifth Council in 1856) and Rangoon (site of the Sixth Council in 1954).

THE DAWN OF MAHAYANA

As Theravada was expanding throughout Southeast Asia during the middle of the first millennium, with Sri Lanka as its hub, Mahayana was spreading northward in two separate strains. One went through present-day Afghanistan, picked up the east-west trade routes entering Central Asia from the Mediterranean, and followed them into China, from where it journeyed on to Korea and Japan (and, in a southern dip, to Vietnam and Indonesia). The other strain, ultimately distinguished as Vajrayana, took the road less traveled and—although shorter—more difficult to negotiate: directly north through the Himalayan Mountains to Tibet.

In sum, Mahayana dispersed itself during the first millennium across almost one-sixth of the world's land mass to become the major religion among an estimated one-third of the world's population. That it could take hold in so many diverse cultures is a tribute to the great adaptability of Buddhism in general and Mahayana in particular. As it came in contact with each preexisting religious, ethical, or social system, it succeeded in changing form to accommodate the best of that system without losing its own essential character.

We'll trace each of the two northern strains of the Mahayana transmission in a moment. First, let's return to its early development in northern India during the first and second centuries C.E. so that we can deepen our understanding of some of the key differences between it and Theravada.

Contrary to what usually happens when a religion starts separating into different sects, Theravada and Mahayana coexisted fairly peacefully during this period—another testimony to the nonviolent, conciliatory nature of Buddhism. The same was true for the diverse schools within each vehicle. Heated debates did take place, irreconcilable differences did develop, and disparagements did get cast. The most glaring example of the latter was the name-calling mentioned earlier: When the more lay-oriented confederation of Buddhist schools first began referring to itself as Mahayana ("great vehicle"), it lumped together the other, more traditional schools—among which Theravada was the largest—under the somewhat demeaning label Hinayana ("little vehicle").

Nevertheless, all these factions stayed connected in working relationships, regarding each other basically as siblings in one larger, family-style sangha. The ever-widening split between the two and later three major vehicles (with the emergence of Vajrayana) is far more a by-product of history and geography than of internecine strife.

Given that the most significant difference between Theravada and Mahayana pivots around the concept of the bodhisattva, why did this particular distinction develop? How did Mahayana, the younger of the two vehicles, justify its reinterpretation? How did that new perspective come to be institutionalized, so effectively that it stayed common among the many Mahayana schools that arose throughout Eastern Asia, despite their myriad other dissimilarities?

As is the case with the vast majority of religious issues, these questions beg two kinds of answers: practical, common-language explanations and official, doctrinal ones. Let's begin with the former, which are closer in nature to the origins of the debate.

Essentially the Mahayana adherents sought to make Buddhism and its promise of liberation more accessible and meaningful to laypeople. This meant putting more emphasis on the compassionate elements of the Buddha's teachings rather than on self-discipline and spiritual refinement.

Some Mahayana leaders declared outright that traditional Buddhism—including the Theravada school—ran the danger of becoming too elitist, while Shakyamuni himself argued for a more democratic spiritual movement. Others were less confrontational. They simply wanted to translate into Buddhist terms some of the more compelling religious beliefs and practices that already existed among the people at large and helped them to feel a sense of spiritual kinship. The common ground among all the various Mahayana groups lay in giving Shakyamuni and other buddhas a more intimate, beneficial, and constant relationship to all of humankind.

It's important to bear in mind that the separation between Theravada and Mahayana began because of differing emphases within the same basic body of beliefs and not because of opposing belief systems. The Theravada Buddhists of the first through third centuries C.E. certainly didn't lack compassion, nor did they fail to exercise or teach it. Their Mahayana counterparts just argued for a religious structure that was more broadly organized around that particular quality.

In turn, defenders of Theravada during that period would often accuse the Mahayana school of watering down the purity of the Buddha's teachings. Some of these critics argued that the more liberal Mahayana perspective on theory and practice could distract individuals from their primary responsibility to free themselves from the endless cycle of life and death. According to Theravada, this personal liberation was the ultimate act of compassion because it helped to liberate all.

The Mahayana Buddhists, however, saw matters differently. They had trouble accepting the notion that Shakyamuni had simply disappeared from the world, leaving it devoid of buddha presence until the far-distant appearance of the next buddha. Instead, might not Shakyamuni have taken on—or returned to—a purer state of being that was still somehow connected to the life of here and now? They didn't imagine him as a god in the all-powerful, maker-breaker way that contemporary Hindus (or, unknown to most if not all of them, Christians and Jews) understood the concept. Nevertheless they did envision him as existing in some sort of beginningless, endless fashion, ever capable of inspiring humans on their path to self-liberation and maybe even of interceding on their behalf.

Eventually the Mahayana Buddhists revealed in scripture their belief that the Buddha persists throughout all time and space as a kind of absolute bodhisattva, still available to the relative world of here and now. Thus we come to the specific doctrinal explanation of how Shakyamuni Buddha—and other buddhas—can function perpetually as bodhisattvas. It's called the Three Body (Trikaya) doctrine.

Although the Three Body doctrine evolved differently in each major Mahayana school, the core idea can be summarized as follows. Mahayana deems Shakyamuni Buddha and historical buddhas in other eras to be "form" bodies *(nirmanakaya)*, which are manifestations in particular human lives of an eternal principle called the "truth" or "essence" body *(dharmakaya)*. A third dimension of buddhahood consists of "bliss" bodies *(sambhogakaya)*, or what we might call archetypes. These buddhas represent qualities of the dharmakaya that can be accessed as living, inspiring images through meditation and devotion, or that can be given life through a human being's own buddha- and bodhisattva-like thoughts, words, and deeds.

THE BURNING HOUSE

The Lotus Sutra, an important Mahayana scripture reputed to contain Shakyamuni's final teaching, states that salvation is available to everyone. It also discusses the Buddha's adoption of *upaya*, "skillful means" or best-possible provisional strategies, to inspire people to seek salvation. By implication, Buddhism as a whole, its various schools and practices, and even certain helpful activities of individual Buddhists can be interpreted as skillful means toward the end of saving people from a world of suffering.

This concept is dramatically illustrated in the Lotus Sutra by the story of the burning house. The owner of an old house returns to find it aflame. He can hear his children playing inside, oblivious to the danger. At first he screams at them to flee the house, but they ignore his cries, not seeing any fire themselves and preferring to keep on playing. Then he tries something else: He calls out to them joyfully that he's brought special carts for them to play with—a different type of cart for each child. Excited by the prospect of these wonderful, one-of-a-kind toys, the children all run outside and thereby save themselves: a much greater gift than they had expected.

An especially well-known sambhogakaya, or archetypal buddha, is the bodhisattva of compassion, Avalokiteshvara (in China, Kuan-yin; in Japan, Kannon). Buddhist practitioners can envision her (or in some schools him) as a symbolic being who connects them more vitally with the essence of loving-kindness. Alternatively, the practitioners themselves can think, speak, or act as Avalokiteshvara in extending selfless assistance to others. They can even encounter Avalokiteshvara in the form of another human being who is especially compassionate to them.

Mahayana often refers to a buddha's or bodhisattva's wise and compassionate use of "skillful means" (in Sanskrit, *upaya*) to help others become enlightened and liberated (see, for example, "The Burning House" on page 52). By implication, all Mahayana Buddhists are encouraged to adopt skillful means to assist themselves and others in realizing the Dharma. Sometimes this practice requires being very straightforward and cutting to the essence of the matter. Other times, it involves a more indirect, creative approach.

Like many formalized concepts or practices in Mahayana, the Three Body doctrine is designed to function as a skillful means of communicating and understanding how buddha nature pervades the universe. The three bodies are not meant to represent a hierarchy, although it's possible to view them that way. Instead, they're intended to reflect three different perspectives on the same essential phenomenon:

- *dharmakaya* (truth or essence body) as the absolute truth or buddha nature;

- *sambhogakaya* (bliss body) as the symbolization of a particular buddha-nature quality (often characterized as a buddha or bodhisattva dwelling in a "buddha paradise"); and

- *nirmanakaya* (form body) as the flesh-and-blood manifestation of buddha nature.

Along with the Three Body doctrine comes the notion that every sentient being has buddha nature, which is not to be considered a separate self or a unique soul, but instead an identity with all other sentient beings as well as with the absolute. Enlightenment thereby entails literally realizing this buddha nature: not just intellectually understanding it or intuitively feeling it, but actually experiencing it with one's whole body and mind.

We'll take a closer look at these beliefs in chapter 3. To gain a better understanding of the different religious contexts in which they present themselves today, let's first track the spread of Mahayana through Eastern Asia and, in the format labeled Vajrayana, through Tibet.

MAHAYANA'S GROWTH IN EASTERN ASIA

While Shakyamuni was dispersing his new message of enlightenment across northern India (late sixth century through early fifth century B.C.E.), the separate teachings of Lao Tse and Confucius were starting to percolate through Chinese life. Almost five hundred years passed before Buddhism began to do the same thing in China, primarily in the format called Mahayana.

By that time—approximately the first century C.E.—Taoism (Lao Tse's philosophy) and Confucianism were well established in China. As Mahayana engaged with them, it quickly and easily incorporated many of their most significant features, translating itself into a spirituality better suited to the needs and temperament of the Chinese people. At the same time, it managed to preserve its own core teachings, thereby proving them all the more universally relevant.

Taoism, as taught by Lao Tse in the Tao-te-Ching ("Book of the Way"), posits the existence of a great Way (Tao) which is featureless in itself but nevertheless constitutes the absolute, natural source of all things. Inferred from Lao Tse's numerous naturalistic stories and verses communicating essential truths about life, the Way also functions as a guiding principle for one's thoughts, speech, and behavior: Being true to the Way constitutes being in harmony with reality.

Mahayana schools developing in China took up this wonderfully simplifying concept on their own terms. Typically they placed even greater emphasis on analogous Buddhist notions of the Dharma, the Middle Way, and nirvana ("emptiness" or "nothingness"), and added Taoist resonances to each of them. They also generated new teaching tales, devices, and images that reflected the earthier character of their Taoist counterparts.

As opposed to Taoism, Confucianism was then—and remains—a philosophical system much more engrained into all aspects of Chinese culture. Confucius first articulated his conservative, commonsense guidelines for living in a series of books that includes the famous I Ching ("Book of Changes"). Over the next few centuries these guidelines worked themselves into every Chinese social, political, ethical, and educational code.

The human qualities promoted by Confucianism include high moral standards, benevolence to all, a love of rationality, and a veneration for tradition, which in part involves honoring one's ancestors. From intermingling with this philosophical system, Mahayana schools tended to develop more points of connection to everyday life—both inside and outside a monastic setting—as well as greater regard for their own customs and teacher lineages.

One important Mahayana sect that grew up in China between 400 and 500 C.E. and survives to this day is the Pure Land school. It elaborates the sambhogakaya dimension of the Three Body doctrine to include an infinite number of buddha fields, the most desirable of which is the western paradise called Sukhavati (Pure Land) presided over by Amitabha, the buddha of limitless radiance.

Pure Land Buddhists believe they will go to this paradisal form of nirvana after their death, to live as bodhisattvas, if they have faith in what Amitabha represents and pay proper homage to him during their time on earth. Among other, more standard Buddhist practices, this means meditating on him and chanting the mantra (power phrase) *nan-mo-A-mi-t'o* ("Glory to Amitabha"). Pure Land Buddhists also venerate Kuan-yin (or Avalokiteshvara, the bodhisattva of compassion), whom they consider either an emanation of, or a companion to, Amitabha.

Building on the need among many Chinese people for a more de-

FROM *THE WHITE LOTUS ODE*

This is an ancient Pure Land invocation attributed to the Chinese teacher Hui Yuan.

What words can picture the beauty and breadth
    Of that pure and glistening land?
That land where the blossoms ne'er wither from age,
    Where the golden gates gleam like purest water . . .
The land where there are none but fragrant bowers,
    Where the Utpala lotus unfolds itself freely . . .
And the ages fly by in an endless chain,
    Never broken by summer's or winter's change.
The burning sun can never more frighten.
    The icy storms' power long ago is subdued.
The clouds full of light and the green mantled forests
    Now cradle all things in their endless peace.
Now the soul is set free from the haunts of darkness
    And rests secure in the dwelling of truth.
See, all that was dim and beclouded on Earth
    Here is revealed, appropriated, accrued.
There ne'er was a country so brightened with gladness
    As the Land of the Pure there far off to the West.
There stands Amitabha with shining adornments,
    He makes all things ready for the Eternal Feast . . .

Adapted from E. J. Thomas, ed., *Buddhist Scriptures.*

votional form of spirituality, Pure Land Buddhism offered them something on a personal level that was similar to the consoling and self-transcending rituals they were accustomed to perform for their heaven-dwelling ancestors. It became particularly popular among those who found Taoism too abstract, Confucianism too sterile, and other forms of Buddhism too complicated or demanding.

Ever since, in all its permutations in different cultures, the strength of Pure Land has been its luminous focus on the hope for salvation. The dazzling, cosmic image of nirvana as a Pure Land where one can go immediately after death inspires people to free themselves from delusive attachment to this contrasting world of impermanence and suffering called *samsara,* with its endless cycle of literal and figurative births and deaths (see "The Burning House" on page 52). The compelling manner in which Pure Land presents this hope has given millions of individuals a means of engaging more emotionally, mentally, and physically with Buddhist teachings than they otherwise might have.

Another major sect of Chinese Buddhism that began in the middle of the first millennium and still exists today is the Ch'an school (from the Sanskrit word *dhyana,* meaning meditation; in Japanese, *zen*). As the name indicates, meditation is its core, all-important practice.

In stark contrast to Pure Land Buddhism, Ch'an began as a movement to strip Buddhism down to the basics, eschewing dependence on rituals and even scriptures to concentrate instead, like Shakyamuni himself, on disciplining the mind and opening it up to enlightenment. At its core, Ch'an is very close in spirit to Taoism, which likewise stresses a natural, introspective approach to realization, as well as the value of personal experience over external doctrine. Unlike many other Buddhist schools, especially Theravada ones, it teaches that enlightenment can come in a flash, either during meditation or, if the mind has been properly prepared for it, at any other moment of the day that strikes just the right chord.

Ch'an is said to have begun in China around 520 C.E., when a legendary monk known as Bodhidharma (in Japanese, Bodaidaruma or Daruma) arrived there from India. In his brief attempt to teach at the imperial court of southern China, he alienated Emperor Wu on several counts. Among other things, he told Wu that his lavish patronage of Buddhist temples had accumulated no merit toward earning him a better life in the future. He thereby expressed, without directly stating, a rejection of the merit system prevalent among Buddhist schools already established in China. Also, when Wu asked Bodhidharma about the nature of the most sacred truth, he replied, "Vast emptiness, nothing sacred," an early indicator of Ch'an's refusal to discriminate between form and emptiness or the sacred and the non-sacred.

Failing to make a favorable impression in southern China, a defiant Bodhidharma retreated to a monastery in northern China. There he sat in meditation, his face to the wall, for nine years straight—allegedly even ripping off his eyelids to avoid accidentally falling asleep. Already a stern, almost wild-looking man, his bulging eyes gave him an even fiercer demeanor, one that has been rendered again and again by Ch'an and later Zen artists as a symbol of the serious commitment and effort that the school's practice requires. He refused to resume teaching until a determined would-be student, Hui-k'o, after keeping vigil for weeks in the deep snow outside the monastery gate, cut off his own right arm to demonstrate his sincerity.

Thus began a lineage of Ch'an (and later Zen) teachers dubbed patriarchs, in symbolic accordance with the Confucian reverence for family ancestors: Bodhidharma being the first Chinese patriarch, and Hui-k'o, the second. Together with their Indian predecessors, these patriarchs serve as a lifeline tracing the transmission of the Dharma from person to person, or, more to the point, mind to mind, down through the centuries since Shakyamuni—a vivid reflection of Ch'an's emphasis on the ageless wisdom of human experience.

Mahayana Buddhism started infiltrating Korea from China around 380 C.E. Over the next few hundred years, all forms of Chinese Buddhism, including Pure Land and Ch'an (in Korean, Son), took root there. During the sixth and seventh centuries various other, older schools of Mahayana spread farther east to the Japanese islands, first from Korea and later from China. Once in Japan, they slowly but surely supplanted the native, shamanistic spirituality called Shinto, the way of the *kami* (gods). Shinto never disappeared altogether, however, and it returned to prominence during the nationalistic era of the late nine-teenth and early twentieth centuries.

Pure Land Buddhism arrived on Japanese shores in a very basic form early in the ninth century. However, it didn't become a significant presence there until the end of the twelfth century, when the monk Honen instituted the ritual of *nembutsu* ("naming buddha"), which en-tails extended chanting of the phrase *namu-Amida-Butsu* ("Glory to Amida Butsu"). His pupil Shinran further popularized Pure Land by introducing devotions to Kannon, the bodhisattva of compassion (in Sanskrit, Avalokiteshvara; in Chinese, Kuan-yin), and to the historical buddha of the future, Miroku (in Sanskrit, Maitreya). These core prac-tices continue in the schools known today as Jodo-shu (Pure Land) and Jodo-shin-shu (True Pure Land, a reformed sect).

A related school arose in Japan during roughly the same period and is now enjoying a renewal of interest both in Japan and America. It was founded by the Buddhist monk Nichiren and ultimately took his name. For years this exceptionally earnest and outspoken man devoted himself entirely to studying the Lotus Sutra, one of the principal Ma-hayana texts. He became convinced that it was not only the supreme expression of Buddhist truth but also a highly magical and even prophetic work, forecasting, for example, that the Mongols would in-vade Japan (which eventually they did).

Nichiren argued so vociferously in public on behalf of the Lotus Sutra that he was jailed and later exiled to the island of Sado, where he began envisioning himself as Jogyo (in Sanskrit, Visishtacarita), the bodhisattva of great action cited in the sutra. The cornerstone of the school he eventually inaugurated is the practice of repeating *namu-myoho-renge-kyo* ("Glory to the Lotus Sutra") as a significant aid toward achieving buddhahood.

Ch'an (in Japanese, Zen) was first imported into Japan about the same time as the monk Honen was refining Pure Land Buddhism— the latter half of the twelfth century. It was the beginning of the Ka-makura shogunate period in Japanese history, when the samurai or warrior class of society held political power. The martial spirit of the samurai (evident, for example, in the self-disciplining code of *bushido*) responded very favorably to the rigor, simplicity, and intense mindful-

ZEN MASTER DOGEN

Born in 1200, Dogen, the founder of the Soto school of Zen in Japan and a towering presence in the history of Buddhism, was eight years old when his mother died. At the funeral, he watched a stick of incense burning down and was suddenly overwhelmed by a sense of the impermanence of life, so much so that he later traced his whole career in the Dharma to this one incident. He went on to become a monk in the Tendai school (a form of Pure Land Buddhism) but at age fourteen transferred to the Rinzai school.

In 1223 Dogen traveled to China to study Ch'an. The experience revolutionized his understanding of the Dharma. One story he afterward told against himself to illustrate what he learned involved an encounter with a Chinese monk who was a cook. When this monk came to Dogen's boat to buy Japanese mushrooms, Dogen pleaded with him to stay and talk about Buddhism. The monk declined, saying, "I'm sorry, but I must return to the monastery and make the meal. Cooking is what I do. It takes up most of my day."

"Why work so hard at being a cook? Wouldn't it be better to meditate and study koans?" asked Dogen.

The monk just laughed. "Good sir," he said, "you seem ignorant of the true meaning of Ch'an."

Dogen confessed that he didn't know what the cook meant at the time, but he eventually understood: Cha'an practice was about applying one's whole body and mind to every activity in life, even the most humble kinds. To do this was the act of an enlightened mind. The same was true of doing *zazen,* a simple, unritualized form of pure meditation that Dogen called "completely natural."

In 1227 Dogen returned to Japan and began teaching Soto Zen, centered around the core practice of zazen rather than koan study. Eventually he developed a monastery in Echizen province that came to be called Eihei-ji. His brilliance, creativity, forcefulness, and integrity in establishing the Soto school and reforming Japanese Buddhist monasticism have given the Buddhist tradition in particular and religious history in general a rich legacy of inspirational and instructional teaching tales. The school he founded remains vigorous, and Eihei-ji continues to rank among the most prominent Buddhist monasteries in Japan.

Despite Dogen's relatively brief life (he died in 1253), his legacy also includes a large body of writings. His principal work, the Shobogenzo (in Japanese, "Treasure Chamber of the Eye of the True Dharma"), a compilation of his major discourses, is widely regarded as a masterpiece of Zen thought and religious literature. In it, he speaks of the value of zazen as follows:

"Multitudes of students have practiced zazen and obtained its fruits. Do not doubt its promise because it is simple. If you cannot find the Dharma where you are, where else can you hope to find it?"

ness of this form of Mahayana and helped it to saturate virtually every aspect of Japanese culture within the next two centuries.

The first branch of Ch'an or Zen to enter Japan was brought back from China by the Japanese monk Eisai. It was (and is) called Lin-chi in Chinese, and in Japanese, Rinzai. It supplements meditation—in Japanese, *zazen* or sitting meditation—with the contemplation of riddle-like questions or stories called koans (perhaps the best-known example being, "What is the sound of one hand clapping?"). The effort to resolve these koans deliberately confounds everyday logic in order to activate a more fundamental, intuitive mode of understanding. This

mental shift is deemed essential because only that form of consciousness can awaken to full knowledge of one's buddha nature or, in other
words, can experience enlightenment.

In 1228 Eisai's student Dogen, considered by many to be the paramount master in the history of Zen, transplanted from China the second major branch of Ch'an, called Ts'ao-tung in Chinese or, in
Japanese, Soto (see page 60). Concentrating even more on zazen meditation and only occasionally using koans, the Soto branch teaches that
zazen is not only a means to enlightenment but also, simultaneously,
the act of enlightenment itself. After all, zazen in itself is the raising of
the *bodhi* (awakened) mind. In addition, Soto disciples train themselves
to carry over that same clear mental focus to every task they perform,
no matter how trivial. It's a way of extending the bodhi mind into all
aspects of one's existence.

Today the Soto school in Japan is about three times larger than the
Rinzai school. Zen in general (the two schools combined) is the sec-
ond most prevalent form of Japanese Buddhism after Pure Land (the
Jodo-shu and Jodo-shin-shu schools combined).

From the eighth through the thirteenth centuries, Mahayana also
spread into Southeast Asia, thanks to Chinese missionaries. In two particular areas—the present-day countries of Indonesia and Vietnam—it
evolved into the major religion.

Indonesia was the first nation to embrace Mahayana wholeheartedly, especially its more mystical or magical dimension, which ultimately came to be distinguished as Vajrayana. Some of Buddhism's
most spectacular monuments were constructed on the island of Java
during the ninth century, including the enormous Borobudor complex: a virtual mountain of interconnected stone terraces symbolizing,
mandala-style, ascending spiritual realms, with dozens of stupas and
hundreds of sculptures adorning each terrace.

The Mongol invasions of the thirteenth and fourteenth centuries put
an end to Mahayana in Indonesia, but during the same time span it
flourished in Vietnam, mainly in the more down-to-earth forms of Pure
Land and Ch'an. It remains the dominant religion in that country.

VAJRAYANA IN TIBET

Tantra, or ritualized magic, exists to varying degrees in all forms of Buddhism, partly as a carryover from preceding religions in India (most notably Hinduism) and partly as a mystical extension of its own basic vision of the universe. However, when Mahayana infiltrated Tibet and mingled with the native shamanic religion called Bon, its tantric elements took on far more meaning and importance. The eventual result was a form of Buddhism so distinct that it became a separate, third vehicle.

On the surface, one glimpses in this vehicle a multitude of engaging personal and communal rituals for transforming one's consciousness, entering into the Buddhist universe, and communing with buddha and bodhisattva presences. They include such ancient mystical practices as creating mandalas (circular cosmograms) in sand or paint, chanting mantras, dancing ecstatically, playing musical instruments, doing great numbers of prostrations, and visualizing while meditating. Below this colorful surface lies a uniquely profound belief in the ongoing presence and accessibility of enlightened beings.

This third vehicle is most commonly called Vajrayana, but it's also known to Tibetan Buddhists as Mantrayana. In addition, they sometimes refer to it as the apocalyptic vehicle, in contrast to the monastic or individual vehicle (Theravada) and the universal or messianic vehicle (Mahayana). The designation "apocalyptic" reflects the vehicle's sense of the immediacy with which one can access buddha reality and, if so prepared, attain enlightenment.

Robert Thurman, Jey Tsong Khapa Professor of Indo-Tibetan Studies at Columbia University, describes how this perception relates to the Tibetan concept of buddhahood in his book *Essential Tibetan Buddhism*:

For the Tibetans, Shakyamuni Buddha, the foremost Buddha of this world-epoch, is not just a dead hero. He is not just an object of belief, a divine being encounterable in another dimension or an altered

state. He is a being believed to have conquered death, just as Jesus
Christ is. But Tibetans are not awaiting Buddha's triumphal return;
they feel He is right now utterly available to them, that in a real sense
He never left them when He withdrew the Ideal Emanation Body
known as Shakyamuni. . . . They find the truth of this teaching in
the presence and deeds of the many people they consider living
Buddhas. (3)

The catalytic cultural process that created Tibetan or Vajrayana
Buddhism began in the mid-seventh century, when Tibet was expanding into present-day China and becoming one of the major
powers in Asia. Greater interaction with its neighbors on all sides
brought more exposure to Mahayana, and one Tibetan king, Songzen
Gambo, became particularly impressed with the religion's ability to
unite so many different kinds of people in peaceful, industrious harmony. According to legend two of his wives, one from Nepal and the
other from China, finally convinced him to embrace Mahayana and
support its spread in Tibet.

So began the translation of the complete Mahayana canon from
Sanskrit into Tibetan, an amazing feat of scholarship that almost single-
handedly transformed Tibetan from a spoken language into a written
one. It's small wonder that the written word and even the written syllable have had an extraordinarily deep spiritual and magical significance for Tibetan Buddhists ever since, and that Tibetan literature has
evolved to be almost entirely sacred in nature.

From the sixth century on, Buddhism gradually became the Tibetan
way of life. No other country in history has absorbed this religion so
thoroughly and, in turn, invested it with so much native character or so
much cultural power. As Vajrayana grew increasingly influential in
Tibet, so did the monastery as the focus of daily life, a position it re-
tained until the mid-twentieth century.

The only similar situation in Western civilization occurred in Europe during the Middle Ages, when Christian monasteries in most
areas served not only as spiritual hubs but also as primary sources of

education, health care, social welfare, and public entertainment. The difference in Tibet was the lack of strong, counterbalancing centers of power equivalent to the royal courts and trade guilds in Europe. Over time, the Tibetan monasteries assumed complete political control of the country, giving Tibet a singularly sacred form of government for centuries.

The key figure in Vajrayana—and, therefore, in Tibetan culture—is the lama (or teacher; in Sanskrit, *guru*). The preeminence of this individual, considered a living buddha, led early Western observers to dub the religion Lamanism, a term that is now deemed misleading if not pejorative. As Vajrayana developed in Tibet, so did various lineages of lamas. The Nyingma school is the oldest, dating from the ninth century and tracing its teachings two hundred years further back to the revered Padmasambhava, one of the historical founders of Tibetan Buddhism.

Born in the present-day region of Kashmir, Padmasambhava journeyed to Tibet as a Buddhist monk, intent upon transmitting the Dharma there. The rest of his story is part fact and part myth, much of it laid out in a poetically elegant biography composed by one of his female students, Yeshe Tsogyel. By all accounts a person of great charm and energy, Padmasambhava is credited with introducing many of Tibetan Buddhism's core teachings, along with the specialized meditative discipline called *dzogchen* ("great perfection"), through which the mind can directly experience primordial emptiness and clarity.

Padmasambhava is also said to have magically tamed the savage nature demons throughout Tibet (no doubt an allusion to the preexisting Bon deities) and to have buried many advanced teachings in various secret places for future discovery. These concealed texts can be interpreted either literally as books or figuratively as concepts. Similarly, the discovery process can be viewed either as a literal excavation in a remote location or as a figurative revelation in the mind of a teacher. For that matter, the entire incident can be taken to symbolize a planting of the seeds for Buddhism's future growth in Tibet. To this day, Padamasambhava is venerated by many Tibetan Buddhists

MILAREPA: "THE COTTON-CLAD"

In Tibetan, the name Milarepa (pronounced mil-ah-RAS-pa) means "Mila the cloth-clad," referring to the thin, ascetic robe he usually wore. He was believed to have the special power of "internal heat" which enabled him to stay warm even during the fiercely cold winters of Tibet. He did not, however, derive this power from Buddhism but from his prior career as a sorcerer.

Milarepa's exotic biography begins with his birth in 1040 to a fabulously wealthy family in western Tibet, near Nepal. When he was seven years old, his father died, and wicked relatives seized all his father's assets. To avenge the robbery, Milarepa learned black magic and conjured a storm that killed thirty-five of his relatives. Guilt over this act led him to the Buddhist teacher Marpa, who subjected him to horrendous ordeals so that he could spiritually purify himself. When Milarepa reached the point of almost killing himself, Marpa transmitted to him the teachings of Naropa, his own master.

Milarepa then went into seclusion and emerged years later as an adept with his own, distinctive, freewheeling style of teaching and demonstrating the Dharma. In addition to a deeper understanding of the doctrines he learned from Marpa, he'd developed yet more wondrous secret powers. He allegedly used them in competition against a priest of the shamanic Bon religion of Tibet in order to gain possession of Mount Kailas, the most sacred mountain in western Tibet, for Buddhism.

Milarepa also had an earthier approach to serving the causes of Buddhism. As he was dying, his student Gompopa begged him for some final teachings. Milarepa countered, "What is required is more effort, not more instructions." Gompopa, clearly disappointed, bid farewell and turned away. Milarepa, taking pity on his student, called after him, "Wait, there is one profound secret that I will share with only you." Gompopa looked back eagerly, at which point Milarepa turned around, pulled up his cotton robe, and pointed to the huge calluses all over his buttocks, the product of years of sitting in meditation. "My beloved disciple," he said with a smile, "this is my final teaching."

Throughout his teaching career, Milarepa wrote songs to convey his messages, and they survive as some of the most lyrical and insightful texts in Vajrayana. He also put in writing many of his guidelines to students. In one of them, he conveys more professorially his belief that effort takes precedence over instruction: "Even a desire for more instruction is a distraction. Too many explanations without the essence is like an orchard of trees without fruit. Knowing many explanations is not knowing the Truth. Too much conceptualization has no spiritual benefit. Only the secret treasure benefits the heart. If you want riches, concentrate on this."

as Guru Rinpoche, "precious guru," and by members of his own lineage as the Second Buddha, still alive in a paradise called Glory Mountain.

The next important surviving lineages to be founded were the Sakya and Kagyu schools in the eleventh century. The latter school claims three famous masters among its early creators: Naropa, a renowned teacher at the Indian university of Nalanda; his student Marpa, hailed as "the Translator" for the many significant texts he imported into Tibet; and Marpa's disciple, Milarepa, perhaps the most celebrated "saint" of Tibet (see page 66).

In the late fourteenth century, the Geluk lineage was established to purify Tibetan Buddhism by revitalizing its ethical standards and reemphasizing its original doctrines. Mongol patrons of this lineage declared its third head to be an incarnation of the bodhisattva

Avalokiteshvara and gave him the title Dalai Lama ("Ocean [or Great] Teacher"). It was the beginning of a succession of Dalai Lamas, each another incarnation of Avalokiteshvara, who ultimately became the most powerful political as well as spiritual leaders in Tibet.

Unfortunately, the present Dalai Lama, the fourteenth in his line, rules in exile. During the early 1950s, Chinese forces invaded Tibet on a massive scale. Intent on eradicating Buddhism in favor of communism, they destroyed hundreds of Buddhist temples and monasteries, slaughtered monks and nuns along with thousands of other Tibetan natives, and forced the teenage Dalai Lama to flee secretly from his palace in the capital of Lhasa across the mountainous Indian border to Dharmsala. This tiny Indian town now serves as the base of the Dalai Lama's worldwide teaching mission. We'll resume this remarkable story later in the book.

QUESTIONS AND ANSWERS

Which vehicle of Buddhism is the most authentic one, in the sense that it comes closest to representing what the Buddha himself taught?
It may initially seem logical to assume that Theravada, historically the oldest vehicle, would best reflect the spiritual teachings and practices that Shakyamuni Buddha espoused. Although the Theravada school itself wasn't formally established until around 244 B.C.E., during King Ashoka's reign, it considers itself the conservative standard-bearer of the official sangha formed by the First Council almost two centuries earlier, just after Shakyamuni's death. It's also responsible for producing the earliest written body of sacred teachings, the Pali Canon, which purportedly records the words of the Buddha himself C.E. as transmitted orally for more than four centuries.

These factors support Theravada's assertion that it is the most genuine form of Buddhism. The other two vehicles, however, have similarly strong reasons to make this claim, based on different criteria.

Mahayana began during the first and second centuries C.E. as a movement within the larger sangha, which included Theravada and many other schools, to restore Buddhism to its original character and vitality. Specifically, Mahayana sought to reform Buddhism by modeling it more closely on Shakyamuni's own career and on the essential elements of his message. Among other things, this meant giving laypeople greater access to the Dharma, putting more emphasis on social virtues like compassion, and investing Buddhist doctrine and liturgy with more of the mystical and intuitive elements that helped shape the Buddha's own path toward enlightenment. Thus Mahayana followers contend that their vehicle not only conveys the Buddha's teachings more accurately but also reflects more vividly the multifaceted spirituality that he himself experienced and inspired.

Vajrayana, which arose out of Mahayana during the middle of the first millennium, was the last vehicle to establish itself, but this very fact helps support its contention that it is the most authentic one. Along with other names already mentioned, Vajrayana is called the "completion vehicle" because it represents to its believers the final, full flowering of Shakyamuni's teachings. Theravada, according to this theory, reflects Buddhism's first, individualistic or monastic stage of growth as a religion. The next evolutionary stage is manifested in Mahayana, the universal or messianic vehicle. Vajrayana, the apocalyptic stage, combines features of both Theravada and the Mahayana and then extends them to a magical new level, so that each individual has even greater opportunity and power to become one with the universe, and so that the universe itself is perceived as one entity—in a sense, a cosmic individual or monastery.

There are additional reasons why Vajrayana claims to be the most authentic vehicle. While the Pali Canon of Theravada is the *first* known collection of Buddhist writings, the seventh- and eighth-century Tibetan translations of Mahayana's Sanskrit scriptures form the *most extensive* library of early Buddhist literature. In addition, they constitute the oldest surviving body of Mahayana scriptures, meaning that Mahayana practitioners in later centuries have had to translate this Tibetan material back into Sanskrit—or into their own native language, such as

Chinese or Japanese—to obtain the most authentic version of their own scriptures. To date, much of this material still awaits its first translation from Tibetan.

Above all, Vajrayana can invoke the argument of historical preservation. For twelve centuries after Buddhism first took hold in Tibet, this remote, mountain-ringed country stayed fairly isolated from the outside world, especially compared to the home countries of Mahayana and Theravada in East and Southeast Asia. As a result, Vajrayana was kept free from the influence of outside religions and philosophies, not to mention outside political, social, economic, and technological develop-

SHANTIDEVA'S VOW

This passage, beautifully expressing the compassionate nature of a bodhisattva, is extracted from the Bodhicharyavatara, a major teaching text in Tibetan Buddhism. It was composed by Shantideva, a Mahayana monk and scholar at Nalanda University in India who lived sometime during the last half of the seventh century and the first half of the eighth.

May I be a balm to the sick, their healer and servitor until
    sickness comes never again;
May I quench with rains of food and drink the anguish of hunger
    and thirst;
May I be in the famine of the age's end their drink and meat;
May I become an unfailing store for the poor, and serve them with
    manifold things for their need.
My own being and my pleasures, all my righteousness in the past,
    present, and future, I surrender indifferently,
That all creatures may win through to their end.

Adapted from Max Muller, ed., *The Sacred Books of the East.*

ments. It can therefore legitimately assert that its style of Buddhism has undergone the least change or contamination over the past millennium.

How does the Mahayana and Vajrayana concept of the Buddha as a bodhisattva compare to the Christian concept of the Christ as a savior?
In certain very broad respects, the two figures are comparable. For example, both Shakyamuni Buddha and Jesus Christ can be considered enlightened individuals who taught people how to lead better lives, who somehow transcended or conquered death, and who continue to exist as eternal forces, available to help human beings follow their teachings.

There are, however, critical differences between them. One pertains to the very nature of their being. Christianity is based on belief in a divinity, God, who was manifested on Earth in the person of Jesus. Buddhism is based on acceptance of the teachings of a human being, Shakyamuni, who realized that he—like all human beings—had an identity far beyond the personal self that is born and dies.

Within the religion of Buddhism, especially in the Mahayana school, this identity is symbolized in part by images of Shakyamuni (as well as other enlightened beings) that can be interpreted as godlike. The goal of Buddhism, however, is enlightenment and release of the self from a life of suffering, not union or relationship with a divinity. The eternal buddhas and bodhisattvas exist solely to help in the enlightenment process.

When the current Dalai Lama was recently asked how Buddhism might explain the notion of an absolute principle like God manifesting in a human form like the Christ, he replied, "In the Buddhist context, this question would be regarded in terms of what is known as the doctrine of three kayas, the three embodiments of an enlightened being. Within this framework, the physical, historical manifestations of enlightened beings are seen, in some sense, as spontaneous emergences from the timeless, ultimate state of the dharmakaya, or Truth Body of a Buddha."

He added, however, that the Three Body doctrine is not any sort of absolute truth, but, rather, a skillful means of pointing to it: "Given that there is such a diversity even among the Buddhist traditions, we should not have the impression that there is one homogenous tradition, one definitive path as it were. Personally, I prefer to relate to Buddha as a historical figure and personality—someone who has perfected human nature and evolved into a fully enlightened human being" (Gyatso, *The Good Heart,* 60–61).

Additional points of distinction between Shakyamuni Buddha and Jesus Christ relate to other doctrinal matters. For example, in Christianity, one is saved from damnation—from paying the price of one's original sin—through the Christ's redemption. In a Buddhist context, salvation lies in freeing oneself from suffering by practicing the Buddha's teachings. Inherently, human beings are all perfect. They simply don't realize their perfection. Individual actions can have harmful effects, but there's no concept in Buddhism analogous to the Christian one of original sin. In addition, Buddhism doesn't involve any belief in a soul, while Christianity maintains that the soul is precisely the entity in need of salvation. Chapter 3 offers more discussion on Buddhist beliefs relating to suffering, self, karma (the law of cause and effect), and the absence of soul.

How can simple activities like chanting "Glory to Amitabha" (Pure Land Buddhism) or "Glory to the Lotus Sutra" (Nichiren Buddhism) help lead to enlightenment?
In any concise summary or limited understanding of a religious tradition, certain isolated activities are bound to seem strange to people who have not witnessed or practiced them in their proper context. For example, people who are not Roman or Anglican Catholic Christians often have difficulty imagining how the chanting of the "Hail Mary" could have any spiritual benefit at all, much less one that's different from other, more easily understood rituals like silent prayer. It's vital to remember that such practices do not exist in a vacuum: There's a larger structure around them that gives them far more resonance and power than outsiders can fully appreciate.

Both of these two Buddhist chants are by no means the only practices involved in their respective schools. They do, however, represent a skillful means of conditioning or, literally, "tuning" the mind to be more open, less chatty, and less caught up in its own linear, rational patterns of processing data.

Most schools of Buddhism, even those with very intricate or exotic-seeming outer trappings, fundamentally rely on a few very simple practices (for example, *zazen*—or sitting meditation—in Zen) because they provide good, clear points of focus. If one can become totally engaged in such a practice, one can sense what it is to have the self drop away, and that's the opening to enlightenment. The process may sound simple, but that doesn't mean it's easy. Chapter 4 offers more discussion on chanting, zazen, and other Buddhist practices.

3 The Path to Enlightenment: Buddhist Beliefs

We are what we think.
All that we are arises with our thoughts.
With our thoughts we make the world.
—the Buddha

What is a Buddhist? What officially defines or qualifies someone as a believer in Buddhism? When authorities estimate the number of Buddhists in the world, what criteria do they use?

If we apply these questions to other major religions, they're much easier to answer. Both Christianity and Judaism have specific rites (like confirmation or bar/bat mitzvah, respectively) and sacraments (like marriage) that initiate, acknowledge, or publicize a person's inclusion in the fold. Christians and Jews are also likely to be enrolled in a specific congregation of believers, which makes them individually more visible and countable.

Muslims don't declare themselves with the same variety of rites or sacraments, but they make up for it

with clarity and conciseness. All it takes to embrace Islam is to say, "There is no god but Allah, and Muhammad is his prophet." The fact that Muslims typically join a mosque also renders them easier to tally.

Aside from monks, nuns, and recently some Western laypeople who take vows, Buddhists are much more difficult to identify, which explains the widely varying estimates of their numbers in the world today (as mentioned in the introduction, anywhere from 200 to 600 million). Like their Hindu counterparts, most lay Buddhists do not engage in any act or ceremony that officially designates their religious orientation, nor do they practice any fixed pattern of observance that is equivalent, for example, to honoring the Sabbath or bowing at prescribed times to Mecca. Most are not formally affiliated with a specific temple or monastery, although they may regularly attend or support one.

Even the words *Buddhist* and *Buddhism* don't really exist outside a Western context. The same is true for *Hindu* and *Hinduism*. The latter two terms were created long ago by people living west of the Indus River, who mispronounced its name "Hindus" and applied that term both to the Indus-area inhabitants and to their religion. In fact, so-called Hindus refer to their own faith as the *sanatana-dharma,* "eternal truth," and to themselves simply as followers of the sanatana-dharma. In like manner, Buddhists outside the West call their faith the *buddha-dharma,* "truth of the enlightened being," and themselves, followers of the buddha-dharma.

Thus most Buddhists can only be described as individuals who believe in the Buddha's teachings—a self-definition that defies easy outside classification. Hopefully they practice the teachings as well (a subject discussed in chapter 4), but the essential element is believing in them, because, as Shakyamuni says in the Dhammapada, "We are what we think."

This chapter looks at major concepts in the buddha-dharma and the variety of beliefs relating to these concepts that exist among the religion's principal schools. Because the core Buddhist teachings emerge directly from Shakyamuni's enlightenment and are meant to assist others to undergo their own enlightenment, let's first consider the nature of this transformational experience:

What does it mean to be enlightened?

How do you achieve it?

How can you tell when it happens?

ENLIGHTENMENT: THE UNCONDITIONED STATE

Strictly speaking, none of these questions is answerable. To formulate a response is to use the mind that is conditioned to think or, in other words, that thinks in terms of conditions. Perhaps one of the best answers was given by the Ch'an master Mumon Ekai (1183–1260). When asked to describe his own enlightenment experience, he replied, "It would be easier for a mute to explain his dreams."

Enlightenment lies beyond the conditions of our phenomenal universe: the realm of time and space, life and death, this and that. To become enlightened is, therefore, to go beyond everyday mind, to see the totality from which all these conditions arise, and to realize our essential oneness with it.

Throughout Buddhism, one is challenged by paradoxes that reflect in diverse ways this great, unknowable, indescribable mystery. Take, for example, the Four Noble Vows that many Zen Buddhists make regularly:

Sentient beings are numberless. I vow to save them.

Desires are endless. I vow to put an end to them.

The dharmas are boundless. I vow to master them.

The Buddha way is unattainable. I vow to attain it.

The extent to which Buddhism is, literally, a faith is that it asks believers to trust in the possibility and value of enlightenment, in themselves as capable of experiencing it, and in Shakyamuni's teachings as a means of preparing their minds for it. And this trust needs to be maintained despite all the inevitable doubts, setbacks, and appearances to the contrary.

Speaking in a more approximate, practical vein, one can describe enlightenment as a state of complete freedom: One's mind is liberated from its limited modes of perception, and one's life is released from the narrow confines of self. It's not so much an experience as it is an opening into a dimension beyond what we literally know as experience.

For this reason, many authorities contend that the Sanskrit word *bodhi* is better translated "awakened" than "enlightened." The latter word suggests the coming of light into darkness, so that things are more visible, which is closer to Western notions of intellectual evolution (reflected, for example, in calling the scientifically advanced eighteenth century the Age of Enlightenment). The word *awakened* more accurately connotes a dynamic change involving the entire mind—not just the intelligence—without erroneously suggesting that any *thing* is illuminated. Nevertheless, the Western world so strongly associates mental or spiritual growth with enlightenment that this word remains the most commonly used one for the raising of the bodhi mind.

So if no thing is revealed, to what does the enlightened mind awake? Buddhist scriptures most often say that it awakens to emptiness (in Sanskrit, *shunyata*). This doesn't mean that the mind enters into some sort of existential void. After all, that would be a thing unto itself, if only "nothingness." Instead, the mind comes face to face with the unconditioned, the unknowable, the impalpable, the nonexistent, the nonapparent, the undifferentiated, or, for want of a better word, emptiness. Rather than being limited to grasping some thing, the mind opens up to experience total freedom.

In the Theravada tradition, this concept of fundamental emptiness applies to the nature of the self: The enlightened mind realizes that the self lacks any fixed or lasting aspects. The self as a discrete, personal entity, with its own limited range of characteristics and mechanisms, is said to "die" in enlightenment.

For Mahayana practitioners, the notion of emptiness broadens to cover the entire universe. The enlightened mind realizes that emptiness permeates not just the self but all things, so that form (apparent reality)

THE HEART SUTRA

The following sutra, the centerpiece of the Prajnaparamita-sutra compilation (hence its name), is chanted daily in virtually every Mahayana and Vajrayana temple and monastery throughout the world. In it, the bodhisattva Avalokiteshvara expresses to Shariputra, one of the Buddha's disciples, the fundamental doctrine of emptiness (*shunyata*) and form pervading the universe. The final incantation, beginning "Gate!" (pronounced GAH-tay), bids one to go far, far out to the other shore of perfect buddha nature. The version below is reprinted by permission from John Daido Loori's *Zen Mountain Monastery Liturgy Manual* in a slightly different format than occurs in the manual.

Avalokiteshvara Bodhisattva, doing deep prajna paramita [practice of the highest wisdom], clearly saw emptiness of all the five conditions [skandha or aggregates], thus completely relieving misfortune and pain.

"Oh Shariputra, form is no other than emptiness, emptiness no other than form. Form is exactly emptiness, emptiness exactly form. Sensation, conception, discrimination, awareness are likewise like this.

"Oh Shariputra, all dharmas are forms of emptiness: not born, not destroyed, not stained, not pure, without loss, without gain. So in emptiness there is no form: no sensation, conception, discrimination, awareness; no eye, ear, nose, tongue, body, mind; no color, sound, smell, taste, touch, phenomena; no realm of sight, no realm of consciousness, no ignorance and no end to ignorance, no old age and death and no end to old age and death, no suffering, no cause of suffering, no extinguishing, no path, no wisdom, and no gain.

"No gain and thus the bodhisattvas live prajna paramita with no hindrance in the mind: no hindrance, therefore no fear. Far beyond deluded thoughts, this is nirvana. All past, present, and future buddhas live prajna paramita [highest wisdom] and therefore attain anuttarasamyak-sambodhi [perfect universal enlightenment]."

Therefore know prajna paramita is the great mantra, the vivid mantra, the best mantra, the unsurpassable mantra.

It completely clears all pain.

This is the truth, not a lie.

So set forth the prajna paramita mantra, set forth this mantra and say, "Gate! Gate! Paragate! Parasamgate! Bodhi Svaha!"

Prajna Heart Sutra.

and emptiness (the featureless absolute) are one and the same, indistinguishable from each other.

The most eloquent expression of this Mahayana belief is the widely chanted Heart Sutra, which states, "Form is no other than emptiness, emptiness no other than form. Form is exactly emptiness, emptiness exactly form." (For the full text, see page 79). A famous poem by the Ch'an master Shih-t'ou Hsi-ch'ien, "The Identity of Relative and Absolute" (in Chinese, "Ts'an-t'ung-chi'i"), seeks to convey this mystery through a series of mind-baffling metaphors, including "The absolute works together with the relative like two arrows meeting in midair."

Many Western scientists see a close, intriguing parallel between the Mahayana world of simultaneous form and emptiness and the world of subatomic physics, where all matter is at once particle and wave, arising out of a universal quantum field. Frithjof Capra writes of this comparison in *The Tao of Physics:*

The conception of physical things and phenomena as transient manifestations of an underlying fundamental entity is not only a basic element of quantum field theory, but also a basic element of the Eastern world view. . . . Buddhists express the same idea when they call the ultimate reality *Sunyata* [sic]—"Emptiness" or "the void"—and affirm that it is a living Void which gives birth to all forms in the phenomenal world. . . . Thus the Void of the Eastern mystic can easily be compared to the quantum field of subatomic physics. Like the quantum field, it gives birth to an infinite variety of forms which it sustains and, eventually, reabsorbs. (197–98)

The relationship between shunyata and the quantum field is only one of many correspondences between Buddhism in general and modern science that has helped to fuel the religion's increasing popularity among Europeans and Americans during the past century. It is as if Buddhism over two thousand years ago tapped into a vision of the universe that science is just now beginning to confirm.

Taking a very broad, Western-style approach to the subject of enlightenment, one can say that it's possible for individuals to undergo different types of it. The particular degree or character of enlightenment they experience at any given time depends on many factors, including the nature of their practice, the stage of their training, and, most crucial of all, the level of their readiness.

Shakyamuni's awakening under the bodhi tree serves as the grand model. As he sat there meditating, his mind opened into full flower—the culmination of a process that took place over hours, days, weeks, years, or lifetimes, depending on your perspective. Most Buddhists agree that this kind of enlightenment happens only once in an era, after the Dharma has long been forgotten and there's no other catalyst except the person's own, innate preparedness and drive. It's no wonder such a powerful individual goes on to become an exceptional teacher, reinjecting the Dharma into history for countless millennia to come until it once again fades from human memory.

Shakyamuni's enlightenment was so profound that it liberated him from having to reenter the cycle of birth, death, and rebirth, called *samsara,* which generates endless suffering. Instead, he could pass at his death into the eternal, unchanging dimension beyond samsara, called nirvana, which is described by some schools simply as the extinction of suffering and by others (for example, Pure Land) as a realm of unadulterated bliss.

The word *nirvana* is often used in Buddhism as a synonym for *enlightenment*. In Shakyamuni's case, it can be said that his realization of nirvana beneath the bodhi tree was the prelude to his eventual death-into-nirvana (in Sanskrit, *parinirvana,* "final nirvana").

Theravada Buddhists maintain that Shakyamuni disappeared at his parinirvana, like a fire being blown out to return to the space from which it came (*nirvana* literally means "extinguished"). Mahayana and Vajrayana Buddhists believe that Shakyamuni progressed from death in this world to life in another mode of existence—an absolute one (nirvana)—that is still involved with our worldly, or relative, one (samsara). Indeed, the two permeate each other to such an extent that they're considered identical, which renders an enlightenment experience ever accessible to the mind that's properly attuned to having one.

According to all three vehicles, it is possible to attain states of enlightenment that may not be as extensive as Shakyamuni's awakening was, but are nevertheless liberating realizations of one's buddha potential. In the Theravada vehicle, arhats become enlightened by virtue of practicing the Dharma taught by Shakyamuni. Although they are not thereby rendered as supremely knowledgeable or powerful as fully enlightened buddhas like Shakyamuni, they do qualify to enter nirvana at death.

It is assumed that an arhat's awakening represents a fourth and final stage of enlightenment: the ultimate release from a self-bound vision of the universe. The other three stages consist of less intense experiences. In the case of an exceptional individual, all four stages may occur during a single life. Otherwise, they are spread over the course of several lives. After undergoing a first-stage breakthrough, a person is called a "stream enterer": someone who is definitely enlightened, but not enough to leave samsara at death or to be deemed an arhat. Experiencing the second stage makes him or her a "once-returner": someone who is so enlightened that he or she need only be reborn one more time. A third-stage breakthrough earns him or her the status of "non-returner": someone who will not be reborn again and may go on to attain arhatship (the fourth stage) before actually entering nirvana.

Mahayana and Vajrayana schools believe in an even wider variety of enlightenment experiences. Some of these are fairly quick and spontaneous. For example, a person who is somehow mentally ripe for it can have a sudden, unexpected flash of insight. Zen Buddhists refer to this kind of realization as *kensho* (literally, "seeing one's nature") or *satori* ("knowing")—a much more profound experience. It may be triggered by years of practice, a skillful teacher's so-called turning words, or even a seemingly ordinary activity like watching a peach-blossom petal fall to the ground. To respond to such a stimulus, however, a mind must already be poised on the verge of enlightenment.

Many twentieth-century Zen practitioners, appreciating the desire among westerners in particular for some sort of description, have attempted to put into words, if only approximately, what such an experience is like. The Japanese Zen master Koun Yamada recalled,

> All at once I was struck as though by lightning, and the next instant heaven and earth crumbled and disappeared. Instantaneously, like surging waves, a tremendous delight welled up in me, a veritable hurricane of delight, as I laughed loudly and wildly, "There's no reasoning here, no reasoning at all! Ha! Ha! Ha!" The empty sky split in two, then opened its enormous mouth and began to laugh uproariously, "Ha! Ha! Ha!"

The American Zen master Bernard Tetsugen Glassman expressed an early breakthrough as follows:

> At the next meal [in the *zendo* or meditation hall]—I was head server—tears were pouring down my face as I served . . . and afterwards, when I went out of the zendo . . . there was a tree there, and looking at that tree, I didn't feel I was the tree, it went deeper than

THE OX-HERDING PICTURES

One of the most clever and widely circulated explanations of the path to enlightenment is a series of ten drawings with commentaries and verses created by the twelfth-century Ch'an master Kuo-an Shih-yuan. The drawings depict various stages of enlightenment in which the images of a man and an ox predominate, the latter symbolizing absolute mind or ultimate reality (as opposed to everyday mind or everyday reality). Through these pictures, the stages in the path are depicted as follows:

1. The man actively seeks the ox in the forest.
2. The man discovers its tracks.
3. The man spies the ox in the distance.
4. The man catches the ox.
5. The man tames the ox.
6. The man rides the ox home.
7. Once home, the man forgets the ox and is left with himself alone.
8. The man forgets the self as well: the total enlightenment experience.
9. The man is returned to the source of his being: pure awareness.
10. The man enters the marketplace to serve with helping hands.

that. I felt the wind on me, I felt the birds on me, all separation was gone.

Alternatively, Mahayana and Vajrayana also recognize enlightenment as a more gradual, more consciously managed refinement in one's awareness of the truth. Tibetan Buddhists, for example, are taught that they enter into an enlightened state whenever they visualize buddhas, and that their experience of this state slowly but surely intensifies with diligent practice. Pure Land Buddhists hold the same belief about chanting key liturgical phrases; Zen Buddhists, about doing zazen. For all of them, the special deed is, in itself, the activity (or, from another point of view, the activating) of the enlightened mind.

In addition, all three vehicles see the officially designated teacher—by virtue of his or her position, the successor to Shakyamuni—as an enlightened being. In the Theravada tradition, that person is an arhat, an individual acknowledged by his or her teacher to be a nonreturner, destined to enter nirvana at death.

The Mahayana and Vajrayana traditions feature a broader range of official teachers representing varying degrees of enlightenment. In Tibetan Buddhism, for example, the Dalai Lama and the heads of the other major lineages are each identified as the latest incarnation of an archetypal buddha who has reincarnated as each preceding head. The formal term for such a reincarnate is a *tulku*. Because the current lineage leaders are bodhisattvas in addition to being buddhas, they will refuse to enter nirvana at death, choosing instead to be reborn to serve again in the same capacity.

Other, lower-ranking teachers in each Tibetan lineage are designated as enlightened by their teachers at the end of their training, but they are not considered to be tulkus (buddha/bodhisattva reincarnations), nor are they necessarily regarded as candidates for nirvana at death. The same is true for all official teachers in Zen Buddhism, which lacks a tradition of reincarnate bodhisattvas.

Commenting unofficially on Buddhist teachers as well as students in his book *Introducing Buddhism,* Chris Pauling, founder of the Friends of the Western Buddhist Order, distinguishes between "capital-E" Enlightenment, representing the totally transformational awakening that Shakyamuni had, and "small-e" enlightenment, reflecting the evolved consciousness of a person who can—and repeatedly does—see beyond the limits of the self and the everyday world:

Some Buddhists are lucky enough to have close contact with a teacher who is near enough to Enlightenment to provide living evidence of its existence, in the same way that the Buddha provided this evidence in his lifetime. But even at a lower level, as we become involved with people who have systematically worked on themselves over a period of years, we begin to meet people who, although they may not be fully Enlightened, are certainly closer to this state than we are. . . . This gives us a firm confidence that real, significant growth *is* possible. (13)

THE FOUR NOBLE TRUTHS

Shakyamuni realized four universal truths during his enlightenment experience under the bodhi tree:

1. All life is suffering.

2. The cause of suffering is desire.

3. Suffering can be ended.

4. The way to end suffering is the Noble Eightfold Path.

Let's consider each of these truths individually.

1. *All life is suffering.*

The most common English rendering of the Sanskrit word *duhkha* (pronounced DOO-kah) is "suffering," but that translation reflects only the most negative aspect of what the root term means. A fuller, more accurate definition also includes the notions of unsatisfactoriness, imperfection, bothersomeness, incoherence, and, most critical, impermanence. The message is that no matter how wonderful life can be—or can appear to be—under certain circumstances, everything in life is intrinsically unsatisfying and ultimately disturbing because it does not last.

On a very basic level, this concept can be related directly to our mortality—the fact that we age, get sick, and die. However, it also refers to more subtle matters: the transitory nature of our pleasures; the fragility of our possessions; the instability of our relationships, fortunes, moods, thoughts, and convictions. Outside our own individual existence—the illusionary world of self—we see that life is filled with the uncertainties and travails of others. And beyond all these disturbing conditions is the constant state of flux pervading the visible and invisible universe.

Given the impermanence of all things, even enlightenment experiences, personal suffering is an ever-present possibility and an inevitably recurring reality as long as we stay bound within the world of samsara. Whether or not we also see great joy in life, this First Noble Truth is the one we most need to acknowledge in order to advance spiritually.

2. *The cause of suffering is desire.*
What causes us to suffer in an impermanent world is not the impermanence itself, but the desire burning within us to attach to things that are not lasting. We harbor this desire (in Sanskrit, *trishna,* also translated "thirst" or "craving") as long as we cling inappropriately to the ego-oriented notion of self. Such a limited, artificial perspective— distinguishing between self and other, instead of realizing the interpenetration of both—easily gives rise to the so-called three poisons, or defilements, of greed, anger, and ignorance. These poisons, in turn, feed desire: the urge to acquire, to overpower, to win.

In distinct opposition to the Hindu belief in a personal self *(atman)* that passes in soul-like form from a lifetime in one body to a lifetime in another, Shakyamuni taught the doctrine of no-self *(anatman)*. Individuals, of course, live as such in the real world, and need to think in terms of a self to a certain degree for basic survival purposes. Nevertheless, the self does not exist as a spiritual or metaphysical entity. Instead, it's simply the name given to a temporary combination (or "personality") of impermanent aggregates.

Buddhism posits five groups of aggregates (in Sanskrit, collectively referred to as *skandha*):

1. *matter.* The eyes, ears, nose, tongue, body, and mind. In Buddhism, each of these items is considered a sense organ.

2. *sensations.* The raw data of sight, hearing, smell, taste, touch, and mental activity.

3. *perception.* The recognition and naming of the sensations listed above.

4. *mental formation.* All mental acts that generate activities—for example, will, judgment, fear, repulsion, pride, and so on. This skandha can manifest the three poisons—greed, anger, and ignorance—or their medicinal counterparts—wisdom, compassion, and enlightenment. Its function links us to our karma (discussed below), which explains Shakyamuni's words quoted at the beginning of this chapter: "We are what we think."

5. *consciousness.* the awareness, registration, and ordering of the perceptions listed above.

This rather technical, numerical categorization typifies the style of many Buddhist writings. It's a reflection of the propensity among ancient Indian philosophers to engage in exhaustive, point-by-point analysis. Specifically, the breakdown of the skandha is meant to illustrate that no entity called the "self" abides—or needs to abide—independent of the skandha. When we delude ourselves with the notion of a fixed self operating as its own agent, we kindle unquenchable, self-oriented desires, which in turn give rise to suffering. In the words of Buddhaghosa, the great Theravada scholar of the fifth century C.E., "Suffering exists, but not the sufferer." For a teaching analogy to the relationship between the aggregates and the self, see "The Analogy of the Chariot" on page 89.

3. Suffering can be ended.

The good-news element among the Four Noble Truths is that suffering can cease. Because suffering is associated with dwelling in samsara,

THE ANALOGY OF THE CHARIOT

The Buddha teaches that the self doesn't exist, except as an ever-shifting combination of five aggregates (see pages 87–88). The monk Nagasena used the analogy of a chariot to explain this doctrine to King Milinda (in Greek, Menander), who ruled northwestern India from Peshawar to Patna in the first century B.C.E. and is said to have converted to Buddhism. The analogy is one of many recorded in an often-quoted Theravada text, "The Questions of Milinda":

Nagasena said to Milinda, "Regarding the chariot you said you rode here, what is a chariot? Is it the pole?"
"No," replied Milinda.
"Or the axle, wheels, frame, reins, yoke, or spokes?"
"No," replied Milinda.
"Is it then all of these separate parts that is the chariot?"
"No," replied Milinda.
"Is the chariot something outside these separate parts, then?"
"No," replied Milinda.
"Then I can find no chariot!"
"A chariot is just a practical designation," said Milinda. "It refers to when all the parts are present, and assembled, and functioning."
"It's the same with the self," responded Nagasena. "It refers to when all the aggregates are present, and assembled, and functioning. It's just a practical designation."

the world of impermanent things, the absence of suffering is associated with realizing nirvana, the state of essential emptiness.

In the Theravada tradition, the emptiness one experiences is literally the absence of any illusion that a separate self exists. In the Mahayana tradition, one becomes aware of the eternal, infinite emptiness of the whole universe. This awakening brings along with it full comprehension that there is no such thing as a separate self.

We've already examined nirvana and enlightenment as virtually interchangeable terms that are, by definition, indefinable. In a well-known Zen allegory, enlightenment is symbolized as the moon, and describing enlightenment is likened to pointing a finger toward the moon. The finger can indicate where the moon is, but it's not the thing itself, nor does it tell you anything about it. Unfortunately, the allegory suggests, people seeking guidance too often look at the finger instead of the moon.

We can only come to know what enlightenment or nirvana is—and means—through experiencing it. The path that we take to get to that stage is laid out in the Fourth Noble Truth.

4. The way to end suffering is the Noble Eightfold Path.

Prior to sitting beneath the bodhi tree, Shakyamuni had known both a princely life of the greatest possible sensual pleasure and a monkish life of the utmost austerity. He finally determined that the path to enlightenment, and therefore to the end of suffering, is the Middle Way. It avoids either extreme and instead strives to balance the interacting forces of samsara (worldly engagement) and nirvana (release from worldly engagement).

The full nature of that path—later formally designated the Noble Eightfold Path—was revealed to Shakyamuni during his enlightenment. It consists of eight parts that are traditionally grouped according to three goals, which in some schools are collectively called the "Threefold Training." Listed below are the three goals (capitalized subheads) and the parts that relate to them (eight numbered items):

WISDOM

1. right understanding

2. right thought

MORALITY

3. right speech

4. right action

5. right livelihood

MENTAL DISCIPLINE

6. right effort

7. right mindfulness

8. right meditation

The Noble Eightfold Path is not a linear one. Although the eight parts are always arranged in the above order, one doesn't start at the first part and progress, stage by stage, to the eighth. Some sources do distinguish parts 3 through 5 as the most elementary ones, that is, the easiest to begin adapting right away, with parts 6 through 8 being the next more advanced ones, and parts 1 and 2 the most sophisticated ones of all. The overwhelming majority of teachers, however, emphasize that all eight parts are equally important and should be applied to one's life simultaneously rather than sequentially.

The customary use of the English word *right* for the Sanskrit term *samyak* is arguably the most accurate single-word translation, but it has the disadvantage of implying a dualism that the Buddha never intended. For example, "right speech" is not meant to be contrasted with "wrong speech," as if one were good and the other bad. Creating such a dichotomy would be in direct contradiction to the nondualistic, Middle Way spirit of Buddhism.

Steve Hagen, a Zen priest teaching at the Dharma Field Meditation and Learning Center in Minneapolis, Minnesota, clarifies the meaning of "right" as applied to the parts of the Noble Eightfold Path in his book *Buddhism Plain and Simple:*

It's better that we understand right as "this is appropriate," "this works," "this is in sync with Reality." Right, on the eightfold path, doesn't mean right versus wrong so much as it means *seeing* versus *not seeing*. It refers to being in touch with Reality as opposed to being deluded by our own prejudices, thoughts, and beliefs. *Samma* [Pali for *samyak*] refers to Wholeness rather than fragmentation. Thus, when I use the word "right" . . . I intend it to refer to what is conducive to awakening. (54)

Let's review the particular meaning of each goal and the parts that relate to it.

WISDOM

In Buddhism, wisdom (in Sanskrit, *prajna*) is acquired not through exercising one's intellectual powers but rather through cultivating truth from one's experiences. It's a matter of developing insight, not gaining knowledge of facts and skills. Wisdom may inspire one to become more well-educated, but it is not the by-product of scholarship in itself.

Right understanding is sometimes referred to as "right view." Teachers commonly interpret it to mean seeing each moment or phenomenon as it actually is, rather than through the filter of preconceptions. Right thought (or, in some versions, right resolve) involves having clear, healthy intentions behind one's actions, so that no harm comes to oneself or to others.

MORALITY

Buddhist morality (in Sanskrit, *shila*) is based on specific ethical precepts that are sometimes taken as vows: for example, during monastic ordination or when a lay Buddhist seeks to declare or reinforce his or her religious commitment. The precepts relating to right speech involve, among other things, not lying or slandering. Those pertaining to right action include not killing, stealing, getting drunk, or behaving in a sexually irresponsible manner. We'll review specific precepts in more detail in chapter 4.

THE ULTIMATE PROBLEM

In a famous exchange with a farmer, the Buddha showed the persistent and pernicious nature of desire, the cause of all suffering. The farmer said to him, "I like to farm, but there are lots of problems. Sometimes it rains too much and my crops get flooded out. Sometimes it rains too little and they dry up. . . ."

The Buddha listened attentively until the farmer finished and changed the subject. "I love my wife," he said, "but she's far from perfect. Sometimes she's cold to me for no reason at all. Sometimes she's so passionate that she wears me out. . . ."

Again the Buddha listened patiently until the farmer once more changed the subject. "My children are wonderful," he said, "but they're always giving me trouble. Sometimes they fight with each other and break things. Sometimes they conspire against me. . . ."

And so it went for quite a while, the Buddha listening quietly and the man continuing to complain. Finally the farmer finished speaking, and the Buddha said, "There's nothing I can do to help you, farmer. We've all got eighty-three problems, and that's that. Maybe you can take care of one, but another one is bound to take its place. And some never change. For example, your farm, your wife, your children, even yourself—all will eventually pass away, and there's nothing you can do about it."

The farmer, outraged, said, "You're supposed to be a great teacher! What good is *that* teaching?"

The Buddha replied, "It may help you with the eighty-fourth problem."

"What on earth is the eighty-*fourth* problem?" said the farmer.

The Buddha answered, "You want not to have any problems."

In addition, Buddhists are encouraged to engage in right livelihood, which means doing work that assists oneself and others to live a healthy, honorable life and to attain enlightenment. Professions that definitely do not fall into this category are those that feature crime, killing, or prostitution. Otherwise, it's a judgment call.

For example, teachers or students who believe that the precept against drunkenness bids one to abstain from alcohol altogether might not consider bartending to be right livelihood. Others who construe this precept as a prohibition against excessive drinking might not rule out bartending as right livelihood, as long as the job entails taking reasonable measures to keep customers from drinking too much.

MENTAL DISCIPLINE

As distinct from wisdom, which involves developing a clearer, more truthful sense of the world and one's experiences in it, mental discipline (in Sanskrit, *samadhi*) refers to training the mind to focus itself in ways that will foster not only wisdom but also morality and, ultimately, enlightenment. The word *samadhi* is sometimes translated as "concentration." This points to one of the core aspects of mental discipline: not squandering one's own life and, indirectly, the lives of others by inappropriately yielding to distractions or succumbing to laziness.

Right effort is the determination to practice the Dharma and to engage in all of life's activities in the manner that best suits the situation, oneself, and everyone else involved. Sometimes this calls for strictness and severity; other times, for a lighter, freer spirit. Right mindfulness is the ability to be completely present in each and every moment, aware of all that one is doing, thinking, and feeling. Among other things, it requires engaging in matters wholeheartedly, rather than reluctantly or superficially, and not brooding unconstructively over the past or future.

Right meditation (or, in some translations, right absorption) refers to stilling the mind, so that it's less inclined to operate restlessly and, in doing so, generate suffering. It's a settling process that traditionally is broken into four successive stages: the letting go of desires; the attaining of peaceful, inner calm (also called "one-pointedness" of mind); the refining of this still cognitive frame of mind into one of pure awareness and well-being; and, finally, the achieving of a state of simple wakefulness and equanimity.

In its earlier stages, right meditation might be beneficially applied to such tightly focused mental activities as contemplation or visualization. In its most advanced stage, the mind falls away into enlightenment. We'll return to the subject of meditation in chapter 4.

KARMA: THE LAW OF CAUSE AND EFFECT

Our thoughts and feelings determine what we do, our deeds have consequences, and the results influence our minds. On an individual level, this is the never-ending cycle known in Buddhism as the law of karma (technically, *karma-vipaka:* in Sanskrit, "action–result"). We know it in the West as the law of cause and effect. For every action, there's a reaction that sets in motion another action, and so on.

Karma functions throughout samsara—the world of time, space, and change. On a macrocosmic level, it's responsible for the formation, growth, and collapse of galaxies. Microcosmically, it governs the dynamism of atomic particles. Indeed, it can be said that no one and no thing exists except as a karmic pattern.

Jack Kornfield, who trained in Asia as a Theravada monk and later founded the Insight Meditation Society and the Spirit Rock Center in the United States, uses an oak-tree analogy to illustrate this idea:

> In one stage of the oak tree pattern, an oak tree exists as an acorn; at a subsequent stage it exists as a sapling; in another stage as a large tree; and in yet another, as the green acorn growing on that large tree. Strictly speaking, there is no such thing as a definitive "oak tree." There is only the oak tree pattern through which certain elements follow the cyclical law of karma: a particular arrangement of water, minerals, and the energy of sunlight that changes it from acorn to sapling to large tree over and over again. (*Path of the Heart,* 273)

In terms of day-to-day human existence, karma shapes the lives that we lead right from the beginning (and even *before* the beginning, as discussed in the "Rebirth" section on page 97). It is generated by all the information and socialization we receive from our family, friends, acquaintances, teachers, mentors, workmates, and the culture at large.

This conditioning creates within us mental and emotional habits that, left unexamined or unbroken, tend to perpetuate themselves by our own conscious or subconscious volition. Karma also proceeds from our more independent, nonhabitual thoughts or feelings, and from the more isolated, unconventional, or exceptional things that we do or experience.

Karma isn't a closed-loop system. A certain kind of conditioning doesn't always have the same repercussions in person after person; nor does a given habit, thought, or deed always wind up causing the same thing to happen. What's more, karma is not an organized system of social justice. We can think good and do good but still get treated badly, thanks to the karma of other individuals or to the collective karma of a whole nation of individuals.

In any event, a deliberate effort toward thinking or doing good in order to be rewarded would not be considered very commendable or, in terms of Buddhism, an example of right intention. The proclivity toward right thinking or right action should come naturally for its own sake, rather than for the sake of being rewarded.

Furthermore, many of the things we think and do have consequences we can't possibly foresee. No thought or deed occurs in a vacuum, and the cross-functioning of countless different, interrelated strains of karma is bound to create a certain amount of unpredictability regarding specific outcomes.

The vitally important spiritual challenge relating to the law of karma is not that we avoid having bad things happen to us. It's that we take mindful and active responsibility for our own lives—for how we think and feel and, by extension, for how we conduct ourselves—rather than functioning blindly and mechanically, or looking toward something or someone beyond ourselves as the determinant of what we do or what we experience.

According to the Buddhist law of karma, wise, wholesome, and compassionate thinking leads to deeds of a like nature. That is the best we can do to help ourselves and the world of sentient beings around us. By implication, living in this manner is its own compensation, whatever else may happen. All other, outside circumstances aside—things that are, at any rate, beyond our control—it's the way of life most likely to bring peace, joy, and enlightenment.

Thus Buddhism leaves us on our own to manage the operation of karma in our personal corner of the universe. It points to concepts that we should consider: for example, right understanding, right livelihood, and other parts of the Noble Eightfold Path. It lays out general precepts, not commandments, to follow, which we'll explore in the next chapter. And it gives us tools like meditation for learning more about how our mind and, therefore, our life work. Nevertheless, it's up to us to make our own decisions—indeed, to make our own thoughts.

Dr. Chatsumarn Kabilsingh, a professor at Thammasat University in Bangkok, Thailand, and a past president of the International Association of Buddhist Women, spoke about this liberating aspect of the law of karma in a 1996 BBC television series, *The Way of the Buddha*: "Buddhism is a religion which has a free spirit. There is no 'have to.' It depends on what you do. If you do good, you carry the result with you. If you do bad, you know it. You will carry the result of that *kamma* [Pali for *karma*] yourself. No one is going to interfere with you. Nobody can take away your bad *kamma* or your good *kamma* for you. You are on your own. You are master of your own life" (Elizabeth J. Harris, *What Buddhists Believe*, 50).

REBIRTH

Many westerners have a great deal of difficulty comprehending or accepting the Buddhist belief that an individual is reborn again and again into different lives—the cycle of samsara—until he or she finally breaks

ANGULIMALA THE ROBBER

The legend of Angulimala, said to have lived during the time of the Buddha, portrays the doctrine of karma, which states not only that our actions cause like results, but also that we can change the way we act.

Ahimsaka was sent at age sixteen to study with a brahmin. He did so well that the other students grew jealous. They told the brahmin an untrue story that Ahimsaka was sleeping with the brahmin's wife. Furious, the brahmin thought up a horrible revenge. He counseled Ahimsaka that to outgrow suffering he would have to kill 1,000 people.

All Ahimsaka's instincts rebelled against this task, but he trusted his teacher so much that he took it up anyway. Living by a forest trail, he slew one traveler after another. To keep track of the number, he cut off a finger of each victim and added it to the necklace of fingers he wore around his neck. That necklace earned him a new name: Angulimala (in Sanskrit, "grisly garland").

One evening Angulimala saw the shadowy form of a man approaching. He leapt out and cried, "Stop and meet your fate!"

But the man, who was the Buddha, slowly continued on his way. Angulimala started running after him to kill him, but no matter how swiftly he ran, he couldn't catch up. And yet the Buddha just kept walking on at a normal pace. "Stop!" Angulimala cried out in frustration.

The Buddha turned and said, "I *have* stopped. It is you who have not."

"What do you mean?" said Angulimala.

The Buddha answered, "I have stopped harming others, while you most definitely have not."

At that instant, Angulimala saw into the horror of his life. He was about to slay himself in remorse, when the Buddha said, "Be patient. Let go of your grief. There will always be time to die, but the time in which to strive and to live is short. Rise and follow me."

Angulimala went on to become a monk. He applied himself diligently to compassionate deeds. Much to his surprise, he found he had a gift for helping women bring new life into the world. However, he was still tormented day and night by visions of his crimes. People in the street continued to revile or attack him because of his past. And he suffered all manner of accidents.

Again, Angulimala was about to kill himself to gain release, when the Buddha came up to him and said, "This is the time for great patience. Make the most of this moment, for your chance for final freedom has come."

Angulimala let all the horrible images, thoughts, and feelings he'd suffered flow through him once again. One by one he let each of them go, and then, if only for an instant, he had a taste of nirvana. He died naturally thereafter, free at last from the cycle of birth and death that had brought such pain.

---

through to nirvana. One of the biggest conceptual stumbling blocks is confusing *rebirth* with *reincarnation*. It's a very understandable problem. Distinguishing between the two notions involves analyzing factors that are abstract and relatively unfamiliar in our predominantly Judeo-Christian culture.

Simply put, reincarnation refers to the transmigration of a soul or personal imprint from one life to another. Thus a key element of an individual's identity travels from carnal body to carnal body (hence, rein-*carnation*). It's an ancient, deeply ingrained belief among the people of India and a cornerstone of Hinduism, in which the self (in Sanskrit, *atman*) is the transmigrating factor.

The Buddha didn't reject the notion of an individual progressing in some manner through numerous lifetimes. In fact, it's a key part of his teaching. During his enlightenment experience, he saw clearly all the previous existences he'd somehow gone through, which, among other things, revealed to him the transcendent greatness of the Dharma in comparison to the brief, fragmentary nature of a single life span.

The modification the Buddha made was to declare that there is no such separate factor as a soul, self, or personal imprint that gets passed along. Instead of the process being a reincarnation, it's purely a rebirth. The quality of one life determines the quality of the next one in a causal way, but the relationship between the two doesn't involve any other kind of transference.

John Snelling, past secretary-general of the Buddhist Society based in England, offers some helpful ways to visualize the concept of rebirth in his book *Buddhism:* "It is rather like a billiard ball flying across the green baize of a billiard table. It hits another ball and that canons on at a speed and in a direction that owes something to the first ball (and also to other incidental factors), but it does not take away anything material or essential from the first ball. Another analogy is of the transmission of a flame from one candle to another" (48).

Thus the link between one life and another is a kinetic impulse or, to use terms closer to Buddhism but still colloquially Western, a karmic energy surge. The karmic aspect relates to the condition of the mind that is dying: not "mind" in the scientific sense of intellectual faculties, but in the broader, more dynamic sense of will, wisdom, and (metaphorically speaking) heart. The cause of the impulse or surge is both the final instant of the life as well as its overall mental history. The Buddha once said to his disciples, "Rebirth arises from two causes: the last thought of the previous life as its governing principle and the actions of the previous life as its basis. The stopping of the last thought is known as decease, the appearance of the first thought as rebirth."

The English word most often used to express this twofold karmic aspect is *habits,* in the most general sense of the term. For example,

Ajahn Amaro, an Englishman who became a monk in Thailand, states, "What is reborn is our habits. That is the essence of it. Whatever the mind holds onto is reborn: what we love, hate, fear, adore, and have opinions about. Our identification with these aspects of mind has a momentum behind it. Attachment is like a flywheel. . . . What is being reborn from life to life is that in us which identifies with objects blindly" (Gyatso, *The Good Heart,* 85).

In referring to habits that get reborn, Amaro does not mean specific, isolated personal idiosyncrasies like a passion for chocolate or a prejudice against foreigners, but rather the overall pattern of thinking and feeling that lies behind such characteristics.

The entire succession of lives that are connected to each other in this manner—for example, all the previous existences that led to Shakyamuni's appearance—can be said to represent an individual strain of life. Strictly speaking, however, they are not different manifestations of the same person, although the language of a folktale, talk, or text may occasionally express them that way for convenience's sake.

From the Buddhist perspective of no-self, even a single lifetime is not lived by one person. Our identity shifts from moment to moment, day to day, and year to year. We are not the same human being physically, mentally, and emotionally at seven years old that we are at age seventeen, twenty-seven, fifty-seven, or any other year. The five aggregates making up a life as it goes along (discussed on pages 87–88) are continually in flux.

Nevertheless, the *illusion* of self—created by our memories, mental conditioning, and sensory inability to detect our body's constant state of change—helps gives us the impression that we are "always" the same person. In fact, according to Buddhism, we die and are reborn from instant to instant to instant.

The physical death that ends one entire lifetime can be viewed as the flickering of a life-impulse that then creates another lifetime. In terms of Western physics, we might envision the two successive lifetimes as two successive particle manifestations of the same wave. Various different branches of Buddhism provide their own interpretation of how, exactly, the process works.

First, let's look at what all these explanations have in common. Every school agrees that the karmic quality of one lifetime determines the nature of the next in terms of progressing toward, or regressing from, nirvana. They also concur that a rebirth can take place in any one of a number of realms of existence (see page 26), from the lowest, hellish world of demons to the highest, heavenly world of devas (or gods).

For example, the death of a human life in which the karmic energy is wholesome can lead either to the birth of another human life more predisposed toward enlightenment or to the life of a *deva*. If the dying life has unwholesome karmic energy, the next life might be either that of another human being further away from enlightenment, or that of a hungry ghost, animal, or demon. This obviously puts a premium on living a mindful life that is committed every moment to following the buddha way, so that the last instant—or effect—of one life can start off—or cause—a worthy new life.

The teachings about rebirth among various branches of Buddhism differ mainly in regard to what the interim period between lives is like. Dr. Walpola Rahula, a Buddhist monk, scholar, and writer who has contributed greatly to the modern West's understanding of the Theravada vehicle, describes death-and-rebirth as a more-or-less instantaneous, natural occurrence that in itself is not anything to wonder about, much less fear:

> The difference between death and rebirth is only a thought-moment: the last thought-moment in this life conditions the first thought-moment in the so-called next life. . . . So from the Buddhist point of view, the question of life after death is not a great mystery, and a Buddhist is never worried about this problem. As long as there is this "thirst" to be and to become, the cycle of continuity (samsara) goes on. It can stop only when its driving force, this "thirst," is cut off through wisdom which sees Reality, Truth, Nirvana. (*What the Buddha Taught,* 34)

Vajrayana beliefs about death and rebirth are encoded in the Tibetan Book of the Dead, reputed to contain the teachings of Padmasambhava, discussed in chapter 2 as one of the founders of Buddhism in Tibet. This remarkably poetic work offers a compelling, detailed examination of the various states of consciousness (or, in Tibetan, *bardos*) that intervene during a forty-nine-day period between the closing of one life and the opening of another.

Many bardo manifestations, such as bliss-inducing white light and other visual phantasmagoria, are similar to images that appear in Western descriptions of illness-related or near-death experiences. Others are distinct reflections of the Dharma: mandala-like visions of the structure of the universe (including, for example, the Trikaya and the six realms of existence) as well as intimations of the lifetime to come—unless the dying person passes from samsara into nirvana during one critical bardo stage.

Although the period of bardos between one life and another includes such awesome, otherworldly events as encountering monsters and reviewing past lives, it is not considered an ordeal to be dreaded but rather a grand rite of passage to be welcomed. The stage-by-stage descriptions in the Tibetan Book of the Dead govern ritual ceremonies, readings, and mindfulness practices that survivors perform for the deceased. These activities both assist the dying life to be reborn and help the living participants to revitalize their faith.

In Mahayana and Vajrayana Buddhism, a bodhisattva repeatedly chooses to be reborn rather than to enter nirvana. It's an act of compassion that he or she continues until all sentient beings are saved. Technically, this kind of rebecoming can be called a reincarnation rather than a rebirth, because the process involves an emanation (*sambhogakaya,* or archetypal buddha) choosing to incarnate again—that is, manifest in yet another human form—rather than one life giving birth to another. The current Dalai Lama, for example, is one of several reincarnated bodhisattvas who head lineages in the Vajrayana tradition. Specifically, he's a reincarnation of Avalokiteshvara, the bodhisattva of compassion, as were the thirteen former heads of his lineage (the Geluk school).

Although nothing that can be called personal transfers from one life to another in the process of rebirth, reincarnation does appear to involve at least a few evidential links between lifetimes, presumably so that mortals can identify and validate the new incarnation. For instance, when Tenzin Gyatso, the current Dalai Lama, was two years old and as yet unidentified, Geluk monks were led to his home by special indicators, including images that appeared in their dreams. These signs were reputedly sent by the previous, thirteenth Dalai Lama, who died the same year that Tenzin Gyatso was born: 1935. The monks then subjected the boy to a test to determine if there were any telltale points of connection between him and the Dalai Lama who had died.

The following account of that investigation appears in *Seven Years in Tibet,* written by Heinrich Harrer, a German explorer who wandered into Tibet when the current Dalai Lama was a young boy and wound up becoming his friend:

> [The presumed fourteenth Dalai Lama] was first shown four different rosaries [actually Buddhist bead-strings called *malas*], one of which— the most worn—had belonged to the thirteenth Dalai Lama. The boy, who was quite unconstrained and not the least bit shy, chose the right one without hesitation and danced round the room with it. He also selected out of several drums one which the last Incarnation had used to call his servants. Then he took an old walking-stick, which had also belonged to him, not deigning to bestow a glance on one which had a handle of silver and ivory. (269–70)

The boy passed the test and became the new Dalai Lama. Some fifty years later, he talked with Father Bede Griffiths, an English Benedictine monk, about the difficulty many Christians have accepting the concept of rebirth. Describing Griffith's personal explanation of the problem as "deeply convincing," he spoke about it at the 1994 John Main Seminar:

> [Griffiths] said that, from a Christian point of view, a belief in rebirth would undermine the force in one's faith and practice. When you

accept that this life, your individual existence, has been directly created and is like a direct gift from the Creator, it immediately creates
a very special bond between you as an individual creature and the
Creator. . . . A belief in rebirth would undermine that special relationship. (Gyatso, *A Good Heart,* 59)

For many Buddhists, however, believing in the doctrine of rebirth provides a means of transcending a painfully narrow, self-oriented perspective on things and envisioning a greater sense of oneness with
time, space, and the universe.

In keeping with all other Buddhist traditions, Zen subscribes to the
basic doctrine of rebirth, but it pays much less attention to the subject
than Tibetan Buddhism does. It focuses more on the realities and po-
tentialities of the existence at hand. Among them are the ever-present
possibility of becoming enlightened *during one's lifetime,* the endless opportunities it offers for saving sentient beings, and the boundless teachings it reveals in its moment-to-moment flow of karma. The literal
beginning and ending of a single life span are regarded as simple in-
stances of change in a constant state of impermanence, not as the birth
or death of anything—hence the Zen saying, "Life is the unborn, death
is the unextinguished."

Abbot John Daido Loori of Zen Mountain Monastery in Mount
Tremper, New York, speaks of the essential "no-thingness" of death
(and, by extension, life) in his Dharma discourse, "Daowu Won't Say":

What is it that dies? There is no question that when this physical body
is no longer capable of functioning, the energies within it, the atoms
and molecules it is made up of, don't die with it. They take on another
form, another shape. You can call that another life, but there is no permanent, unchanging substance, nothing passes from one moment to
the next. Quite obviously, nothing permanent or unchanging can pass
or transmigrate from one life to the next. Being born and dying continues unbroken but changes every moment. Life and death are nothing but movement. (*Mountain Record* 16, no. 4 [summer 1998]: 7)

For all Mahayana and Vajrayana practitioners, not only the self but also life and death are fundamentally illusory, whatever real challenges they may present in ordinary, day-to-day existence. This insubstantiality is poignantly conveyed in a passage of the Diamond Sutra that is often quoted at memorial services:

> Thus shall you think of all this fleeting world:
> A star at dawn, a bubble in a stream;
> A flash of lightning in a summer cloud,
> A flickering lamp, a phantom, and a dream.

Because Buddhism denies the lasting nature of anything personal, it's nearly impossible for *any* individual—Buddhist or non-Buddhist—to grasp the concept of rebirth in an intellectual way. As with most other teachings in their religion, Buddhists can come to understand rebirth only by "taking it within"—that is, meditating on it; studying it in an intimate, teacher-student relationship; and above all living with it on a day-to-day basis so that it is "real-ized" (or made real) in their personal existence.

QUESTIONS AND ANSWERS

Given the First Noble Truth, "All life is suffering," is it fair to say that Buddhists have a fundamentally pessimistic or negative view of life?
Two of the most prevalent misconceptions about Buddhism are based on partial, oversimplified understandings of its message. Ironically, they contradict each other.

On the one hand, many people associate the religion with a blissful, above-it-all, what-me-worry attitude. It's easy for them to see their perspective confirmed in the fat, jolly, so-called buddha statues that are ubiquitous in gift shops, lawn ornament stores, and garage sales. Actually, this figure doesn't represent Shakyamuni or any other buddha at all, but instead an eccentric, much-beloved tenth-century Chinese Ch'an (Zen) monk named Pu'tai (in Japanese, Hotei). Although a homeless beggar, he radiated joyfulness and allegedly worked miracles to help people. This kind of goodwill and compassion is indeed taught in Buddhism, but it shouldn't be confused with any sort of lighthearted stance apart from, or in spite of, the realities of the world.

On the other hand, many people hold the distorted notion that Buddhism portrays life as round after round of ceaseless misery. In addition to citing the First Noble Truth, they may point to the frequently reprinted depictions of Shakyamuni as an emaciated, near-skeletal beggar (which, in fact, he was during his preenlightenment period of asceticism) or to the popular images of grotesquely horrifying demons from Vajrayana iconography.

Each interpretation of Buddhism—as a happy or a despairing religion—is an extreme one, at odds with Shakyamuni's teaching of the Middle Way. The truth is that Buddhism takes a practical approach to the inherent uncertainties and dilemmas of life. If anything, it is essentially optimistic: The Third Noble Truth says that there can be an end to suffering, and the Fourth Noble Truth shows the way to end it.

Although Buddhism teaches that life is full of suffering, it doesn't deny that life can also bring countless moments of beauty and pleasure. Like every other religion, it expresses praise and gratitude for such experiences throughout its scriptures, and many of its stories, sayings, and customs abound in humor and sheer delight. It does, however, warn that clinging to happiness—or to anything—and wishing it would last forever inevitably results in frustration, disappointment, and sorrow, which, in combination with experiences that are directly painful, can lead to a life that's constantly unsatisfying.

According to Buddhism, the solution lies first in accepting the pervasiveness of this upsetting instability in life. If we don't face it, or worse, if we actively resist admitting it, we'll simply breed more suffering. Externally, we'll fail to address in a constructive manner the situations that are hurting us and our world. Internally, we'll build up ever greater reservoirs of alienation, hopelessness, guilt, and depression.

Properly regarded, suffering can be a stimulus toward becoming a

LETTING GO
(a Zen teaching tale)

Once two Zen monks were walking together through the woods. They came to a broad, shallow river and began hitching up their robes for the walk across to the other side. Suddenly, a short distance away, a beautiful young woman dressed in wedding finery stepped out of the forest and paused before the river. By observing the troubled expression on her face and the way she paced backed and forth, the monks could tell that she needed to get across, but couldn't without ruining her clothes.

The older monk said to the younger one, "I will offer to carry her across."

Shocked, the younger monk said, "But what about the rules? We've taken a vow of chastity! Why, we're not even supposed to touch a woman!"

The older monk said, "And what about compassion? Just look, there are tears on her face!" Without hesitating, he went over to the woman, offered to assist, received her grateful smile, and helped her climb onto his back. Then, following behind the clearly disgruntled younger monk, he carried her across the river. When they reached the other side, he set her down. She thanked him, bid farewell, and went on her own way farther north.

The two monks traveled on for half a day in silence, the younger monk scowling all the way. Finally the younger monk burst out to the older one, "You should not have carried that woman on your back. You know the rule!"

The older monk smiled, "Young man, I set down that woman on the bank of the river hours ago. It seems that you're still carrying her."

less selfish, more enlightened being. As Thich Nhat Hanh often says, "Out of suffering, compassion is born." If any one image in Buddhism accurately reflects this positive, healing response to life's difficulties, it's the serene expression that appears on so many representations of Shakyamuni's face during meditation.

In putting so much emphasis on the nothingness of self, life, and death, Buddhism seems to teach nihilism: that nothing matters because nothing exists. Is this true?

In fact, the opposite is true. Buddhism teaches that one's own life and death—as well as life and death in general—are of supreme importance. What "doesn't matter" (except that it needs to be avoided) is *attachment* to them, or to any aspects of them, as "things," because they have no lasting existence. However, that doesn't mean they lack significance.

Through the way we think, act, and conduct our lives, we work toward liberating ourselves from suffering, which benefits the whole universe. By constantly being mindful of self, life, and death—until it becomes second nature—we learn how to advance further along the path to peace and enlightenment. Zen master Dogen was alluding to this fact when he wrote in the "Genjokoan" fascicle of his Shobogenzo,

To study the buddha way is to study the self.
To study the self is to forget the self.
To forget the self is to be enlightened by the ten thousand
    things.

Nihilism is an extremist philosophy based on the belief that nothing has any value, that all is chaotic, anarchic, and meaningless. Buddhism doesn't have such a blank perspective. To assume that its teaching about the essential emptiness of things signifies that things don't matter is to think in overly dualistic terms—something Buddhism cautions against. In *Buddhism Pure and Simple,* Steve Hagen offers a Judeo-Christian

THREE QUESTIONS

Once a king decided that if he knew the answer to three questions, he would be the master of life itself:

• When is the best time?

• Who is the most important person?

• What is the most vital thing to do?

He resolved to visit a mountain-dwelling hermit said to be an enlightened being. Leaving his attendants some distance behind, he approached the hermit, who was digging a garden in front of his hut. The hermit listened to the king's three questions, but then simply resumed digging. The king was flustered and started to leave, but watching the hermit work so hard, he said, "You must be tired. Let me give you a hand."

The king dug for several hours until he was exhausted. He said to the hermit, "If you can't answer my questions, please tell me so that I can be on my way."

The hermit replied, "Do you hear someone running?" Just then, a man came stumbling out of the woods, clutching his stomach, and passed out. The king ripped open the man's shirt, saw a bloody wound, and bandaged it. Then he carried him into the hermit's hut, where all three spent the night.

The next morning the wounded man said to the king, "You don't know me, but for years I thought of you as my enemy. During the last war, you took my lands and I swore vengeance. When I saw you climbing this mountain, I decided to kill you on your way back, but your attendants spotted me and gave me this wound. I escaped, but if you hadn't helped me, I would have died. Please, I beg of you, forgive me!"

The king was astonished. "I forgive you," he said, "and I promise to restore your lands." The two men embraced. Then the king turned to the hermit, who was sowing seeds in his garden. "I must leave," the king said. "Can you give me no answer to my questions"?

The hermit laughed, "Your questions have already been answered! If you had not delayed to dig my garden, you would have been attacked by that man. Therefore the best time for you then was the time you were digging; the most important person was myself; and the most vital thing to do was to help me. Later, when the wounded man appeared, the best time was the time you spent tending his wound, for otherwise you would not have gained his friendship. He was then the most important person, and the most vital thing to do was to help him. Remember: The best time is always right now, the only moment you can control. The most important person is always the one you are with. And the most vital thing to do is always to make that person happy."

---

analogy: "Many people think, 'The Buddha said there is no self; therefore Buddhism is a religion of nihilism.' This is like thinking, 'Since you don't believe that God is a handsome, elderly gentlemen with a long, white beard who lives in the clouds, you must be an atheist' " (125).

Isn't the doctrine of karma fatalistic, binding us in one continuum from birth to death and from one life to another?
The law of karma is a natural law of cause and effect, not a moral law of right and wrong. Technically, there's no such thing as "good karma" or "bad karma." Although individual actions or results may be considered good or bad in themselves from a relative point of view, no one is locked into the deterministic playout of a certain kind of karma. If we

find ourselves suffering or inflicting suffering upon others, we can always change our thoughts and actions so that the end product will be less suffering.

To say that the law of karma works like fate or destiny presupposes some sort of a deity or power that exercises judgment and metes out fortunes accordingly. Buddhism lacks this kind of a justice system. Instead, it assures us that our thoughts and actions do have consequences, and leaves it up to us to take the proper responsibility for them. Even if we're born into an unsatisfactory situation, we have the power to free ourselves.

Karma refers to volition, to acts that we *will* to take place. Much that happens in our lives results from other causes that are not karma-related. John Snelling speaks of this issue in his book, *The Elements of Buddhism:*

> Were someone to fall ill, a censorious person might declare, "Ah well, that's the result of past karma. He's merely reaping what he sowed." This, however, is to ignore the fact that non-karmic forces are also in play. Our bodies, being organic, are subject to growth and decay regardless of how we behave. Beyond that, anything—literally *anything*—can happen. So indeterminacy or uncertainty is built into the basic workings of the Universe. The Buddha himself may have been implying something like this when he rebuked his loyal attendant, Ananda, for saying that he fully understood karma. (47)

In the same vein, Pracha Hutanawatr, a Thai monk and prominent member of the International Network of Socially Engaged Buddhists, told Elizabeth J. Harris, author of *What Buddhists Believe,* that he considers the law of karma to be "proactive, not reactive": "If you look at the concept of kamma [Pali for karma] carefully, it is far too simplified to say that you are poor because you have done something bad in the past. I don't agree with that. The doctrine of kamma gives you the courage to work and change society and change your life. If you take the doctrine fatalistically, that is not Buddhism" (107).

TRUST IN HEART

The teaching of nonseparation, nondualism, or "Not Two" is expressed in this poem of Seng Ts'an, the Third Ch'an (Zen) Patriarch, who died in 606 C.E. The poem is also known as "Faith in Mind." In the Chinese and Japanese languages, *heart* and *mind* are often used interchangeably.

The Perfect Way is only difficult for those who pick and choose;
Do not like, do not dislike; all will then be clear.
Make a hairbreadth difference, and Heaven and Earth are set
    apart;
If you want the truth to stand clear before you, never be for or
    against.
The struggle between "for" and "against" is the mind's worst
    disease. . . .
Do not try to drive pain away by pretending it's not real;
Pain, if you seek serenity in Oneness, will vanish of its own
    accord. . . .
Thoughts that are fettered turn from Truth,
Sink into the unwise habit of not liking.
"Not liking" brings weariness of spirit; estrangements serve no
    purpose. . . .
The One is none other than the All, the All none other than the
    One.
Take your stand on this, and the rest will follow of its own accord;
To trust in the Heart is the "Not Two," the "Not Two" is to trust
    in the Heart. . . .

Adapted from E. A. Burtt, ed., *The Teachings of the Compassionate Buddha*, 227–30.

4 Walking the Way: Buddhist Practices

With a quiet mind
Come into that empty house, your heart
And feel the joy of the way
Beyond the world.

—the Buddha

Shakyamuni had a disciple named Malunkyaputta who repeatedly pestered him to answer philosophical questions, especially in regard to his own core teachings. Not interested in pursuing such mind-agitating matters, Shakyamuni finally asked him, "Did I ever tell you, 'Come, lead the holy life under me, I will explain these questions to you?' "

"No, my teacher," Malunkyaputta replied.

Then the Buddha told him a story: "Suppose a man is wounded by a poisoned arrow. Imagine that when he is brought to a doctor, he says, 'I will not allow this arrow to be removed until I know what caste the bowman belongs to; what his name is; what his family is like; whether his skin is black, brown, or golden; and where he lives. I will not allow this arrow to be re-

moved until I know the kind of bow he used, the type of arrow, the sort of feather on the arrow, and the class of metal on the tip.' I tell you, Malunkyaputta, that man would die before he could discover any of these things."

This often-quoted story reflects the absurdist structure of many Buddhist parables, a style that can easily perplex westerners. On the surface, the situation seems ridiculous. Of course the poisoned arrow should be pulled out immediately! The very ludicrousness of the parable makes it linger in the mind—which is precisely the point.

Once people have heard the tale, they're likely to return to it mentally again and again, each time saying to themselves, "How stupid! *I* would certainly never waste valuable time with such questions!" Nevertheless, human nature being what it is, someday they're almost certain to find themselves doing essentially the same thing on a less obvious level.

For example, a man may be slowly but surely ruining his life by drinking too much alcohol on a regular basis. Before actually giving it up, however, he may procrastinate by overly rationalizing or intellectualizing the dilemma, endlessly pursuing questions like: "Why do I do it?" "How can I make up for it?" "Under what circumstances might it be okay to drink?" "How many drinks can I get away with?" "What particular occasions or beverages cause the most trouble?" "When would conditions be the best for me to quit?" "What's 'normal drinking' for a man like me?" If he can recall the parable during such moments, it just might help him to get beyond playing mind games with himself and do what he knows deep down is right—stop drinking alcohol.

The story of Shakyamuni and his mind-agitating disciple Malunkyaputta is open to a variety of different interpretations, but it is commonly used in Buddhist teachings to point out the danger of getting caught up in the mental world of logic, reason, and intellect and therefore losing touch with what is natural, intuitive, instinctive, and physical. It's easy to confuse the two categories. Indeed, referring to the parable, we may be inclined to say that pulling out the arrow is the *ra-*

tional thing to do, but that's not really accurate. In truth, it's the *instinctive* thing to do—a human being's natural impulse toward life and health. The rational thing, literally speaking, is to begin mentalizing, to start asking questions, which the parable, admittedly, takes to an absurd level.

Buddhism seeks the Middle Way, the right balance between extremes. The opposite poles indicated in this parable can be characterized in various, interrelated terms: mind and body, thinking and doing, reason and instinct, theory and practice. However you express the two coordinates, each one needs to be given its proper weight and attention in our lives. Jeopardy lies in favoring one too much and the other too little.

After the creation of the Pali Canon, Buddhism's earliest collection of scriptures (c. 50 B.C.E. to 50 C.E.), the debate over such issues of balance sharpened. For the first time, written texts enshrined large portions of Shakyamuni's teachings in a permanent, authoritative, and easily replicable form, one that could function as a uniquely valuable and versatile spiritual training medium. As a result, a key question arose that continues to exist for each and every Buddhist school and practitioner: To what extent is it necessary or even helpful to master these teachings *intellectually*—indeed, to exercise one's powers of rationality in general, as opposed to putting one's faith more directly into practice?

During the first century C.E., one group of Theravada monks, the Dhammakathikas, argued that learning should be the basis of the religion. Another group, the Pamsukulikas, countered that practice should be. The opposing perspectives were eventually translated into the two basic training tracks of Theravada Buddhism: *gantha-dhura* (in Pali, "the vocation of books") and *vipassana-dhura* (in Pali, "the vocation of insight").

Theravada Buddhism, at least in Asia, still tends to emphasize learning over practice as the basis of the religion, an understandable position given Theravada's emphasis on monasticism and its long history as an educational force throughout India and southeast Asia (in many areas,

the only formal one). Mahayana and Vajrayana Buddhism are more inclined to stress practice over learning, but that doesn't mean they belit-
tle an intellectual mastery of the Dharma. The Dalai Lama once
expressed their combined benefit this way:

> Generally speaking, what seems to be true is that in one's own spir-
> itual practice, any faith or conviction that is based on an under-
> standing attained through a process of reasoning is very firm. Such a
> conviction is firm because you have convinced yourself of the effi-
> cacy or validity of the idea in which you have placed your faith. And
> this conviction is consequently very powerful in motivating you
> into action. This is why, according to Buddhism, intelligence is con-
> sidered very important in one's spiritual path. (Gyatso, *The Good
> Heart,* 64)

The Dalai Lama quotes an ancient Tibetan proverb to back up his
statement: "Someone whose faith is not grounded in reason is like a
stream of water that can be led anywhere."

Nevertheless, each of Buddhism's three vehicles acknowledges that
what we learn from the teachings needs to be supplemented by what
we come to know experientially, through listening to all that our heart,
gut, and physical activity tell us. Referring specifically to meditation as
"the practice of enlightenment" and "an entry into the true depth dis-
covered by the ancient Orientals," Kosho Uchiyama, a Japanese Zen
master and abbot of Antaiji monastery from 1965 to 1975, warns
against thinking of learning and practice as competing disciplines:
"The true depth of the East isn't a denial of human reason. It's not
some kind of depth within the fog of anti-intellectual unlimitedness
and nondefinition. . . . It must be a true depth that emerges only *after*
the intellect itself can be sufficiently convinced that the unlimited
transcends that intellect." Uchiyama compares meditation to sleep because both involve "letting go" of rational consciousness or, as he puts
it, "opening the hand of thought": "Thinking means to be grasping or
holding on to something with our brain's conceptual 'hand.' But if we

open it, if we don't conceive, what is in our hand falls away" (*Opening the Hand of Thought,* xviii–xix and 9).

The crucial difference between sleep and meditation, however, is that meditation constitutes a greater state of wakefulness rather than a lesser one. Let's now take a closer look at this key practice in all three vehicles of Buddhism.

MEDITATION: THE MEANS AND THE END

Essentially, meditation in Buddhism involves "stilling" oneself physically, mentally, and emotionally. The underlying assumption is that our normal, agitated lives, with their myriad distractions, attachments, and changes, keep us from experiencing who we really are.

In meditation, we enter into the possibility of enlightenment—or, as Zen and various other Mahayana and Vajrayana schools see it, into the very act of enlightenment. We can realize the fundamental truth of our emptiness as individual selves and of our oneness with the universe.

Individuals who engage in a Buddhist meditational practice are likely to reap numerous other benefits, regardless of the depth of their religious commitment. It's the kind of discipline that, over time, can reduce one's chaotic mind-chatter and make one more alert, focused, aware, internally well balanced, and capable of staying in the present moment.

From a Buddhist perspective, however, these psychological benefits are by-products of the main purpose, which is to free the mind to realize the truth. Some forms of Buddhist meditation employ skillful means (*upaya*)—such as specific contemplations or visualizations—to purify, train, or even trick the mind away from its ordinary, self-imprisoning occupations. Other forms call for the mind to plunge more directly into the absolute. The selected meditational practices described below reflect this spectrum of styles.

In virtually all types of Buddhist meditation, the individual is directed to maintain a certain posture, one that has proven over the centuries to be the most stable physically, and therefore the most conducive to stillness in body and mind:

1. Sit comfortably in one of the following positions (beginning with the best possible):
   • full lotus (legs crossed with each foot resting on the opposite thigh);
   • half lotus (legs crossed with one foot resting on the opposite thigh; the other foot, on the floor);
   • Burmese (thighs spread so that the knees are resting on the floor and both feet are tucked next to each other on the floor, close to the body);
   • kneeling with a cushion or bench supporting the buttocks; or
   • sitting in a chair with the feet flat on the floor and the back away from the back of the chair.

   (NOTE: In certain schools, institutions, or formal circumstances, the latter two, less traditional postures—kneeling and sitting—are not used. In some cases, the purpose is to limit practitioners to those postures that promise the most physical stability. In others, it's to ensure that everyone in a group of meditators is adopting relatively the same posture and, therefore, not creating a visual difference or distraction.)

2. Keep the spine as straight as possible, centered between the hips at the bottom and the ears at the top.

3. Hold the head up, as if the top of it were supporting the sky.

4. Clasp the hands loosely together at the waist in the particular position (mudra) that's appropriate for the meditation. In many schools, the standard meditation mudra is made by placing the left fingers on top of the right (palm-sides-up) and touching the thumbs together above them, so that a hollow "O" is formed between the linked thumbs and the stacked fingers.

5. Leave the eyes slightly open and unfocused rather than closing them, which can lead to sleep or chaotic imagery. (NOTE: Certain meditations call for focusing the eyes on a specific object or closing the eyes altogether.)

As with any Buddhist practice, final instructions for meditation need to come from a teacher, who can then advise on the experience one has during the meditation.

Here are descriptions of widely practiced forms of meditation in different schools of Buddhism:

shamatha meditation. Early in Buddhism's history, meditational practices were divided into two categories: *shamatha,* which means "calm abiding" in Pali and Sanskrit; and *vipassana* (in Pali) or *vipashyana* (in Sanskrit), which means "insight." Although the meditations in all three vehicles can still be classified into one or the other of these two categories, the names themselves more strictly describe the two types of meditation most commonly practiced by Theravada Buddhists.

Shamatha meditation involves focusing the mind on something in particular that can thereby function as a clarifying influence, keeping other thoughts and feelings at bay. Frequently shamatha meditators are directed to "abide with" their breath. In Sri Lanka, for example, the most widespread practice is mentally to observe the breath at the tip of one's nose. Other focal points might be the sound of rain or traffic outside, the pain in one's legs, or even the nature of a Buddhist virtue such as compassion (in Pali and Sanskrit, *karuna*) or loving-kindness (in Pali, *metta;* in Sanskrit, *maitri*).

vipassana meditation. As distinct from shamatha meditation, vipassana (insight) meditation leads practitioners toward a more open awareness of their own thoughts and feelings—one that's liberated from conditioned responses, psychological tendencies, rationalizations, dramatizations, judgments, and other self-oriented modes of perception. In the process, practitioners develop a more intuitive under-

standing not only of themselves but also of their true connection
with everything else.

Jack Kornfield, founding teacher of the Insight Meditation Society,
based in Barre, Massachusetts, characterizes this form of meditation as
"a systematic training and awakening of body, heart, and mind that is
integrated with the world around us." Referring both to Buddhism in
general and insight meditation in particular, he notes,

> An integrated sense of spirituality understands that if we are to bring
> light or wisdom or compassion into the world, we must first begin
> with ourselves. The universal truths of spiritual life can come alive
> only in each particular and personal circumstance. This personal ap-
> proach to practice honors both the uniqueness and the commonality
> of our life, respecting the timeless quality of the great dance between
> birth and death, yet also honoring our particular body, our particular
> family and community, the personal history and joys and sorrows
> that have been given to us. In this way, our awakening is a very per-
> sonal matter that also affects all other creatures on earth. (*A Path with
> Heart,* 9–10)

zazen. The sole form of meditation in Zen, *zazen* (literally, "just-sitting
meditation") is designed to free the mind from *any* kind of thinking or
feeling in the ordinary sense of these activities. To this end, it has much
less content than other forms of meditation. Indeed, at its most advanced level, it has none.

Taisen Deshimaru, a Japanese Zen master who made it his life's mission to transmit Zen to the West throughout the latter half of the
twentieth century, once used a particularly apt analogy: "During zazen,
brain and consciousness become pure. It's exactly like muddy water left
to stand in a glass. Little by little, the sediment sinks to the bottom and
the water becomes pure."

Beginners in zazen are sometimes advised to follow their breathing
as a means of taming their mental restlessness, but eventually they are
expected to outgrow the need for this device. They may then move on

to *shikantaza* ("nothing but sitting"), the central practice of the Soto school of Zen, or to zazen combined with koan study, the central practice of the Rinzai school.

Koans are teaching questions or tales that confound rational or emotional logic: for example, "What is your original face, the one you had before your parents were born?" Sitting with a koan is not like focusing on the breath or some other meditational object. Instead, it's a means of breaking through the everyday mind to a higher level of awareness. A koan functions as what John Daido Loori calls a "lancet of inquiry." In other words, it's more accurately labeled a meditation catalyst rather than a meditation focus.

In his book *The Eight Gates of Zen,* John Daido Loori quotes Master Dogen in referring to the ineffable nature of zazen:

> "When ordinary beings see it, they are sages. When sages see it, they are ordinary beings." Although we may speak of zazen in terms of counting the breath, following the breath, being the breath, "just sitting," koan inspection, and various other names and descriptions, we should bear in mind that they are just that—descriptions and intellectualizations of zazen—they don't yet reach zazen itself. . . . Zazen means to be intimate with the self. To be intimate with the self is to realize the whole phenomenal universe as the self. (84)

mantra meditation. In many schools of Buddhism, a *mantra* (in Sanskrit, a power-laden syllable or series of syllables) may be used as a meditational device. The meditator's constant, silent repetition of the mantra simultaneously clears the mind of extraneous thoughts or feelings and concentrates its attentiveness, thereby training it to be free from random distractions or attachments.

In some schools, almost any syllable, word, or expression can serve as a mantra, and meditators often choose—or are assigned—a particular mantra for a certain spiritual purpose. Typically the mantra does not have an explicit meaning, but rather a subliminal one.

For example, meditating on the word *buddha* (a Theravada practice) may induce the practitioner to merge with the indefinable qualities that he or she associates with the word. Pure Land Buddhists can meditate using their standard chanting mantra, *nan-mo-A-mi-t'o/namu-Amida-Butsu* (in Chinese and Japanese respectively, "Glory to Amitabha/Amida Butsu"); and Nichiren Buddhists can do the same with *namu-myoho-renge-kyo* (in Japanese, "Glory to the Lotus Sutra").

In Tibetan Buddhism, the mantra *om-mani-padme-hum* (in Sanskrit; in Tibetan, *om-mani-peme-hung*), which roughly translates as "jewel in the lotus," is by far the most popular one for meditation. It's also widely used for many other devotional practices, such as chanting, inscribing on slips of paper to be turned in a prayer wheel, or painting on a flag to be flapped in the wind (see "The Lesson of the Mani Man," below). As the mantra of Avalokiteshvara Bodhisattva, it essentially conveys the attitude of compassion, but has many other complex resonances. The six written syllable characters, for instance, are associated with the six realms of existence.

THE LESSON OF THE MANI MAN

This ancient Tibetan tale points to the wisdom of not dwelling on the future and not thinking in dualistic terms like good and bad. It also testifies to the steadiness of mind that can be gained from doing simple, repetitive activities like turning the prayer (or *mani*) wheel, whether it's a small, hand-held wheel mounted on a stick or a big drum filling an entire room.

Inside the wheel are slips of paper covered with a mantra. Turning the wheel stirs the mantras and thus "recites" them. For example, a hand-held wheel may contain twelve sheets, each covered with 2,460 tiny inscriptions, resulting in 29,250 recitations per turn. By making an easy 120 turns a minute, one can recite the mantra 3,542,000 times. The same principle applies to mantras written on flags that flap in the wind, or carved into stones that are read by the wind as well as every passerby.

Once there was an old man who lived with his son and one horse on a small piece of land. He used every spare moment to turn his homemade prayer wheel, and so he was called the Mani Man.

One morning the Mani Man woke up and the horse—his one valuable possession—was gone. His neighbors gathered to wail with him over the loss, but he just kept calmly turning his wheel. "We must give thanks for everything," he said. "Who can tell what is good or bad?"

After a week, the horse came trotting home, and in its wake were two wild mustangs. Again the neighbors rallied, this time to celebrate, but the Mani Man, turning his wheel, only said, "I am grateful, but who knows what the future will bring? We must simply wait and see."

Two days later, while training one of the mustangs to carry him, the son fell and broke his leg. The neighbors rushed to commiserate with the Mani Man, but he sat quietly at his son's bed, turning the wheel and refusing any sympathy. "My son's life continues to be a blessing to me," he said. "What has happened cannot be called good or bad."

The next day, a military recruiter appeared at the Mani Man's door and commanded, "We have come for your son! All healthy young men are needed to fight in the war!" Because the son was bedridden, he could not be taken. The neighbors, whose own sons had been whisked away to almost certain death, couldn't help expressing their envy to the Mani Man. Turning his wheel as always, he simply reminded them, "Nothing is known. We shall see."

Ringu Tulku, a Tibetan Buddhist who lives in Sikkim but teaches extensively in the West, explains the literal meaning of *om-mani-padme-hum* as follows:

> *Om* is the [seed] syllable or the sound which is believed to be the source of all sounds, because it is a sound which can be made without making any movements of your tongue or lips. *Mani* in Sanskrit means the wish-fulfilling jewel and *padme* is the lotus flower. The wish-fulfilling jewel is the representation of compassion. . . . Padme, the lotus flower, is usually regarded as a symbol of purity. . . . Even if they grow in dirty places, no speck of dust or stains can be seen on the petals. Therefore, this represents wisdom, which is a state where all negative things, all defilements, all ignorance, just go away. . . . *Hum* is a word which means "I am"—I am compassion and wisdom. (Harris, *What Buddhists Believe,* 84)

visualization meditation. Another widespread form of meditation in the Pure Land schools of Mahayana and in Vajrayana features visualization. Practitioners mentally envision an image (for example, a particular buddha or bodhisattva) that represents an enlightened state of being they aspire to achieve. In the process, they can not only "imagine" themselves into that kind of state but also teach themselves a new way of seeing—one that goes beyond the conceptual limits of everyday vision.

In Pure Land, practitioners who choose to meditate almost always visualize Amitabha (Amida), archetypal buddha of light, and/or his western paradise, the heaven that symbolically represents the bliss of one's final release from the cycle of samsara. When they do, they typically reconstruct in their mind iconic images that appear in books or artworks or that are described to them by their teacher.

Tibetan Buddhists engage in a similar but more intense and multidimensional form of visualization called deity yoga. The word *deity*—a clumsy but closest-possible translation of the Tibetan term *yidam*—doesn't refer to anthropomorphic superpowers but rather to principles and concepts that are cast into godlike formats to facilitate clear and vibrant visualization. In addition to buddhas or bodhisattvas, practitioners may imagine, for example, terrifying demons, perhaps to assist them in taming uncontrollable emotions. To perform this kind of visualization, the meditator usually needs to cooperate closely with his or her teacher, especially at the more advanced levels of tantric (or magical) practice.

OTHER WAYS TO BE MINDFUL

Meditation may be the purest extension of right mindfulness, but other Buddhist practices also provide special training in this regard, so that mind *and* body learn how to be wholeheartedly present in the moment. Among them are:

walking practice. In Zen, people typically engage in mindful walking *(kinhin)* between periods of zazen, repeating the same circuit over and over again with evenly paced steps (either fast, slow, or in between, depending on the school or teacher). Thus they can apply to a physical activity the same total absorption that they've just invested in a mental one. It's a means of reinvigorating themselves without breaking the kind of concentrated focus they've been developing in meditation.

In his 1991 book *Peace Is Every Step: The Path of Mindfulness in Everyday Life,* the Vietnamese Zen master Thich Nhat Hanh outlines a very compelling walking practice that combines meditation with breath control. The meditation part is disarmingly simple: "Walking meditation is really to enjoy the walking—walking not in order to arrive, but just to walk." In this spirit, it can be done anywhere (preferably someplace beautiful where interruptions are unlikely) and with anyone who is similarly inclined. Walking at a slightly slower pace than normal, practitioners coordinate breathing with steps, so that, for example, they take three steps with every in-breath and three steps with every out-breath. To assist the process, they can even say to themselves as they step, "in, in, in, out, out, out." Although the process may initially seem awkward, it can quickly become second nature.

Nhat Hanh employs a number of motivational metaphors to communicate the type of mindframe one should have during walking meditation. He urges us, for example, to "walk as if you are kissing the Earth with your feet. We have caused a lot of damage to the Earth. Now it is time for us to take good care of her." Alluding to Shakyamuni's first steps as a newborn infant, he asks us to suppose that "every step makes a flower bloom under our feet."

In a more contemporary vein, Nhat Hanh spins a delightful backstory that can be summarized like this: Imagine that you're an astronaut and you've crash-landed on the moon. Gazing at big, blue, beautiful Earth suspended in the sky above you, you yearn to be there once again and despair that it will never happen. Then, miraculously, you're able to repair the spaceship and return. How would you feel as you first set foot back on Earth? How intensely would you experience all that was going on around you?

chanting. Various mantras or sutras can be chanted in service or in individual practice to attune the mind and body to a certain teaching or state of being. So can a short, songlike composition called a *dharani* (in Sanskrit, literally "holder"). Dharanis typically consist of repetitive words and syllables that are not designed to make sense as texts but, rather, to produce beneficial mental associations and physical vibrations.

Throughout history, chanting (or singing) has been a central practice in every major religion. Its presence in Buddhism can therefore easily be understood as yet another extension of the natural human tendency to vocalize spiritual thoughts and feelings and to derive inspiration from doing so. However, the current use of chanting in the fast-growing, highly visible Soka Gakkai school of Buddhism has generated a great deal of dispute among outsiders, so it deserves mentioning in this context.

The Soka Gakkai school, founded in 1930 in Japan, is a branch of

Nichiren that has become increasingly popular not only in Japan but also in America, thanks in part to vigorous proselytizing, an activity fairly rare in Buddhism. Like all other branches of Nichiren, it supports chanting *namu-myoho-renge-kyo* as a means of releasing one's inner Buddha nature. Some practitioners, however, also chant for material benefits, such as more income or a favorable turn of fortune in a lawsuit or relationship, and it's this activity that has stirred up controversy.

The assumption of critics is that the people who chant for worldly success are led to believe in the virtue and efficacy of this approach by their teachers or by the lack of any doctrinal guidelines to the contrary within the school itself. More likely, it's simply the inevitable sort of thing that happens in any newly organized religious school that attracts people who are new to religion in general.

Whatever the case, Charles Prebish, associate professor of religious studies at Pennsylvania University, examines this chant-for-gain tactic at its face value in his book *Luminous Passage: The Practice and Study of Buddhism in America* and poses the important question, "Does it work?"

Are the goals of chanting achieved for its proponents? No doubt it would be just as presumptuous to assume that it did *not* work as it would to believe all the positive testimony I have collected in the past two decades. It might be fairer to argue that irrespective of whether specific goals are attained, in very many cases strong and positive subjective changes can be witnessed in the behavior of individuals. . . . At the very least, it is *not* a passive activity. Coupled with the positive expectation of the practitioner, it allows him or her to proceed into the world with an attitudinal shift that is necessarily beneficial and productive. (125)

On a more scientific note, recent neurological studies have shown that religious chanting in all traditions tends to follow a beat of two to four seconds, which corresponds to a basic pulse in brain activity. This alone could account for the overall healing, enlivening, and enriching effects of chanting.

* * *

bowing. In virtually every human culture, bowing is a means of expressing respect or veneration for a person, institution, idea, or spiritual power through humbling oneself. The head or body is lowered into a less self-important, freestanding, confrontational posture, and the hands are clasped or moved in a way that indicates submissiveness.

Over the past few centuries, Western civilization has increasingly emphasized individualism, and so it has gradually come to disparage bowing except for religious prayer. Even in this context, bowing usually involves only a slight lowering of the head and joining of the palms with, perhaps, a dropping to the knees in certain formal or intense situations.

Eastern civilization, which has placed a comparatively higher value on collective harmony over the same time period, has continued to honor the custom of bowing in many spheres of human endeavor. Accordingly Buddhism has developed and still offers a wide range of bowing activities to suit various religious purposes. Although these activities may seem alien to Western observers, who often misinterpret them as demeaning exhibitions of adulation or self-abasement, they present to Buddhists unique opportunities to exercise the combined mental, physical, and spiritual quality of mindfulness.

The simplest and most frequent bow is the gracious one that Buddhists make to greet, thank, or take their leave from one another. With the hands joined palm-to-palm a few inches in front of the mouth (fingertips pointing straight up and wrists bent at right angles to the forearms), the body is bowed slightly from the waist.

This bow can be made informally, during any one-on-one or group encounter, or formally, during moments of a service or ceremony when individuals come together or take their leave from each other. It can also be performed to an image of, or offering to, Shakyamuni or some other buddha or bodhisattva. In each of these applications, the palms-together gesture has the same meaning: Besides conveying respect, it expresses the bower's oneness with the object of the bow and, by extension, the oneness (nonduality) of all things in the phenomenal universe.

Another, fuller bow of gratitude is commonly made to an altar image of Shakyamuni Buddha or to a teacher. In either case, the bow is actually intended to express gratitude for—and oneness with—the teachings, not the individual (Shakyamuni or the teacher functioning as his representative). With hands palm-to-palm as described above, the person bows at the waist, drops to the knees, and touches the forehead to the floor, while simultaneously lifting the hands, palm-side-up, on either side of the head, a few inches into the air. The person then rises to the feet again by reversing the process. Typically this kind of bow is done in a series (for example, three or more bows in succession).

In addition to representing the humbling of the self, the gesture of touching the floor reminds the individual of his or her connection to the earth and to the ground-of-all-being. The accompanying gesture, the lifting of the hands, is given various symbolic interpretations, depending on the school or teacher. In an allusion to the ancient, iconic importance of the footprint in Buddhism (see page 24), Theravada practitioners often describe it as placing the Buddha's foot on top of one's head (i.e., acknowledging his role as the master teacher). Mahayana practitioners tend to say it indicates—or invites—the raising of the *bodhi* (enlightened) mind.

An even more elaborate bowing activity is the Vajrayana practice of prostrations. In its simplest prescribed format, it consists of a total of 100,000 full-body bows performed in repetitive intervals over a set period of time. The practice is typically part of one's officially becoming a Buddhist (known in Vajrayana as "taking refuge [in Buddha, Dharma, and Sangha]"), but it can also be performed at other times—either ceremonial or self-chosen occasions—to intensify one's practice.

A proper prostration begins by raising the hands over the head, palm-to-palm, in salutation, and then laying the body completely down, so that forehead, chest, hands, and knees are touching the ground. The exact procedure for accomplishing this "laying down" maneuver varies from individual to individual. David Lewis, a practitioner in the Nyingma tradition, describes in *The Complete Guide to Buddhist America,* edited by Don Morreale, how he learned to do it smoothly, quickly, and safely up to 3,000 times a day during a two-month retreat:

> I was using a polished hardwood board for the prostrations, along
> with two cloth pot holders to expedite the sliding of my hands along
> the wood. . . . I placed a pad for my knees on the board, and would
> slide down like a falling tree, not letting the knees touch until my
> chest had taken the brunt of the impact. Consequently my knees
> rarely hurt and the stale airs were shocked from my body. After a
> while the force of falling became the force of rising and the prostra-
> tions entered an effortless and blissful space.

The specific purpose of Lewis's prostrations retreat was to achieve spiritual purification. This principle, known as *vajrasattva,* is embodied in a *sambhogakaya* of the same name, whose symbolic, all-white image Lewis visualized as he prostrated. True to the character of the experi-ence, he only started realizing its positive effects after about thirty thousand repetitions:

> I was beginning to comprehend how the prostrations were working
> on me, and how subtle and inborn were the obstacles I was hoping
> to clear. How great are those practitioners who have accomplished
> the compassion to work for others on this level of penetration! I had
> touched the very fiber of *bodhisattva beingness* and though it was not
> mine to keep at this point, at least through raw effort a kind of self-
> initiation was pointing out this truth. My respect for teachers in gen-
> eral moved from idealism to recognition, and I felt a deep satisfaction
> in belonging to the sangha. By the time I had accomplished one
> hundred thousand prostrations, I had lost twenty pounds, my sweat
> had become sweet instead of salty, and I felt ready for the next hun-
> dred thousand. (225–26)

* * *

The procedures discussed above represent some of the more obvi-ous, formal, and intense ways to practice mindfulness. In fact, we can

ZEN WAYS

As Zen Buddhism evolved in Japan, it affected every aspect of Japanese culture. The result was the emergence of many refined art and body practices through which one can express, experience, or cultivate various aspects of Zen sensibility, for example, simplicity, intimacy, a love of nature, internal and external harmony, whole mind-and-body focus, the interpenetration of form and emptiness, and seeing into the essence of the matter. Among these practices are:

aikido. A dynamic defensive activity involving body movement and sparring with a short staff or sword.

brush painting. The fully engaged process of tapping and releasing energy to create an especially powerful composition.

haiku. A seventeen-syllable poem (in three lines of 5-7-5) capturing the essence of a subject.

ikebana. The arrangement of flowers in a spiritually and aesthetically satisfying manner.

karate. A weaponless form of self-defense aimed at disarming an opponent or rendering his/her hostile motions harmless.

kyudo. A form of archery combining spiritual and physical training.

No drama. A style of theater aimed at the direct communication of experience and emotion.

pottery making. An approach to making pottery that conveys special respect for the materials and the process.

shakuhachi. The playing of a bamboo flute in harmony with the breath and the emotional force moving the breath.

tea ceremony. The especially graceful and aware preparation of tea and management of the tea-partaking interchange between host and guest.

Zen gardening. A meditative approach to creating, tending, and enjoying a garden.

bring this quality to every moment of our lives, no matter what we're doing or experiencing. The challenge lies in keeping ourselves fully aware of, and intimately involved in, what is occurring *as it happens.* Among other things, this means avoiding distraction, lethargy, or passivity in favor of attention, wakefulness, and commitment. When we live in this manner, we see more clearly into the nature of our existence and, therefore, of the universe.

COMPASSION: ACTUALIZING THE TRUTH

Among the most compelling and useful symbols in Buddhism is one that is borrowed from Hinduism and invested with its own special meaning: the image of Indra's Net. Specifically, Indra is the supreme Hindu god, but throughout Indian culture in general, he is regarded as the great, mythical "Father of Everything." In the Buddhist Avatamska Sutra, his net is perceived as covering the universe; indeed, it constitutes the universe. At each of the net's intersections is a jewel (phenomenon, entity, or being) that reflects all the other jewels in the net. In fact, each jewel only exists as a reflection of the others; and within every jewel, the reflecting process goes on ad infinitum.

The literal description of Indra's Net corresponds to what is known in Western science as a hologram: a laser-produced image that appears three-dimensional despite being flat. No matter how many times a hologram is cut into pieces, each resulting fragment reflects the entire original image.

What concerns us in this book, however, is not the scientific reality of Indra's Net but the spiritual truth it conveys metaphorically. Think of each jewel in the net as an individual life or phenomenon in the universe. The net as a whole, therefore, depicts how the entire universe, including every sentient being, is reflected in each person's life, or, alternatively, how each person's life is interwoven in an endless network of cause and effect with everything else, including all other lives, in the universe.

On a superficial level, the image of Indra's Net presents one more way of conceiving the doctrine of no-self. Despite our apparent existence in separate "skin bags" (as Zen expresses it), we are actually one with everything in the universe. The notion that we are individual selves is simply a convenient illusion, one that helps us survive in the world of samsara.

On a deeper level, the image of Indra's Net suggests that we have a responsibility to think and act for the benefit of everything in the universe. The care we give to this endeavor is simultaneously for our own good as well as the good of others.

This message is implicit throughout Buddhism, but is especially evident in the Mahayana and Vajrayana vow to "save all sentient beings." Although some may see the task as being impossibly heroic, people who believe in the Buddhist principle of universal interdependence know that they can work toward fulfilling their vow in every thought they have, every word they speak, and every action they take.

There may even be a scientific correlative to the notion of saving all beings through one's own individual efforts. Robert Thurman draws a connection between this Buddhist belief and the concept of "morphic resonance" in biology, first developed by evolutionary biologist Rupert Sheldrake to explain a statistical pattern he observed among primitive life forms.

Specifically, Sheldrake's research indicated that when a large number of species members adopts and then embodies a certain pattern of behavior, it can accelerate the rate at which others adopt and embody it—whether or not any overt interaction occurs between the two groups. He hypothesized that the same kind of imperceptible transference might occur among humans, as a result of the resonances created by individual (and, eventually, group) beliefs and activities.

While acknowledging that Sheldrake's hypothesis remains controversial within the scientific community, Thurman asserts that it not only makes "intuitive sense," but also relates very closely to the Buddhist doctrine of interdependence. In *Inner Revolution* he discusses this issue, using the analogy of sensation-processing "software programs" in the human brain: "Once certain programs have become routine in our brains, we can articulate those programs to other people through language, image, song, rhythm, or a multitude of other means. Why might we not also radiate the patterns of those programs so that they can 'hang in the air' and be directly received by other brains?" He then proceeds to translate the belief behind this theory into practical terms: "If we would be activists for good, for the positive, we must assume responsibility for our minds as well as our speech and our physical activities, otherwise our negative mental habits will drag down the entire community of beings. On the other hand, when we break through into the liberty of heart, mind, and spirit in the process of enlightenment, we free others at the same time" (27–28).

Referring to the two most important Buddhist qualities—wisdom and compassion—teachers often say that while the *recognition* of truth is wisdom, the *activity* of truth is compassion. By compassion, they don't mean empathy or sympathy, both of which imply a passive, self-and-other point of view. The precise meaning of the original Sanskrit word *karuna* suggests a more active, immediate, and pure expression of caring or help, a natural inclination toward fostering the welfare of the universe. At first one's practice may inevitably involve thinking and doing good in a conscious, deliberate manner (i.e., telling oneself that it is right, kind, loving, or "Buddhist" to do so). The goal, however, is to reach the stage where one instinctively thinks and acts compassionately, without any mediating considerations.

TWO BANQUET HALLS

A Zen story tells of a fellow who dies and finds himself in a shimmering realm. He says to himself, "I must have lived a better life than I thought." A glistening being appears and guides him into a regal banquet hall. There an immense circular table is laden with delicacies. He sits down at the table just as other people are doing so. But when he picks up his fork to eat, someone comes from behind and straps boards to his arms so he can't bend his elbows. He can still get food on his fork, but he can't get his fork to his mouth.

Looking around, he notices that everyone else is in the same predicament, and the hall is filled with grumbling and groaning. He calls over to the glistening being, "This must be hell! What is heaven?"

The glistening being takes him to another banquet hall that looks just like the first, with the same big, circular table laden with the same food. Again he sits down just as others are doing so, and again boards are strapped to his arms so he can't reach his mouth with his fork. He thinks, "What's going on? This is the same thing as before!"

Then he looks around the table and notices something different. Instead of people grumbling and groaning as they try unsuccessfully to get food to their mouths, each person is holding his or her arm straight out to the right, to feed the person at the next seat. He does the same, and the hall is quickly filled with the sound of people happily eating.

To assist in one's mental and physical self-training, Buddhism offers a variety of moral and ethical precepts. Although they resemble the Judeo-Christian Ten Commandments in style, they are not commandments in the strict sense of the word because there is no commander or almighty god in Buddhism to lend them authority. Instead, they are principles or codes of conduct that one takes up on his or her own in order to lead a wiser, more compassionate life.

Here are the five basic precepts common to all Buddhist traditions:

1. *Avoid causing harm to other sentient beings.* This precept may also be expressed in terms like "Do not kill" or "Affirm life." In general, it means to refrain from life-damaging violence of all kinds, whether it's in one's thoughts, words, or deeds. More specifically, it asks one not to take another person's life or even one's own.

   Some schools, teachers, or practitioners interpret the precept quite literally to mean not eating meat, which obligates them to be vegetarians. Others say that it allows for the eating of meat, provided one is mindful about it rather than thoughtless, gluttonous, or wasteful.

   Those who believe the precept permits meat eating cite the Middle Way approach to food consumption (versus the ascetic one) as well as scriptural evidence that Shakyamuni himself ate meat as part of his commitment to consume any food put into his begging bowl. It's even said that a bite of spoiled boar's flesh led to his death (although some texts claim it was mushrooms). This is hardly a good recommendation for meat eating, but it does not in itself constitute a prohibition.

   Mahayana practitioners often argue that vegetables, too, are sentient beings, so it's actually not more virtuous to be a vegetarian. In Tibet, where it's very difficult to grow crops, meat has always been an essential part of the diet for everyone, including Buddhists.

   The difference of opinion over meat eating in Buddhism underscores that the precepts are guidelines rather than commandments. They need to be incorporated into a person's life in the manner that most wholeheartedly expresses his or her own commitment to practice, a commitment that includes his or her relationship with a particular school and teacher.

2. *Avoid taking anything that is not freely given.* This precept may also be expressed in terms like "Do not steal" or "Be generous." In addition to warning against outright theft or greed, it also bids one to refrain from manipulating or exploiting people or from making unreasonable demands on them. Its general purpose is to encourage the practitioner to let go of possessiveness, craving, and attachment.

3. *Avoid sexual misconduct.* Buddhism is remarkable among the major religions of the world for not flatly proscribing certain nonviolent sexual activities that often meet with social disapproval, like masturbation, sex without marriage, or homosexuality. It tends to affirm the beauty and "rightness" of nature and, by extension, of sex, which can be an especially intimate and valuable way of going beyond self to relate to another.

   In this spirit, Buddhism counsels people to refrain from abusive or manipulative sex as well as from sexual obsession, jealousy, or deception. Among the acts that are clearly harmful to oneself as well as one's partner are rape, molestation, and, at least in many situations, adultery.

   Most schools of Buddhism require that monks and nuns take vows of chastity, but the rationale is that sex in a monastic setting can distract one from spiritual work and disrupt group harmony, not that it's in any way intrinsically evil. In some schools, monks and nuns are allowed to marry or even to pursue stable, monogamous relationships without marrying.

4. *Avoid untruthfulness.* This precept is sometimes phrased "Do not lie" or "Be truthful." It obviously applies to what one says or writes, as do many other precepts in Buddhism relating to slandering, gossiping, boasting, being frivolous, or expressing negative opinions.

   However, the precept is also intended to govern how one thinks and behaves. It encourages people to be straightforward in all aspects of their life, so that they don't mislead others as well as themselves in any way that might be harmful.

Teachers often caution against interpreting the precept too dual-istically, as if *true* and *false* were always polar opposites, and one must consistently choose the former over the latter. In some situa-tions, wisdom and compassion may dictate a skillful approach that isn't, in a strict sense, "true."

For example, suppose a man whom you know to be extremely sensitive to criticism asks you to comment on his poetry, some-thing that is very special to him. You may truly believe it is awful, but it may well be better under the circumstances not to express your true opinion quite so openly to your friend. If you're certain that a woman in distress is facing some horrible times ahead and she cries out to you in her pain, "Will things turn out okay?," the best course of action may be to comfort her by saying, "Yes, I'm sure they will."

When Buddhists find themselves in such situations, the precept urges them to consider, "Am I motivated toward a certain untrue response in order to protect myself, to make myself look better, or to advance my own cause?" If they are, then they are definitely in danger of violating the spirit that lies behind the precept: maintain-ing one's own integrity and respecting the integrity of others.

5. *Avoid clouding the mind with drugs.* This precept is alternatively phrased in terms like "Refrain from intoxicating drinks and drugs." Some schools or teachers interpret it to mean total abstinence from alcohol or any other kind of mind-altering drug, especially if it's expressed in the latter language. Others say it allows for limited al-cohol or drug consumption, as long as one doesn't become inebri-ated or mentally fuzzy.

By extension, the precept relates to other kinds of induced men-tal druggedness as well, such as zoning out for hours watching tele-vision, playing computer games, or doing one's work on automatic pilot. In addition, it obliges one not to encourage others to cloud their minds with drugs, either at all or in excess, depending on how it's understood. The point is to actualize the positive version

of the precept: Maintain and promote clear mindfulness at all
times.

The actual number of precepts an individual Buddhist adopts varies
from tradition to tradition and, within each tradition, from context to
context. Laypersons generally vow to enact the basic five precepts just
discussed above and, possibly, three to five others in Buddhism relating
to specific doctrinal points—for example, "Avoid spreading the poison
of anger"—or to secular activities deemed unwholesome—for example, "Avoid wearing cosmetics."

Monastics also embrace the same five basic precepts along with additional ones. Theravada monks and nuns typically commit themselves
to five more precepts that apply to monastic life in particular: for example, "Avoid possessing luxuries." Mahayana monks may vow to
maintain up to 250 precepts, including the basic five plus a host of others applying to finer points of appropriate behavior: for example,
"Avoid gossiping," "Avoid insulting," "Avoid expressing skepticism."
Mahayana nuns may agree to follow up to 348 precepts. Many of the
extra ones, now merely ceremonial in nature, reveal the negative attitudes toward women that prevailed in the ancient patriarchal societies
of Asia: for example, "Avoid engaging in seductive magic." We'll look
more closely at issues relating to women in Buddhism in chapter 6.

Taking up the precepts means committing oneself to living more
mindfully moment by moment, day by day, and year by year, which is,
in fact, the practice of enlightenment. One cannot passively follow the
precepts. Instead, one much actively make them part of one's constant
endeavor to think, speak, and act as wisely and compassionately as possible. Each new thought or action presents a new challenge: Given the
context at hand, how do the precepts apply? How can I employ them
in the most skillful manner?

As one lives with the precepts, posing and answering these questions
becomes second nature, thereby positively transforming not only one's
own life but also the life of the universe. John Daido Loori expresses
this idea eloquently in *The Heart of Being:*

The possibilities that compose the spectrum of human experience are your possibilities. All space and time come alive in each of us. How we practice and realize our lives depends on what we invoke, what we call forth. Regardless of whether we appreciate this fact or not, we are ceaselessly invoking. So what will it be? Will it be greed, or will it be compassion? Will it be anger, or will it be wisdom? Will it be ignorance, or will it be enlightenment? It is all in our hands. How do we invoke vow, and practice that vow in our lives? We should examine this question thoroughly and keep examining it forever. (34)

THE TEACHER-STUDENT RELATIONSHIP

Becoming a Buddhist means quite literally becoming a student. To learn what the religion means and how to practice it, an individual needs to establish a close, dynamic relationship with a teacher. There is no central, instructional text that by itself can reveal the Dharma to a reader.

Even more to the point, Buddhism asks one to break through the narrow confines of self, which demands going beyond self-education to accept the more objective and enlightened guidance of a master. As a spiritual path that manifests itself solely in the way that individual practitioners come to think, speak, and act, it can be examined and understood only in the living context of an ongoing teacher-student relationship.

In many respects, the teacher functions to reparent the student into a new way of being. It's not that the teacher *gives* the student life. Actually, one of the most dangerous misconceptions would-be Buddhists can have is that they can *get* anything from a teacher—a craving-driven attitude that denies one's innate powers and encourages overdependency on others. Instead, a teacher facilitates training, so that the student can evolve naturally to achieve his or her own full spiritual potential.

Atisha, the great eleventh-century Indian Buddhist scholar credited with the so-called second spreading of Buddhism into Tibet, is famous for writing that the "instruction of the mentor" is even more important than a knowledge of all the sutras and commentaries, because he or she represents, as Shakyamuni did, the "immediate application" of the teachings. Atisha likens the mentor to a doctor who diagnoses the patient (the student) and prescribes the medicine (the Dharma). Without a doctor's personal intervention, the analogy implies, it's useless for sick people to carry around a bag full of medicine.

Throughout Buddhist history, the ideal means of entering into a teacher-relationship has been to join a monastery as a monk or nun (usually, but not always, men and women are trained in separate monasteries). There resident teachers can observe and interact with students on a daily basis in many different contexts, including one-on-one instructional encounters, classroom-style gatherings, discourses, liturgical services, special ceremonies, work assignments, meals, and casual contact.

In addition to declaring that they "take refuge" in the Three Jewels (Buddha, Dharma, and Sangha), monastics typically agree to lead a life of chastity, poverty, stability, and various other conditions that are appropriate to their vocation. Their days are spent meditating and performing other spiritual practices as well as studying with their teacher.

In many Asian monasteries, especially Theravada ones, monastics also emulate Shakyamuni and his disciples by begging for food or money throughout the local region, an activity usually performed in silence by outstretching a bowl. In Mahayana monasteries in Asia, monastics may also or alternatively grow their own food or do their own manual labors. Theravada monasteries tend to depend more on laypeople to do these activities.

The teacher-student relationship for laypeople in Buddhism has historically been much less intimate. Individuals, families, and communities can join in support of a given monastery and can take advantage of public hours, services, and ceremonies to confer with teachers, hear them speak, or observe their conduct. Teachers also speak publicly on occasion or visit the homes of faithful or needy believers. However, the opportunities for nonmonastic Buddhists to sustain close, frequent, face-to-face interaction with a teacher are fairly rare.

As a result, Buddhism has continued to be primarily a monastery-based religion, as opposed to Christianity, for example, which began transforming itself into a more lay-oriented, church-based religion as the Middle Ages gave way to the more individualistic Renaissance era (1200–1600 C.E.). Now that Buddhism has spread into the Western world, it shows signs of following the same pattern. Many Western teachers operate out of temples or lay centers rather than monasteries, and many Western students can have almost as much access to these teachers as monastics do in a monastery. This subject is discussed more extensively in the next two chapters.

Among Buddhist teachers in general, there are many different styles that vary according to official status, personality, or both. At one end of the spectrum is what Chogyam Trungpa, the well-known Vajrayana teacher and founder of the Naropa Institute in the United States, calls a "spiritual friend." This kind of teacher guides the student very gently, informally, and unceremoniously, as if the two of them were near equals in virtually every respect (and, in fact, this style is naturally appropriate for a teacher who doesn't have many formal credentials).

At the other end of the spectrum is what Trungpa calls the guru, which is the proper Sanskrit term for teacher and is used as such in Hinduism and in some schools of Buddhism, especially Vajrayana ones. An equivalent term in Theravada is "venerable [one]"; in Zen, "master" (in Japanese, *sensei* and, for a senior teacher, *roshi*); and in Tibetan Buddhism, *lama* and, as a special honorific, *rinpoche*. This kind of teacher relies heavily on using the traditional training mechanisms and the authority of his or her position in the religious hierarchy as teaching tools.

In between are myriad variations on these two themes, including teachers who are as a rule—or as best fits the situation—taskmasters, nurturers, visionaries, scholars, servants, commanders, inspirers, placators, challengers, collaborators, innocents, sophisticates, saints, or rebels. Unfortunately, as in every other religious or educational context, there are also individuals who bear the title "teacher" but who lack the skill, training, experience, character, or self-control to fulfill that role effectively (for more discussion of teacher-related problems, see "Questions and Answers," on page 148).

Finding the right teacher thus becomes both critical and complicated. It doesn't just involve evaluating his or her background, although that step is certainly advisable. It's also not simply a matter of choosing someone with a matching personality (which may not be demanding enough) or a counterbalancing one (which may be too demanding). Ultimately, the wisest course for the seeker may be to trust in his or her own heart, gut, or instincts—a type of self-reliance that, after all, is a fundamental part of what's involved in following the Buddhist path.

According to most expert commentators, a student's relationship with a Buddhist teacher tends to go through several common, developmental stages that are similar to the phases of a romance. First there's the courtship: The student yearns to get close to the teacher and gain his or her approval, which, paradoxically, sometimes causes the student to fear the teacher and hold back. Next, a power struggle emerges: The student overtly or subconsciously battles the teacher for control of the relationship—the last stand of the student's ego. Then the relationship enters a partnership phase, which can take one or more of several forms as time goes by. The student may participate actively in whatever the teacher offers, give up and follow the teacher passively, or remain as resistant to the teacher as possible without actually breaking off.

Hopefully the partnership stage is eventually overcome, and along with it, any remaining vestiges of quasi-romantic attachment. The student outgrows the need to relate to the teacher as "the other," the administrator of the teachings, the key to the treasure. Instead, the student sees both the teacher and him- or herself as valuable individuals who share the wealth of the teachings.

In *A Path with Heart,* Jack Kornfield writes that the best teachers help us learn "how to love and be loved," and then how to go beyond that "to love the truth, love life":

The genuineness of a teacher and teachings becomes a sacred vessel that holds the truth that leads us to awaken our heart. The respected Zen master Suzuki Roshi was described by his student Trudy Dixon in this way: "Because he is just himself, he is a mirror for his students. When we are with him, we feel our own strengths and shortcomings without any sense of praise or criticism from him. In his presence we see our original face, and the extraordinariness we see is only our own true nature." (232)

QUESTIONS AND ANSWERS

Meditation appears to represent a turning away from the world, or even a rejection of it. Is this true?
Contrary to what meditation looks like, it is not intended to be either an immediate means of escaping the world or a gradual process of learning to release oneself from worldly matters. Teachers consistently warn students that using it for these reasons goes directly against its essential purpose in Buddhism: to free the mind, so that it can see into the truth of the self and the universe, and ultimately to enlighten the individual, so that he or she can be more vitally present in every moment of life.

Meditation is definitely the act of looking within rather than without; and to facilitate it, meditators value a peaceful environment that is not likely to present many distractions. Over time, meditation can also teach a person not to become so painfully attached to specific people, places, or things in life.

However, none of these facts constitutes a rejection of the outside world. When we take the time to look within, we can't help confronting what is truly going on in "our world," something that's all too easy to do when we're caught up in the busyness of the day. And when we learn to avoid becoming attached to various self-oriented desires, we're able to engage in life more skillfully and to become more intimate with the people, places, and things we experience.

Many Buddhists assert that meditation can lead to the most intense and positive kind of social activism. Indeed, they claim that meditation may be a prerequisite for it. Venerable Yos Hut Khenmacaro, a Cambodian Buddhist monk deeply engaged in the grassroots reconstruction of his war-ravaged country, attributes much of the activist fervor that he and other monks feel both to the monastic way of life and to meditation. In the 1996 BBC-TV series *The Way of the Buddha,* he said, "We have strengthened ourselves through increasing our own education in Dhamma and Vinaya [in Pali, the Dharma and the monastic codes] but also through insight meditation. In this way we could become mindful within ourselves and create peace within our hearts in order to help create peace for others around us and within the whole society" (Harris, *What Buddhists Believe,* 67).

How does the Buddhist concept of compassion relate to the Christian concept of love? To the concept of romantic love?

The Buddhist concept of compassion (in Sanskrit, *karuna*) does have similarities to the kind of love that Christian theologians call *agape* (in Greek, "spiritual love" as opposed to *eros,* "sexual love"). Both karuna and agape can be characterized as pure, selfless love that transcends petty human preoccupations. Nevertheless, significant differences exist between the two notions.

According to Buddhist doctrine, karuna flows freely and spontaneously from the individual who realizes that there is no such entity as a separate self and, therefore, no such duality as self and other. Unlike the Christian concept of agape, it is not an act of loving someone *as* oneself, or expressing the love that is in one's soul, or being an agent of God's love. Nor is it a sacrifice of one's own self-interest that is symbolically akin to the Christ's sacrifice on the cross. In Buddhism, there is no self, soul, or God—nothing to relate to, or to give up, in the expression of compassion. Instead, it's perceived as simply and absolutely the natural thing to do.

People who know little about Buddhism tend to assume that all those smiles they see on buddha statues reflect a very generalized benevolence—one that is cool, detached, and even elitist. In fact, the concept of karuna asks believers to become totally one with every individual they encounter, and to manifest unconditional love to each person who is suffering in the manner that will most help him or her.

Often when karuna is enacted, it does not have the outward appearance that we're culturally conditioned in the West to associate with love. It may not look passionate, graceful, affectionate, sentimental, sweet, joyful, heroic, or renunciatory. Depending on the need involved, it can even seem stern: what modern psychology calls "tough love." And yet it may well be the deepest, most genuine, and most effective expression of compassion for that particular situation.

Another common misconception is that Buddhism's emphasis on nonattachment and universal compassion casts a negative light on two people entering into their own special love relationship. In fact, Buddhism points to a much more committed love between two people than the type popularly designated as "romantic" love.

A romantic relationship feeds on the separation between the two partners. Each engages in desiring, wooing, fighting against, and making love with the other. In other words, each regards him- or herself as *attached* to the other. From a Buddhist perspective, the ideal love relationship between two people is one in which they truly merge into a compassionate oneness, so that there is no remaining vestige of self-and-other mentality to breed suffering.

The teacher has a great deal of authority in Buddhism. Isn't that dangerous for students? How does a student avoid or cope with teachers who abuse their power, or who don't live up to their teachings?
Buddhism, like other religions, has its fair share of horror stories about teachers. Human nature being what it is, there are inevitably a few teachers who wind up manipulating their students for selfish purposes, exploiting them financially, enticing them into inappropriate sexual liaisons, or otherwise taking unethical advantage of their trust.

Fortunately, the positive stories—the ones about teachers guiding their students to enlightenment and giving up their own personal agenda in favor of their students' needs—far outweigh the negative ones. It's important to keep in mind several key factors built into Buddhist doctrine and practice that work in favor of healthy teacher-student relationships.

First and foremost, Buddhism revolves around the principle of achieving freedom, of being one's own authority, or, as Shakyamuni put it, being "a lamp unto yourself." With this end in view, a teacher's training, a student's path, and the teacher-student relationship are each carefully designed to encourage a student's autonomy.

Even in Tibetan Buddhism, where devotion to a teacher is especially emphasized, official doctrine explicitly cautions the student not to focus on the personality of the teacher as an object of hero-worship. Teachers, like their grand predecessor Shakyamuni, are to be venerated for what they represent, not for who they are as individuals. Instead of blindly imitating the teacher, the student is advised to apply the teacher's message wisely and skillfully to his or her own life.

Buddhism is based on the notion that everyone is equally valuable and intrinsically good—that certain people aren't "better" than others. The Dharma extends this concept to the student-teacher relationship. The student *chooses* a teacher and retains control over that choice. Leaving, defying, or even denouncing a teacher is not associated with sacrilege or damnation. From the standpoint of the Dharma, it may even be a step toward spiritual growth.

Rita M. Gross, professor of comparative studies in religion at the University of Wisconsin–Eau Claire and author of *Buddhism after Patriarchy,* notes that spiritual *authority* is often confused with spiritual *power.* In Buddhism, she maintains, teachers are granted the authority to teach, but not the power to determine a student's fate.

Gross deplores teachers who abuse that authority, and as a feminist, she particularly laments the injustice of male teachers pressuring their female students for sex. Nevertheless, she points out that the probability of student collusion in alleged teacher-based misbehavior is often unfairly discounted by people who mistakenly assume that the teacher holds reign over the subordinate or incompetent student.

In Gross's essay "Helping the Iron Bird Fly: Western Buddhist Women and Issues of Authority in the Late 1990s," she opposes in particular the frequent comparison of sexual encounters between Bud-

dhist teachers and students to those between bosses and secretaries or
between professors and students:

> Secretaries and academic students rarely choose their bosses or pro-
> fessors in the way that Dharma students choose a spiritual mentor,
> and they usually cannot exercise the degree of discrimination that is
> required of a Dharma student vis-à-vis his or her guru. Most espe-
> cially, I reject the comparison of the guru-student relationship to the
> therapist-client relationship, which is so inegalitarian that sexual re-
> lationships would almost always be exploitative. . . . The guru is not
> a therapist and the meditation student is not a therapy client. (Pro-
> bish and Tanaka, eds., *The Faces of Buddhist America,* 243)

Second, all sorts of institutions and rituals are connected with the
process of teaching that help prevent it from becoming dangerously
isolated, informal, or manipulative. One of the biggest safeguards is that
the relationship between teacher and student occurs in the context of
a sangha, whose members all educate each other through a cooperative
system that commentators sometimes refer to as "mutual polishing."
For each student, this multidirectional group process counterbalances
the one-on-one dynamic he or she has with the teacher. The presence
of an alert sangha also makes it more difficult for secretive, unusual, or
disruptive activities to take place between a teacher and his or her
student.

In addition, most Buddhist schools require students to go through
sobering, socially distancing protocols whenever they formally interact
with a teacher. Typically the student bows to the teacher—a gesture of
respect—at the beginning and end of every face-to-face teaching encounter. Often doctrine requires that such encounters stay within a
specific format. For example, koan study between a Zen teacher and
his or her student generally precludes any conversation that doesn't relate specifically to the koan currently under consideration—something
of which both parties are fully aware from the beginning.

Such conventions help keep real or presumed social intimacy between teacher and student from interfering with the kind of mind-to-

mind intimacy that leads to enlightenment. In other words, they assist the student in maintaining the most effective perspective possible in regard to his or her teacher—not too near, but not too distant. An ancient Tibetan saying expresses the idea well: "A teacher is like a fire: If you stand too close, you get burned; too far away, you grow cold."

Finally, the teacher is not officially set up to be a godlike figure or even to stand in place of one. The teacher's authority lies in being a representative of the great teacher, Shakyamuni. Like the Buddha, a teacher is only human and may occasionally exhibit personality traits that are not perfect and that some people might find objectionable. He or she may smoke, drink too much, poke fun at people from Indiana, have no appreciation of music, or be grumpy in the morning. Such less-than-ideal behaviors, however, do not in themselves indicate that the person who displays them doesn't know the Dharma, doesn't strive to live it, or can't inspire students to learn it and awaken.

In the same essay quoted above, Gross dismisses the myth that the teacher is—or should be—a perfect role model:

> This principle that the guru is not an authority on all issues needs to be much more thoroughly assimilated, for in my view much of the disappointment many people express about their teacher's conduct results from theistic expectations of the guru, from confusing the guru with God, or from longing for him or her to be the perfect mummy or daddy one never had. It is also my view that the demand for a perfect guru is . . . resistance, in the form of the statement, "Unless I find a guru and a spiritual scene that I totally approve of, I won't practice meditation with them." (241–42)

The Zen master Philip Kapleau points out that westerners, brought up in a Judeo-Christian tradition of dualities (good and evil, God and Satan, saint and sinner), are likely to project unrealistic expectations on any teacher who claims to be enlightened: "In the West a roshi is expected to [have] flawless conduct. . . . But this idealistic view can blind one to the merits of a teacher. . . . A Japanese long experienced in Zen once told me, 'My roshi does have character flaws, yet of the teachers I have had he is the only one who taught me real Zen and I am exceedingly grateful to him' " (quoted in John Wellwood, "On Spiritual Authority," *Shambhala Sun,* 8, no. 1 (September 1999): 47).

Part of the difficulty may be that westerners often mistakenly assume that an Eastern spiritual leader is meant to be an ideal person whom the student can aspire to become—in other words, that enlightenment automatically turns one into a perfect individual in every way. Believing this concept, they justify for themselves what they mistakenly assume the student is meant to be: totally submissive to the teacher.

In fact, the situation in Buddhism is much more human and humane. Apart from their ceremonial roles, teachers are meant to be exactly who they are: human beings who have attained a certain degree of realization and remain engaged in a struggle to apply what they've learned in their day-to-day lives. Allowing their students to witness who their teachers really are is yet another way of helping their students learn the Dharma for themselves.

In a similar manner, students are expected to present themselves to teachers as openly and honestly as possible, without hiding behind any mantle of subservience. It's certainly risky for the student to reveal him- or herself so nakedly, and in rare cases a teacher may take unscrupulous advantage of it. However, in the presence of a genuine master, such self-exposure provides a uniquely powerful opportunity for personal growth.

BUDDHIST HOLIDAYS

Buddhism encourages students to give each day—and, for that matter each moment—equal importance. Accordingly, holidays are less significant in Buddhism as occasions for special religious expression than they are, for example, in Christianity, Judaism, or

Islam. This is particularly true among non-Asian Buddhists in the West, where the mainstream, Judeo-Christian culture does not reinforce the observance of Buddhist holidays.

Although various Buddhist cultures, schools, or organizations may have their own additional festivities during the year, regular Buddhist holidays in both Asia and the West revolve around the major events in the Buddha's life. They include:

Shakyamuni Buddha's birthday. In many cases, especially in Mahayana and Vajrayana schools, this day is celebrated on or around April 8, according to the Western calendar. It's traditionally a day devoted to honoring children. In some Buddhist schools, a special ceremony is held in which children pour water over an image of the Buddha placed under a woven canopy of grass and flowers.

Traditionally, Theravada schools celebrate Wesak, the full-moon day in spring on which the Buddha's birth, enlightenment, and death are all supposed to have occurred. In the Western calendar, this day usually falls in May but some years in June. Of the three events honored on Wesak, Shakyamuni's enlightenment is considered the most important.

Shakyamuni Buddha's enlightenment. In many Buddhist schools, especially Theravada ones (see Wesak, above), Shakyamuni's enlightenment is honored in the spring: May or June. In Zen, it's celebrated on or around December 8. Some Zen groups associate it with the winter solstice, a time when light comes back into the world. Typically the day is observed by meditating and, possibly, making a special donation of time, energy, or money to the temple, monastery, sangha, or community in general.

Shakyamuni Buddha's paranirvana. Most Theravada schools celebrate Shakyamuni's death, or final entry into nirvana, on Wesak in May or June (see above). In many Mahayana schools and most

Vajrayana ones, it is celebrated on or around February 15. For some predominately Buddhist countries in Asia, including Tibet, this day represents New Year's Day. February 15, 2000, in the West began the year 2486 in these countries, which date their yearly calendar from 486 B.C.E., the traditional year of the Buddha's paranirvana. There are no official customs associated with this day, other than feasting and celebrating life itself.

5 The Dharma Comes to the West

When the iron bird flies, and horses run on wheels, the Tibetan people will be scattered like ants across the world, and the Dharma will come to the land of the red man.

—Padmasambhava, c. 775 C.E.

In 458 C.E., a Chinese Buddhist monk named Hui-shan led a daring sea voyage up the coast of Asia, across the Bering Strait, and down the coast of North America. He came ashore in the region we now call Mexico but he dubbed Fu-sang, after a plant with dark leaves widely cultivated there. In a nearby village at the base of a volcano, he and his five priest-companions lived among the natives, whom he described as "red-skinned." Besides spreading the Dharma, the six monks taught methods of farming, building, and health care that were, in Hui-shan's words, "far superior" to those in use. They returned to China the following year, and Hui-shan submitted a lengthy report of the journey to the imperial archives.

Was Hui-shan's journey the first contact between

Buddhism and the Americas, and at the same time one of the religion's earliest forays into the Western world? It's only one of many provocative questions relating to Buddhism's history outside Asia. Because of the quiet, subtle, pacifist nature of Buddhism and, typically, of its spokespeople, Buddhist thought and practice could possibly have infiltrated the West at various times during the centuries after Shakyamuni's death without attracting much attention, at least as far as official, written records were concerned. In the words of John Daido Loori Roshi, current abbot of Zen Mountain Monastery in Mount Tremper, New York, "The dharma [universal way, law, or truth] has *always* been in the West. The question is, when did the Dharma [specifically, the Buddha's teachings] arrive?"

Hui-shan's document describing his fifth-century voyage was rediscovered in the mid-eighteenth century by the French sinologist Joseph de Guignes. It was de Guignes who determined that the band of monks visited Mexico—rather than some other place—via the route described above. Hui-shan only wrote that it was a land "twenty thousand miles [i.e., Chinese miles, shorter than Western ones] from China in an easterly direction." Otherwise, all the facts cited above are taken directly from the report.

Many additional details in Hui-shan's account and in pre-Columbian American history can also be interpreted to mean that he visited an area in or near Mexico. Putting them all together, de Guignes further speculated that Hui-shan could have traveled south to an area he then named Gautama-mala, "The Beads of the Buddha" (i.e., Guatemala), and east to an area he called Maya, after the mother of Shakyamuni (i.e., the homeland of the Mayan Indians).

Ever since de Guignes published his theory, scholars have embellished on it. For example, Hui-shan recorded that the local inhabitants greeted him as if he were "a heavenly being" and treated him accordingly for the rest of his visit. They may have continued to revere him for a long time after he was gone. Several folklorists who have said so have noted that the native Americans dwelling along Mexico's west coast have always called themselves the Huichols.

And that's not all. For generations the Huichols' neighbors have referred to them colloquially as "Chinois" because of their distinctly Chinese appearance. Peace-loving by nature, the Huichols are often seen carrying traditional healing bowls called "sakai-mona." They also conduct an annual spiritual dance in which the performers *(chinelos)* dress up as old white men with canes. Although the origin of the dance is unknown, it is said by Huichol medicine people to go back over a thousand years.

Some archaeologists, anthropologists, and historians have seen indirect evidence of Hui-shan's Buddhist mission to the North American continent not only among the Huichols but also within other Native American cultures ranging as far away from Mexico as the Mississippi and Ohio River valleys. More tangible support for their claims has come from the discovery of Buddhist design elements (e.g., seated meditators, lotus plants, swastikas) on temples, artifacts, and rocks throughout Mexico and the southwestern United States, including southern California.

The late-nineteenth-century American scholar Charles G. Leland speculates that early Buddhist influence may account for both the artistic style and the peaceful character of a geographical chain of native tribes extending from Central America northward into the mound-builder region of the midwestern United States. The folklorist Henriette Mertz, in her 1972 book *Pale Ink: Two Ancient Records of Chinese Exploration in America,* even argues that Hui-shan may have inspired the myth of Quetzalcoatl, culture hero of the ancient inhabitants of western and central Mexico. As the legend goes, Quetzalcoatl suddenly appeared on the western coast from across the ocean. Light-skinned (in contrast to the dusky- or "red-skinned" natives) and averse to violence, he lived among the people for a brief time, teaching them to farm, weave, smelt, heal, use manners, and practice spirituality. Then he disappeared from whence he came.

As exciting as it is for westerners to believe that Hui-shan visited the Western Hemisphere as opposed to some Eastern land, the evidence is entirely circumstantial, and so the theory itself remains controversial. Nevertheless, it's intriguing to think that Buddhism may have subtly influenced the development of peaceful Native American cultures.

It's also logically consistent, at least in the abstract. Both worlds—Buddhist and Native American—uphold the importance of spiritual illumination through mental and physical discipline, and both are characterized by egalitarianism, gentleness of spirit, simplicity of lifestyle, a reverence for nature, and a veneration for ancestors.

All we can say for sure, however, is that we know very little about any contacts between Buddhism and the West for the first 1,500 years of the religion's existence. Living in an era when we can instantly communicate with every inhabited region on the globe, we have to strain to imagine just how isolated the East and the West appear to have been from each other during this time. Most likely some episodes of cross-fertilization occurred between the two worlds every now and then, but what form any such exchanges took is shrouded in mystery, speculation, and outright fantasy.

Indeed, as far as recorded history is concerned, the process of Buddhism's assimilation into the Western world has just begun. The earliest credible, substantial reports of the religion printed in the West date only from about two hundred years ago. As a result, even today many aspects of Buddhism still seem problematically alien, fabulous, and raw to the Western mind.

Given this state of affairs, it's little wonder that so many Americans and Europeans continue to find it difficult to understand Buddhism or to accept it as a major, serious, and vital development in human history. Others, however, in company with de Guignes, Leland, and Mertz, believe that it may long ago have had a much more significant impact on Western civilization than we'll ever be able to prove. Let's briefly examine some of the tantalizing hints.

A BUDDHIST ROLE IN SHAPING CHRISTIANITY?

Spreading from Asia five centuries before Hui-shan's voyage and heading in the opposite direction—that is, toward the Mediterranean Sea—Buddhism may have contributed to the way Christianity evolved and, by extension, to the development of Western Europe.

Again, the evidence is small, but it's definitely more considerable and convincing than the total body of clues supporting a Chinese Buddhist connection to America a millennium before Christopher Columbus.

Although no record exists of any direct contact between Buddhists and Europeans prior to Jesus' lifetime, word of Buddhism as it grew into a major religion almost certainly traveled along the ancient trade routes connecting Europe and Asia. During Ashoka's reign over much of northern India (272–236 B.C.E.), he sent Buddhist missionaries westward along these same routes. Allegedly some of them even reached the Mediterranean coast. As mentioned earlier in this book (see page 8), many of the jataka tales—stories of the Buddha's previous lifetimes—were presumably converted into Aesop's fables around this period in history.

In the first century B.C.E., Milinda (or, in Greek, Menander), the Greek ruler of northwestern India roughly two hundred years after its conquest by Alexander the Great, engaged in a famous question-and-answer dialogue with the Buddhist monk Nagasena (see page 89). Milinda may have even converted to Buddhism himself. In any event, some historians believe that Buddhist concepts filtered from Milinda's colony back to Greece to inspire the Neoplatonists, many of whose ideas were later mirrored in Christianity.

It is known for certain that Buddhist priests were living in Alexandria, Egypt, around the time of Jesus Christ. Many authorities suggest that the vigor of Buddhist teachings then circulating in the eastern Mediterranean world may have helped to shape certain aspects of the religion that evolved in the Christ's name, such as its emphasis on compassion, nonviolence, and (in the broadest sense) selflessness.

A few experts even claim that the Buddha's life story offered the gospel writers a narrative model for organizing their official versions of the Christ's biography. In fact, the two sagas bear many striking similarities: for example, the renunciation of the father's business; the years of searching in the wilderness; the accommodation of the existing religious tradition (in Shakyamuni's case, Hinduism; in Jesus's, Judaism);

the teaching career of sermons and parables; and the close, complex relationships with disciples.

Finally, many historians maintain that Christian monasticism, which is commonly thought to have evolved in Egypt during the fourth century, was somehow patterned after Buddhist monasticism. Certainly no other model for the institution existed at the time, and there are striking similarities between Christian and Buddhist monasticism to this day.

WEST MEETS EAST: FROM MARCO POLO TO EUROPEAN IMPERIALISTS

Regrettably, most of the history of West meets East from the Western point of view shows a prejudice against predominately Buddhist Asia as non-Judeo-Christian and, therefore, pagan and backward. This bias persists to varying degrees among many westerners today, making it hard for them to see Buddhism as a legitimate religion, or if they do, as much more than an organized form of idolatry, self-abasement, and world-rejection.

For the balance of the first millennium, the decline of the Roman Empire, the rise of Islam, and the Mongol invasions severely cut down communication between Western Christendom and Eastern Buddhist lands. It wasn't until around 1200, with the growth of nationalism and a mercantile middle class in Europe, that trade relations between the two worlds finally started picking up again.

From 1271 to 1295, the trader-adventurer Marco Polo traveled throughout Asia, where he had especially strong encounters with Theravada in Sri Lanka and Vajrayana in the Mongolian court of Kublai Khan, a recent convert. Polo's journals speak favorably about the character of "Sagamoni Borcan" (his transliteration of "Shakyamuni Buddha" in the Mongol dialect), saying, "For a certainty, if he had been baptized a Christian he would have been a great saint before God." Regardless of this commendation, however, it's clear that Polo considered Christianity to be superior to Buddhism in every respect.

Despite journeys by numerous other enterprising westerners after Polo, steady or extensive interaction between the two continents didn't reoccur until the sixteenth century, when the major European powers began earnestly exploring and colonizing diverse parts of Asia. Much of this activity was motivated or accompanied by Christian missionary ventures. As a result, the majority of Europeans over the next four centuries tended to regard (or, more to the point, disregard) the Asian people even more emphatically as godless inferiors, and the religion of Buddhism as a primitive form of devil-worship.

There were, however, exceptions. During the same period that Europe was reconnecting with Asia, it was also discovering the Americas, and both areas, with their very different but equally exotic civilizations, stirred the imaginations of many Western artists, writers, and thinkers. The French *philosophes* of the eighteenth century, for example, extolled Native Americans as "noble savages" and Buddhists as "great sages."

During the 1770s and 1780s, while England was simultaneously losing political control over America and gaining it over India, the English intelligentsia began focusing far more intently on Asia than it ever had before. Sir William Jones, a justice in British-occupied Bengal, formed the Asiatick (sic) Society in 1784 for the express purpose of studying "all matters relative to Man and Nature" in that part of the world. Regrettably, its research during his lifetime had little to say about Buddhism, which had virtually disappeared from India centuries before.

Even Bodh Gaya, the site of Shakyamuni's enlightenment, was by that time devoid of any Buddhist temple or shrine and usually any pilgrim. Jones's friend and eventual biographer, Lord Teignmouth, referred to the downtrodden village rather contemptuously—and erroneously—as "the birth place of Boudh, the author of a system of philosophy which labors under the imputation of atheism."

Nevertheless, Jones's first-ever translations of Hindu manuscripts from Sanskrit into English, as well as his commentary comparing them to the literature of ancient Greece, elevated the study of Asian cultures and religions to a new level of seriousness. When the English translations were cast into French, they inspired the French linguist Eugene Burnouf, an expert in Pali and Tibetan as well as Sanskrit, to give similar attention to Buddhist works. In 1844 he published his classic *L'introduction a l'histoire du Buddhisme indien (An Introduction to the History of Indian Buddhism),* which contained a full translation of the Lotus Sutra.

THE DHARMA APPEARS IN ENGLISH

Buddhism's entry at last into widespread Western consciousness during the eighteenth and nineteenth centuries took place simultaneously with Europe's settlement of the so-called New World and the birth of the United States. It makes sense, therefore, that the "new" Eastern religion went on to flower most extensively in America—the final frontier of Western expansion.

The trend began in 1844, the same year Burnouf published his landmark work in France. Across the Atlantic Ocean in Concord, Massachusetts, Henry David Thoreau incorporated an English translation of part of Burnouf's version of the Lotus Sutra into the last edition of his literary magazine, *Dial.* The translation itself was done by Elizabeth Palmer Peabody, an American publisher as well as a self-taught student of Buddhism. Entitled "The Preaching of the Buddha," this article was the first printed appearance of the Dharma in the English language.

Thoreau, the great American transcendentalist, never formally claimed to be a Buddhist himself, but he did shock many of his contemporaries by including the Buddha among his eclectic pantheon of personal heroes and role models. Taking a very Buddhist attitude toward the controversy, he wrote in his 1849 work *A Week on the Concord and Merrimack River,* "I know that some will have hard thoughts of me, when they hear their Christ named beside my Buddha, yet I am sure that I am willing they should love their Christ more than my Buddha, for the love is the main thing."

Among the Americans who picked up Thoreau's enthusiasm for the Buddha was the poet Walt Whitman, who in his 1860 poem "Passage to India" yearns for a return to the "primal thought of old occult Brahma . . . and the tender junior Buddha."

The rest of the nineteenth century saw other fruits of Burnouf's pioneering work on both sides of the Atlantic. The German philosopher Arthur Schopenhauer responded to it in an 1861 revision of his masterpiece, *The World as Will*. Among other things, he writes that the ideal condition of "suspended will" would be "identical with the Nirvana of the Buddhists."

In 1881 the English publisher Max Muller was moved by Burnouf's lasting achievement to create *Sacred Books of the East,* a series of annotated translations of Hindu and Buddhist scriptures. In collaboration with T. W. and Caroline Rhys-Davids, he simultaneously established the Pali Text Society (PTS), which brought most of the Pali Canon into print over the next forty years.

Meanwhile, other events were drawing the attention of British and American cognoscenti to Buddhism. In 1879 Sir Edwin Arnold published *The Light of Asia,* an English verse adaption of Shakyamuni's life story as recounted in the Lalitavistara. It proved surprisingly popular in both the United States and Europe, and even more remarkably among the educated Sri Lankans, who had long been discouraged from practicing "heathenistic" Theravada by their British rulers.

MADAME BLAVATSKY AND THE WHITE BUDDHISTS

The very next year, Sri Lanka witnessed the first known conversion of westerners to Buddhism. The two converts were Americans: Helena Blavatsky, more commonly called Madame Blavatsky, and Colonel Henry Steel Olcott. History has since dubbed the pair "the White Buddhists," but as far as their careers are concerned, they were quite colorful.

Olcott and Blavatsky met in 1874 at the Eddy Farm in Chittenden, Vermont. At the time, the farm was an early center of Spiritualism, a movement promising communication with the dead through séances that attracted many followers in America and Europe over the next five decades. Immediately recognizing each other as intellectual soul mates, they went on to cofound the Theosophical Society in 1875.

Olcott stated in the society's inaugural address that its mission was "to collect and diffuse knowledge of the laws which govern the universe." Several years later, Blavatasky wrote that it was created "at the direct suggestion of Indian and Tibetan Adepts" who were, in her words, "Esoteric Buddhists." They allegedly corresponded with her via "magically transmitted" letters that Olcott, widely admired for his integrity, verified as authentic. Olcott even claimed to have witnessed a manifestation of one of the Adepts, whom he described as follows: "He was so grand a man, so imbued with the majesty of moral strength, so luminously spiritual, so evidently above average humanity, that I felt abashed in his presence, and bowed my head and bent my knee as one does before a god or a god-like personage" (quoted in Rick Fields, *How the Swans Came to the Lake,* 90).

Olcott and Blavatsky soon began calling themselves Esoteric Buddhists, followers of the "Master-Adept, Gautama Buddha" who, in their view, was one among numerous masters of the same, basic truth. "Our Buddhism," Olcott explained, "was identically the Wisdom Religion of the Aryan Upanishad, and the soul of all the ancient world faiths. Our Buddhism was, in a word, not a creed but a philosophy."

In response to another master's magical directive, Olcott and Blavatsky journeyed to India in 1878. On May 17, 1880, they sailed into the port of Galle, Sri Lanka (then called Ceylon). It was a triumphal entry, much more so than they had expected, even though they had publicized it in advance. All along the deep harbor, thousands of local Theravada Buddhists, accustomed to having their religion disparaged, waved flags of greeting from piers and fishing boats specially decorated in honor of the visit. A week later, the celebrated pilgrims knelt before a Theravada priest, took refuge in the Three Jewels, and accepted the Five Precepts.

Afterward, Madame Blavatsky was more often called a White Buddhist (a press moniker that stuck) than an esoteric one, but there's no indication she actually practiced her newly official religion. Instead, she put most of her rapidly diminishing energy into occult healing endeavors, finally dying in 1891 after several years of crippling illness.

Olcott, who lived robustly until 1907, took his vows more seriously. He immediately composed the *Buddhist Catechism,* a concise, user-friendly book expressing the basic tenets of Buddhism in a way that conformed well with Theravada doctrine (several priests served as advisers) and yet spoke intelligently to his fellow westerners. It was soon translated into many different languages for the benefit of Buddhists and non-Buddhists alike. He also worked hard to nurture the revival of Theravada in Sir Lanka, campaigning successfully for the legalization of Buddhist customs on the island—as opposed to the British-enforced observation of Christian ones—and raising enough money to establish three Buddhist colleges and 250 Buddhist schools there.

EASTERN BUDDHISTS COME TO THE WEST

As the phrase "White Buddhists" suggests, the discussion so far in this chapter of eighteenth- and nineteenth-century encounters between East and West has been limited to the point of view of westerners learning about Buddhism. It's important to keep in mind that during this same time period, when Buddhism in the abstract was first becoming known to modern Western minds, many flesh-and-blood Buddhists were coming from Asia to live among westerners.

Isolated Buddhist individuals or groups had been filtering into Europe since the mid-1700s, a by-product of imperial expansion into Asia. Beginning in the mid-1800s, however, the United States became an especially popular and relatively more accessible destination for Chinese people—most of them presumably Buddhists—seeking jobs or other opportunities in life that were unobtainable in their homeland.

The first boatload of Chinese men was lured to California by the gold rush of 1849. Thereafter, the volume of Chinese emigration to "Gold Mountain" (as California and later the United States came to be called in China) increased exponentially. The 1870 census reported 63,199 Chinese immigrants in the country, most of whom lived in the western states, and the vast majority of whom were men. They represented 10 percent of the population in California at that time, and an even higher percentage in Montana and Idaho.

Along with the Chinese people came their temples and shrines. The first few were constructed in San Francisco in the early 1850s. Over the next half-century, hundreds sprang up throughout the American West, welcoming not only Buddhists but also Taoists and followers of various Chinese folk religions.

To people of European, African, or Native American descent, these establishments remained virtually invisible. Far from attracting any converts, they didn't even draw curious visitors or taunting brick-throwers. Non-Asian Americans simply dismissed them as "joss houses," literally "luck houses," but figuratively something more like "mumbo-jumbo" or "woo-woo" halls. Apparently the contempt that non-Asians harbored for such places was mixed with just enough fear to make them keep their distance.

As demeaning as this attitude was, the religious isolation it created for the Chinese seemed to suit them as well. Their temples and shrines could thereby serve as precious retreats where they could gather to be among their own kind and reconnect with their heritage, undisturbed by domineering, unsympathetic outsiders. In some respects, the same kind of division still exists within the modern American Buddhist scene, with so-called ethnic (Asian-descent) and nonethnic believers maintaining what amounts to separate religious identities and institutions. We'll look into this subject more deeply later in this chapter and in chapter 6.

Unfortunately, the near-total estrangement between the Chinese and mainstream cultures in nineteenth-century America also led to very blind and shamelessly blatant forms of discrimination. In 1882 the U.S. Congress passed the Chinese Exclusion Act, barring further immigration of people from China, and other anti-Chinese legislation quickly followed.

It wasn't until the mid-twentieth century that the climate between the two cultures improved and the discriminatory laws began to be repealed. Meanwhile, most second- and third-generation Chinese Americans—as well as immigrants from other areas of Asia and their descendants—tended to abandon their ancestral, "non-American" religion, which in most cases was Buddhism.

Nevertheless, eleven years after the Chinese Exclusion Act was passed, Buddhism formally debuted in America and, for that matter, the modern world. The occasion was the World's Parliament of Religions, the spiritual component of the Columbian Exposition, popularly known as the Chicago World's Fair—the same event that brought us peanut butter and the Ferris wheel.

MAKING IT OFFICIAL: THE 1893 WORLD'S PARLIAMENT OF RELIGIONS

If one were asked to decide which single milestone best marked the beginning of the global age, or at least public recognition of it, the Columbian Exposition of 1893 would be an excellent candidate. Its governing concept grew out of the fact that all of the continents on Earth were now vitally interconnected for the first time in history by trade, economics, politics, missionary work, scientific expeditions, classroom education, tourist travel, the press, the telegraph, and even the telephone. Officially, it commemorated the four-hundredth anniversary of Columbus's "discovery" of America, bringing the Old World and the New World together, but in actuality it seemed to celebrate the emergence at last of what we can now call a "One World" planet.

Granted, the exposition presented Western culture, the hub and chief beneficiary of this web, as the pinnacle of human accomplishment. The majestic and aptly named "White City," built from scratch on the shores of Lake Michigan to contain the event, paid architectural tribute primarily to the empires of Greece, Rome, and Renaissance Italy—with a token nod to Egypt. Still, the exhibits within that grandiose global village reflected a wider range of Earth's people, places, and products than had ever been showcased before.

To complement this material display, the exposition's organizers also sought to convey in some reasonably public manner a wide spectrum of the world's spiritual faiths. Thus they set up a week-long World's Parliament of Religions and invited selected religious leaders from around the world to speak.

Again, first prize was given to the West. In justifying the parliament's existence, the chairman, Dr. John Henry Burrows, a Protestant Christian minister, declared, "Since it is as clear as the light that the Religion of Christ has led to many of the chief and noblest developments in our modern civilization, it did not appear that Religion, any more than Education, Art, or Electricity, should be excluded." Continuing the same metaphor, however, he became somewhat more ecumenical: "Religion, like the white light of Heaven, has been broken into many colored fragments by the prisms of men. One of the objects of the Parliament of Religions has been to change this many colored radiance back into the white light of heavenly truth" (quoted in Fields, *How the Swans Came to the Lake,* 102–21).

On the parliament's opening day, the honor of giving the final speech was allotted to Anagarika Dharmapala, a Sri Lankan Theravada Buddhist and friend of Olcott. Declaring Barrows "the American Ashoka," Dharmapala announced that the gathering was "simply the re-echo of a great consummation which the Indian Buddhists accomplished twenty-four centuries ago." It was a nice balancing act: honoring his host and creating a bridge between cultures while at the same time asserting the dignity and historical priority of his own religion.

Also among the Buddhists at the parliament was the Zen master Shaku Soen. Unlike Dharmapala, he didn't speak English, the official language of the event. Also, his talk, entitled "The Law of Cause and Effect as Taught by Buddha," focused on doctrine rather than diplomacy, leaving many troubling questions hanging in the air: for example, "From morning to evening we are agitated by the feelings of pleasure and pain, love and hate. . . . Why is the mind subjected to constant flux?"

As a result, Shaku Soen didn't have the same strong, favorable impact on the general audience that Dharmapala did. Few even saw Soen. It was Barrows who actually stood onstage and read the speech, from an English text prepared by Soen's young multilingual student, D. T. Suzuki. Yet Soen, his message, and especially his student had more impact on the future of Buddhism in the West than any other part of the whole conference, thanks to someone they did impress quite profoundly: the Illinois-based writer and publisher Paul Carus.

THE TURNING OF THE DHARMA IN AMERICA: 1893–1900

The first tangible evidence of just how much Soen and Suzuki impressed Carus appeared in 1894, a year after the World's Parliament of Religions: Carus's book *Karma: A Story of Early Buddhism*. Commenting on the "joy and intensity" of his own "awakening to Buddhism" at the parliament, he points out in the epilogue how compatible Buddhism is with "contemporary styles of thought" and particularly with his own, self-composed spiritual philosophy, the "Religion of Science." He writes,

> [The "Religion of Science"] may be categorized as Positive Monism, that is to say, a unitary world-conception, which endeavors to become a systematised statement of facts. . . . [It] is in agreement with Buddha's teachings, so lucidly set forth in his farewell address to the disciples . . . : "Hold fast to the truth as your lamp. Seek salvation in the truth alone." . . . The "Religion of Science" is, like Buddhism, a religion which bases man's hopes for a deliverance from evil upon enlightenment. (quoted by Martin J. Verhoeven in Prebish and Tanaka, eds., *The Faces of American Buddhism*, 213–14)

Distorted as Carus's opinion was, especially in equating Buddhist truth with scientific fact, many westerners agreed with him that Buddhism's intellectuality, lack of deity worship, and cosmic air of modernity made it a very compelling *philosophy*—one that need never be encumbered with all the "mythologizing aspects" (as Carus put it) of an outright religion.

Carus popularized this notion even more effectively in his next book published the same year, *The Gospel According to Buddha*. Translated during the following decade into many Western and Eastern languages (including Suzuki's Japanese version), it went one step further toward integrating Buddhism into the Western world by noting affinities between Shakyamuni Buddha and Jesus Christ as "successive saviors of the world."

Eager to take whatever advantage they could to spread the Dharma in the West, Soen and Suzuki publically reinforced Carus's widely appealing argument. In 1897 Suzuki moved from Japan to Carus's home in LaSalle, Ilinois to work with Carus on translating, editing, and printing Buddhist and Taoist texts. Over the next eight years, their many publications promoted an image of Buddhism that held sway among educated westerners for a long while to come and, rightly or wrongly, still lingers today: that of a rational spirituality, tailor-made for what the *New York Times* dubbed in 1900 "A New Age of Progress."

A half-century later, when Western people's faith in science and the intellect wasn't so blindly positive, Suzuki recanted his early association with Carus's overly streamlined perspective on Buddhism. In the 1959 essay "A Glimpse of Paul Carus," he wrote, "I now think that a religion based solely on science is not enough. There are certain 'mythological' elements in every one of us, which cannot be altogether lost in favor of science."

But 1959 is a giant leap ahead of 1893. In the intervening years, different schools of Buddhism infiltrated the United States and Europe in all sorts of distinctive ways. For clarity's sake, the rest of this chapter focuses separately on each major vehicle of Buddhism and how it evolved in the West during the past one hundred years, rather than going through the century chronologically and discussing all things Buddhist that happened along the way.

First, however, let's return to the immediate aftermath of the 1893

World's Parliament of Religions to consider yet another turning point in the history of Western Buddhism. At the conclusion of a follow-up talk Dharmapala gave a week later for the Theosophical Society of Chicago, he asked Charles T. Strauss, a New York City businessman raised in the Jewish faith, to join him on the stage. There, repeating the words of Dharmapala, Strauss took refuge in the Three Jewels. The ceremony was brief but groundbreaking. It made Strauss the first known person of non-Asian descent to become a Buddhist on American soil.

THERAVADA: TO BE OR NOT TO BE MONASTIC

Until the World's Parliament of Religions, the only vehicle of Buddhism known to most informed westerners was Theravada, the one most commonly encountered by the European colonizers of Asia. Vajrayana was virtually locked inside the mountain fortress of Tibet, where it stayed until the Chinese invasions and subsequent Tibetan diaspora of the 1950s. The main homelands of Mahayana—China, Korea, and Japan—remained comparatively independent and uncharted by westerners until aggressive traders finally broke through isolationist barriers in the second half of the nineteenth century. As these latter three nations began emerging more and more on the world scene, so did other varieties of Buddhism.

Nowhere was this development more evident than in the United States. Being the closest Western country to these Mahayana nations, it was the most active in seeking to explore, convert, or do business with them (Britain's colony in Hong Kong notwithstanding). It was also the primary Western target of similar efforts made by these nations, as well as the most common Western destination of people emigrating from them—legally or illegally.

Because of this situation, the Sri Lankan teacher Dharmapala's presence at the parliament, commanding though it was, ironically marked the end of Theravada influence in America for many years. Meanwhile, Japanese Zen eventually grew to represent Buddhism as a whole in the minds of most United States citizens of non-Asian descent.

Theravada's emphasis on monasticism also complicated matters. It still does. Accustomed to democratic institutions and individual freedoms, westerners in general, and Americans in particular, tend to gravitate more to Mahayana and Vajrayana because of the greater latitude these two vehicles give for lay practice, on either a personal or a group basis.

Also, while teachers in the latter two vehicles can use a comparatively wide range of strategies and contexts to communicate with students, Theravada instruction depends much more critically on the establishment of a monastery (in Pali, *vihara*) with a reasonably large sangha in the strictest sense of the term—a community of *male* monks. Regrettably, a Theravada sangha cannot officially include women. The lineage-based tradition of nuns in this vehicle died out by the twelfth century. Among westerners, this exclusion has been an especially significant stumbling block (for more on women's issues relating to Buddhism, see chapter 6).

It wasn't until 1966 that the first vihara in America was founded, the Buddhist Vihara Society of Washington, D.C., created to serve the rapidly expanding Sri Lankan community there. In 1972, five Theravada monks from Thailand established the Wat Thai center in Los Angeles, offering programs for both Asian and Western Buddhists.

Over the next decade, two distinctively Western-style Theravada institutions arose that were nonmonastic in nature: first, the Insight Meditation Center (now Insight Meditation Society, or IMS) in Barre, Massachusetts, and then the closely associated Spirit Rock Center in Marin County, California. Besides being the most well known Theravada-based organizations in the United States today, they are also among the most popular conduits of Buddhism in general, attracting many people whose main interest may originally have been meditation or self-help rather than the religion itself.

Focusing on vipassana practice as the heart of a broader, almost nonsectarian form of Buddhism, IMS was fathered by two Americans, Joseph Goldstein and Jack Kornfield. Before they met for the first time in 1974, each of them had trained with different Theravada teachers in

Southeast Asia after working in the Peace Corps there. Goldstein studied with the scholar Anagarika Munindra in Bodh Gaya, India, which by the 1960s had once again become a place of Buddhist teaching and pilgrimage. Kornfield's teacher in Thailand was Achaan Chah, who, as a traditional "forest monk" (in Pali, *bikkhu*), roamed through the jungles, begged for food, and often slept under the stars. To study with Chah, Kornfield himself had to become a forest-dwelling bikkhu, a path he couldn't sustain logistically when he returned to the United States.

THE DULLARD

In his book *Insight Meditation,* Joseph Goldstein recounts an incident when his Indian teacher, Munindra, talked about two different kinds of meditation subjects: one for intelligent people and another for stupid people. At first, Goldstein admits, his Western sensibilities were shocked at the casual use of the word *stupid.* Later, he realized "it was freeing to learn that for spiritual practice there is no preference regarding intelligence."

After all, Goldstein explains, intelligence can sometimes be a barrier to enlightenment if it involves having too much ego or placing too much importance on rationality over character and compassion. Buddhaghosa's fifth-century Visuddhimagga even offers various categories of meditation subjects suitable for people with varying degrees of intelligence.

This appreciation reminded Goldstein of one of his favorite stories about the Buddha. Once the Buddha had two disciples who were brothers. One was an arhat who was very smart. The other was a dullard with a sweet heart and a strong faith in the Dharma. The arhat, in an effort to accommodate his brother's stupidity, assigned him as a meditation practice just a simple, four-line verse of the Buddha's teachings to memorize. The dullard tried and tried to commit the lines to memory, but they wouldn't stick. Finally, in exasperation, the arhat brother said, "It's hopeless! It's probably better for you to leave the order."

The dullard slowly walked away from the sangha with his head and his spirits hanging low. Suddenly the Buddha came up beside him. "Wait!" he cried. "I've got another meditation subject, just for you. Take this white handkerchief, stand out in the hot sun, and rub it."

The dullard did as the Buddha said. As he was rubbing the handkerchief in the hot sun, it started getting dirty from the sweat of his fingers. The grime awakened memories of previous lifetimes, when he'd practiced and seen impurities come out from his body. The breadth and depth of his vision opened his mind, and he was enlightened. Along with the enlightenment came intelligence as well as psychic powers, some of which he subsequently used to play good-humored tricks on his brother.

Commenting on the story, Goldstein concludes, "I feel great affection for the dullard."

In 1974 both Goldstein and Kornfield came independently to the Naropa Institute in Boulder, Colorado, to teach Theravada meditation techniques. Naropa had just been opened by the Tibetan master Chogyam Trungpa Rinpoche as a school for East-West spiritual and intellectual studies. Based on the model of Nalanda, the renowned Buddhist university in ancient India, it was named for the eleventh-century Vajrayana scholar who taught many important students there, including Marpa, Tibetan Buddhism's "Great Translator."

In the spirit of Nalanda, the Naropa Institute was designed to serve as a crossroads for many different schools of thought inside and outside

Buddhism—a function it continues to serve. The two Theravada in-
structors Goldstein and Kornfield responded well to its collegiate atmosphere and to each other's humanistic way of communicating the
Dharma. They soon forged a partnership leading to the creation in
1976 of the Barre center, whose cofounders were Sharon Salzburg and
Jacqueline Schwartz. In 1981 Kornfield moved to Marin County, California, and joined James Baraz, Sylvia Boorstein, and Anna Douglas in
founding the Spirit Rock Center there.

Rather than being organized along the hierarchical lines of a Theravada vihara, the two centers are governed democratically by a lay sangha
in cooperation with a body of vipassana teachers. They don't attempt to
recreate the full structure of Theravada training. Instead, they support the
practice of insight meditation in particular as a source of enlightenment,
while making other teachings available on a more selective basis.

The arrangement has a built-in appeal to individualistic westerners,
who often have difficulty establishing—or committing themselves to—
the kind of close teacher-student relationship that's more traditional in
Buddhism. It also fulfills another valuable purpose. In addition to giving nonmonastic westerners access to Theravada, it offers monastery-
educated easterners and westerners a place to teach it. Goldstein once
referred to the project as starting a new lineage "outside the monastic
continuum—a new experience of the Dharma unfolding."

At the other end of the Western-oriented Theravada spectrum in
the United States are several small but promising monastic communities established during the past decade. Among them are the Abhayagiri
Monastery in Redwood Valley, California, the Metta Forest Monastery
in San Diego, California, and the Bhavana Society of High View, West
Virginia.

Meanwhile, the number of U.S.-based ethnic Theravada temples has
risen dramatically since the 1970s, due mainly to increased immigration from Sri Lanka, Thailand, Myanmar, and Cambodia. There are
now around 150 temples scattered throughout the country and averag-
ing three or four resident monks apiece, almost all of whom are Asian
nationals.

In Europe, where Mahayana and Vajrayana influence has been comparatively slight until recent years, Theravada has remained the most familiar and pervasive form of Buddhism. England has seen the most significant Theravada activity, due to the British Empire's strong connections with Sri Lanka, Myanmar, Thailand, and other predominantly Theravada regions of Southeast Asia.

In 1907 the Theravada monk Ananda Metteyya (an Englishman named Alan Bennett), founded the Buddhist Society of Great Britain and Ireland as a venue for his teaching. It was transformed into the Buddhist Society in 1924 under the new leadership of Christmas Humphreys, a prolific writer on Buddhism in general who did much to popularize the religion throughout the Western world. Still, the basic perspective of the organization (and of Humphreys himself) was Theravada in nature. Two years later, the first Buddhist temple in Europe, the London Buddhist Vihara, was set up in the Chiswick section of West London.

The relatively new nation of Germany was also providing a European home for Theravada Buddhism in the early part of the twentieth century. Profoundly impressed by Schopenhauer's references to the Dharma, Karl Eugene Neumann studied Sanskrit and Pali and, after visiting India and Sri Lanka in the 1890s, set about translating the Pali Canon into German. His works fueled much discussion in the German-speaking intellectual world, famous for its love of philosophical debate.

One reader of the Neumann translations, Georg Grimm, was moved in 1915 to write *The Doctrine of the Buddha, the Religion of Reason,* which in turn helped inspire Hermann Hesse to compose his 1922 novel *Siddhartha,* a work that became a classic among British and American youth after it was translated into English in the 1950s. From 1923 to 1924 another Neumann-stoked convert to Buddhism, Paul Dahlke, built an elaborate Buddhist temple in Berlin. Called Buddistisches Haus (Buddhist House), it remains one of the largest Buddhist complexes in the West.

From the 1930s through the 1950s the Buddhist scene in England

and the rest of Europe remained stagnant as immigration from Asia dwindled and the continent became embroiled in economic depression, war, and reconstruction. Social and intellectual ferment in the 1960s brought a renewal of English interest in Buddhism, leading in 1967 to the creation of the Friends of the Western Buddhist Order (FWBO) in London.

Although designed to be a broad-based Buddhist school for westerners independent from any particular Asian branch of Buddhism, the FWBO has a distinctly Theravada cast. It was founded by the Venerable Sangharakshita, an Englishman who received Theravada training in India; its vocabulary is mainly Pali; and its frame of reference (if not practice) is classic Theravada monasticism.

The difference, however, is purely Western. The order itself (surrounded by a larger, less intensely involved network of friends) consists of members who are not traditional monks, but not exactly laypeople either. Male members each assume the title *Dharmachari,* and female ones, *Dharmucharini,* both terms meaning "Dharma-farer." They take precepts and, perhaps, an optional vow of chastity, but individually they pursue a variety of different lifestyles. Some reside together communally in centers; others have their own homes. Some work exclusively for the order; others hold part-time or full-time jobs in which they consistently strive to apply and extend their Buddhist beliefs. A few join the order's mission to revive Buddhism among the caste of so-called untouchables in India.

All FWBO friends and members subscribe to the order's positivistic expression of Buddhism, one that is more in keeping with Western idealism. For example, the first precept is given a more proactive spin as follows: "I undertake to refrain from harming living beings. With deeds of loving kindness I purify my body." Commenting on this upbeat style in a 1985 essay, Dharmachari Vessantara, a prominent order member, writes,

> Whilst we don't ignore the Buddha's teaching on dukkha (in Pali, suffering), we stress that Buddhism is a Path leading to higher and

more satisfying mental states. For instance, one traditional formulation of the Dharma which we often talk about is the "spiral path." It
begins when you see the unsatisfactoriness of ordinary mundane life,
which gives you confidence in the Buddha's analysis of the human
predicament. With that confidence you practice the precepts and
meditation wholeheartedly. This purifies your mind and leads to
higher mental states: joy, rapture, calm, and bliss. (quoted in Clive
Erricker, *Buddhism,* 174–75)

Later years saw the advent in England of other, more strictly Theravada institutions. In 1977 the American-born Ajahn Sumedho, who
was ordained in Thailand by the Theravada master Achaan (or Ajuhn)
Chah, founded a small monastery in London that moved the next year
to Chithurst in Sussex and took the name Cittaviveka (in Sanskrit and
Pali, "silent mind").

Six years later, a second center for monks, nuns, and laypeople was
established in Hertfordshire. Called Amaravati (in Sanskrit and Pali,
"deathless realm"), it has created a uniquely successful model for the
transplantation of traditional Theravada into a Western setting. A body
of seriously committed monastics—including men *and* women—en-
joys the support of both residential and nonresidential laypeople and
reciprocates regularly with teaching events.

MAHAYANA: PEACEFUL LEGACY OF WAR

The history of Mahayana among westerners for most of the past century has been predominantly the history of Zen in the United States.
Given Mahayana's emphasis on compassion, it's ironic that American
interest in Zen has repeatedly been stimulated by war.

In 1905 Japan's victory in the Russo-Japanese War and resulting
emergence as a world power galvanized American attention on this
little-known nation. After all, Japan was just across the Pacific and not
too far from U.S. concerns in the Philippines, Guam, Alaska, and
Hawaii. President Theodore Roosevelt himself brokered the treaty that

ended the war. Sensing the prime moment had come to awaken more Americans to Japan's major spiritual tradition, Shaku Soen, the Japanese spokesperson for Zen at the World's Parliament of Religions, traveled once again to the United States to meet with key supporters.

The following year Soen was joined by his pupil D. T. Suzuki, who had been working and living with the publisher Paul Carus in Illinois since 1897. Crisscrossing the country by train, the two of them gave talks on Zen—and Japanese culture in general—to hundreds of religious, academic, private, and public audiences over the next three years, with Suzuki translating Soen's Japanese words into English ones. Afterward both men returned to Japan, but Soen's teachings stayed behind to represent Buddhism to interested Americans for decades to come.

At the end of the 1920s Nyogen Senzaki, also a student of Soen, journeyed to California and established *zendos,* or meditation halls, in San Francisco and Los Angeles, the latter of which survived until his death in 1958. In 1930 yet another one of Soen's students, Shaku Sokatsu, later ordained as Sokei-an, came to New York City and founded the Buddhist Society of America (after 1945, the First Zen Institute of America).

World War II brought devastation at American hands both to the people of Japan and to U.S. citizens of Japanese descent living along the West Coast—among them Nyogen Senzaki—who were interred in detention camps for the duration of the war. It also thrust many Americans into direct, mostly adversarial contact with Japanese natives, as combatants, prisoners of war, or agents of occupation.

However, out of this horrendous maelstrom came a much greater awareness of Zen among Americans. D. T. Suzuki returned to the United States in 1950 and taught intermittently at Columbia University for the next eight years. He also produced many highly readable books and articles that have continued to make Zen more accessible to westerners. Meanwhile, the Korean War and its aftermath made even more U.S. citizens familiar with Zen in the form of *Son* (the Korean word for Zen). By the late 1950s Zen had entered into mainstream consciousness and Main Street talk.

Admittedly, most of the interest in Zen was intellectual rather than spiritual. Abstract artist Franz Kline claimed that it helped inspire his black-and-white "form-and-emptiness" paintings. The composer John Cage, who studied with Suzuki at Columbia, said that it influenced his similarly spare, atonal compositions.

THE BEATS AND BUDDHISM

Discard such definite imaginations of phenomena
as your own self, thou human being, thou'rt a
numberless mass of sun-motes: each mote a shrine.

These words come from the only overtly Buddhist book by American writer Jack Kerouac (1922–1969) published during his lifetime, *The Scripture of the Golden Eternity* (1959). He wrote two others in the 1950s: *Some of the Dharma,* published posthumously in 1997, and *Wake Up,* a life of the Buddha yet unpublished, although serialized during the 1990s in the magazine *Tricycle.*

Several of Kerouac's other works also draw on Buddhist themes: the haiku collection *Mexico City Blues* (1959) and the novels *Dharma Bums* (1958), *Tristessa* (1960), *Visions of Gerard* (1963), *Desolation Angels* (1965), and *Satori in Paris* (1966). In these books he may have misled people about the true nature of the religion, but he also started many on the path to discovering it for themselves.

Kerouac became instantly famous after his 1957 novel *On the Road* was hailed as "the voice of a new generation"—one he called "beat," meaning both down-and-out and "beatific." Overwhelmed by his celebrity, he started a long, slow decline into alcoholism and public buffoonery that lasted the rest of his short life and did much to discredit him as a serious artist, not to mention a committed Buddhist.

Nevertheless, Kerouac's attraction to the Dharma was sincere. Often linked with Zen, the most familiar form of Buddhism in

America at the time, he didn't subscribe to any particular school. In 1954 he was so moved by Ashvaghosha's second-century *Life of the Buddha* that he began studying Dwight Goddard's 1937 sutra anthology, *A Buddhist Bible*. He went on to devour every Buddhist text available in English and French (his first language, as a child of French-Canadian descent).

Throughout the 1950s, Kerouac practiced his own program of "American Buddhism" for months at a time: asceticism, celibacy, daily chanting of the Diamond Sutra, and daily, cross-legged meditation (painful because of football-related knee injuries). In his pocket he carried a notebook with the precepts printed on the first page. On the other pages, he recorded his own day-by-day reflections on them. Meanwhile, he frequently wrote about Buddhism in letters to his Beat-associated friends, who included:

Allen Ginsberg. Poet; Tibetan Buddhist; student of Trungpa Rinpoche in the 1970s and, later, Gelek Rinpoche; in 1971 joined Anne Waldman, another Beat-influenced poet, in founding the Jack Kerouac School of Disembodied Poetics at Naropa Institute.

Diane Di Prima. Poet; Zen student of Shunryu Suzuki in the 1960s; later Tibetan Buddhist student of Trungpa Rinpoche.

Gary Snyder. Poet; Zen Buddhist; studied Rinzai Zen in Japan, 1956–1969; in 1982 founded Ring of Bone Zendo in California.

Philip Whalen. Poet; Zen Buddhist; head monk at SFZC's Tassajara center from 1975 to 1987; in 1991 became abbot of Hartford Street Zendo in San Francisco.

In literature, Zen was reflected in, and promoted through, numerous different works by existentialist and so-called Beat writers. Among the latter, Jack Kerouac gave it the most publicity in his best-selling 1958 novel *Dharma Bums,* which offers a thinly fictionalized account of the poet Gary Snyder's early involvement in Zen (see "The Beats and Buddhism," page 180).

Zen was also popularized during this period by Allen Watts, a British-born American writer. Watts had been mingling with Buddhist groups and studying Buddhism in his own, independent way since the late 1920s. One of his best known works, the essay "Beat Zen, Square Zen, and Zen," appeared in a special 1958 "Zen" edition of the *Chicago Review,* along with Jack Kerouac's "Meditation in the Woods" and D. T. Suzuki's translation of *The Sayings of Rinzai.* As Watt's essay reveals to anyone well versed in Zen, his particular understanding of it (which he calls "Square Zen") is scarcely traditional, but like the equally unorthodox, even outright inaccurate forms of Zen expressed by many of the Beats, it provoked much healthy curiosity about the religion.

In 1959 Robert Aitken and his wife Anne founded the Diamond Sangha in Honolulu, Hawaii. Aitken was first exposed to Zen in a Japanese prisoner-of-war camp during World War II, and afterward he devoted more and more of his life to the religion as time went by. He ultimately studied in Japan, received transmission, and become one of American Zen's most prolific and respected writers.

The 1960s and early 1970s proved a major turning point for Zen in the United States. It was during this time of social upheaval, liberation politics, and widespread psychospiritual experimentation that legions of young Americans took it upon themselves to study Zen. Much of the overall revolutionary climate of the era as well as the interest in Zen was spurred by America's controversial involvement in Vietnam.

Since 1955, the United States had been backing the corrupt but at least anti-Communist South Vietnamese government led by Ngo Diem, a stauch Roman Catholic Christian in a predominantly Zen Buddhist country. In the summer of 1963, forty Buddhist demonstrators were killed and thousands were arrested after Diem's regime refused to allow the flying of a religious flag on the Buddha's birthday. To protest this latest event in the ongoing persecution of Buddhists, a monk named Thich Quang Duc sat down in a Saigon street in front of a barrage of media photographers and camera crews, doused himself with kerosene, set himself afire, and, as he sat in motionless meditation amid the flames, quickly burned to death.

The image of Quang Duc's startling self-immolation flashed around the world and imprinted itself indelibly in the minds of all who saw it. Diem, trying to discredit the move, pointed out that no true Buddhist would violate the first precept by committing suicide—a remark that only underscored the poignancy of Quang Duc's act and the callousness of Diem. Madame Nhu, Diem's sister-in-law, showed even more effrontery by dismissing the death sarcastically as "a barbecue."

By the end of that summer, six more monastic Buddhists killed themselves the same way. In November—the month President John F. Kennedy was assassinated—a military coup overthrew and murdered Diem. So began the war in Vietnam that wrought so much havoc in America as well, but simultaneously gave it yet another mass exposure to Buddhism.

As the war progressed, the institutional seeds were sown in the United States for the dynamic growth of Zen practice that occurred throughout the rest of century. One of the first and most prominent Japanese Zen masters helping to effect this transplantation was Shunryu Suzuki.

Suzuki arrived in San Francisco in 1959 to be the chief priest for the ethnic Japanese Zen community there. To his surprise, the majority of the people who showed up to sit at the Soto Zen Mission on Bush Street were Americans of European descent, newly enthusiastic about embracing Zen as their religion. In 1961 he inaugurated the San Francisco Zen Center (SFZC) to serve this rapidly increasing population.

During the 1960s, as the Vietnam War intensified and increasing numbers of young countercultural Americans flocked to the Bay Area, the SFZC turned itself into one of the most progressive and popular Zen institutions in the Western world. In 1968 it established another, mountain-based center at Tassajara Hot Springs, which has since evolved into a monastery. In 1970 Suzuki's book *Zen Mind, Beginner's Mind* became an instant Western Zen classic that continues to be popular as an introductory text to the religion.

The next year Suzuki died, and Danin Katagiri, who had come to the United States in 1964 and had assisted at SFZC ever since, left to found the Minnesota Zen Meditation Center in Minneapolis. In 1972 SFZC expanded even further by creating Green Gulch Farm and Zen Center in Marin County. That same year, the Korean Zen master Seung Sahn settled in Providence, Rhode Island, and founded the Providence Zen Center, now headquarters for what is known as the Kwan Um School of Zen.

Meanwhile, Hakuyu Taizan Maezumi—like Shunryu Suzuki, one of the most important early transmitters of Zen from Japan to America—was building a strong home base for Zen in Los Angeles. Having moved to the city in 1956, Maezumi began offering weekly public zazen sessions at the Soto Zenshuji temple in the early 1960s. They were so successful that they motivated him to found the Zen Center of Los Angeles (ZCLA) in 1967.

Maezumi's career as a teacher and leading figure in the "Zen boom" of the 1960s and early 1970s is remarkable in several ways. His broad-based aspirations for Zen in America gave him an academic mission as well as a religious one, and so he led ZCLA to create the Kuroda Institute, a forum that continues to offer some of the best available scholarly programs on Zen and Buddhist topics.

Also, unlike most Japanese priests who receive a single transmission in a particular Zen school, Maezumi received three transmissions representing both major branches of Zen—Soto and Rinzai—and each of the three principal teaching lineages now in America. This rich background helped him to establish at ZCLA one of the strongest and most comprehensive training matrices in the country. By the time of his death in 1995, he had transmitted to twelve Dharma heirs, all of whom have created their own Zen communities in different parts of the country (see "Invocation of a New Millennium" on page 205).

Philip Kapleau was another significant U.S.-born pollinator of Zen in America during the Vietnam War period. He first became acquainted with Zen as a court reporter at the 1946 war-crimes trials in Tokyo, where he met D. T. Suzuki. Later, he studied with Suzuki at Columbia and then returned to Japan for formal training.

Making an extremely rare concession for a Zen master, Kapleau's teacher, Hakuun Yasutani, permitted Kapleau to take notes on what was said during *dokusans* (private, one-to-one encounters between teacher and student). These notes were incorporated into Kapleau's very successful and influential 1965 book, *The Three Pillars of Zen*. The following year Kapleau established the Zen Meditation Center in Rochester, New York, from which he recently retired as leader.

The Vietnam War also brought Americans in contact with many Vietnam-born Zen Buddhists. Some were independent spokespeople for the religion, like the now internationally well known monk Thich Nhat Hanh, who first came to the United States in 1965 to promote the cause of peace in his homeland (see page 225). Others were refugees, especially after the fall of Saigon in 1975. Twenty years later, researchers counted approximately 160 Vietnamese temples and centers throughout America—most of them, in keeping with Vietnamese tradition, offering a mix of both Zen and Pure Land Buddhism to ethnic Vietnamese members.

The history of ethnic Japanese Buddhism in America revolves primarily around Pure Land Buddhism—Jodo-shu and, to a much greater degree, Jodo-shin-shu—rather than Zen. In 1899 Japanese immigrant followers of Jodo-shin-shu in San Francisco created the Young Men's Buddhist Association, modeled after the Young Men's Christian Association. It was transformed in 1914 into the Buddhist Mission of North America (BMNA), an umbrella organization for all the small temples that had arisen by then in the Bay Area.

Over the next two and a half decades, the BMNA grew to represent most Americans of Japanese descent living along the West Coast, which meant most Japanese Americans in the nation. Then tragedy stuck. In 1942 over 100,000 such individuals—the overwhelming majority of this population—were sent to internment camps by the War Relocation Authority. There, as part of an effort to Americanize itself, the Buddhist Mission of North America changed its name to the Buddhist Churches of America (BCA).

After World War II ended and the camps were closed, dispersing now homeless, job-seeking Japanese Americans throughout the United States, the BCA went through a period of nationwide expansion. That era lasted until 1980, when BCA membership began to decline due to the increasing secularization of its younger members.

In 1963 Nichiren Buddhism finally established itself in the United States when the Japanese immigrant Masayasa Sadanga created Nichiren Shoshu of America (NSA) in Los Angeles. Intent upon making the NSA a truly American group, Sadanaga changed his name to George Williams, adopted zealous proselytizing techniques, and used them to attract people of all backgrounds to NSA, not just those of Japanese descent.

As a result, NSA grew rapidly all across the country. According to a report quoted by Charles S. Prebish in his 1999 book *Luminous Passage: The Practice and Study of Buddhism in America,* the NSA attracted an average of 7,500 new members per month in 1969; and among the total members for that year, "41 percent were Caucasian, 30 percent Asian, 12 percent black, and 13 percent Latin American" (25).

In 1975 the NSA founded Soka Gakkai International (SGI) as a lay group affiliate. The relationship between the two organizations was stormy from the start and steadily deteriorated until 1991, when SGI split away and became SGI-USA.

Today SGI-USA is a uniquely democratic, non-priest-oriented form of Mahayana involved in a number of ambitious social and educational projects. As an official nongovernmental organization of the United Nations, it works to promote world peace. It also operates Soka University of America (which, along with other programs, offers a master's degree in second- and foreign-language education) and the Boston Research Center for the Twenty-first Century (which, among other things, sponsors interfaith and cross-culture symposiums).

Chinese Americans constitute the other major ethnic group in the United States that is associated with Mahayana Buddhism (most Korean immigrants and their descendants have been Christians). As discussed above, Chinese immigration into the United States was severely restricted for most of the twentieth century until the Immigration Act of 1965, which opened the country's doors wider for all immigrant groups and created the more multicultural nation we enjoy today. Over the next twenty years, more than 400,000 Chinese resettled here, most of them from Taiwan. Although it's not known how many of them were Buddhists, around 150 Ch'an and/or Chinese Pure Land temples or centers were established during that period, primarily in California.

The year before the 1965 act, C. T. Shen, a wealthy, China-based shipper who moved to America in 1952, established the Buddhist Association of the United States (BAUS) to promote Ch'an in this country. In 1980 he and his wife donated land in Kent, New York, for BAUS to build the Chuang Yen Monastery. A gigantic work-in-progress, it now features one of the finest libraries for Buddhist studies outside Asia and a thirty-seven-foot-high statue of the Buddha, the biggest one in the Western Hemisphere.

On the other side of the continent, in Hacienda Heights, California, sits the largest Buddhist monastery in the Western Hemisphere, the Hsi Lai Temple, completed in 1988. A project of the Fo Kuang Shan Monastery in Taiwan, it's actually meant to serve all schools of Buddhism—not just Mahayana, but Theravada and Vajrayana as well. It thus reflects and expands the tradition among many Asian-based Mahayana monasteries of offering separate wings, buildings, and/or shrines for other sects to use. In addition, it's chartered to include nonethnic Buddhists as well as ethnic ones.

Hsi Lai received a great deal of unfavorable media attention in the years following the 1996 U.S. presidential election, when it was determined that some of the members, knowingly or not, took advantage of Vice President Al Gore's campaign appearance there to raise illegal contributions to the Democratic Party. Since then, Hsi Lai supporters have worked hard to erase the unfairly negative image of Buddhism that this incident gave to the American public. Pointing out that the name Hsi Lai means "Coming to the West," they claim that the experimental institution may demonstrate how Buddhism as a whole can best go about doing that.

Because of Europe's distance from East Asia and its lack of strong ethnic Chinese, Japanese, Korean, or Vietnamese communities, Zen has had much less impact there during the twentieth century than it has had in the United States. Again, England has seen the most activity.

The London branch of the English Buddhist Society began offering Zen meditation courses in addition to its Theravada programming during the 1960s. In 1971 Reverend Master Jiyu-Kennet established Throssel Hole Priory, a center for Soto Zen monastics and laypeople, near Hexham in Northumberland. A smaller center was later founded in Reading, Berkshire.

In 1982 France became an international destination for Western Zen students and sympathizers when Thich Nhat Hanh established a large Zen center called Plum Village near Bordeaux. Surrounded by vineyards and fields of wheat, corn, and sunflowers, it continues to be his home base and a regular sponsor of Zen retreats, lectures, and special events.

VAJRAYANA: THE DHARMA OF THE DIASPORA

As indicated previously, it's a striking paradox in twentieth-century history that warfare functioned time and time again as the most significant agent in bringing Zen Buddhism, a religion based on compassion and nonviolence, to America. An even starker irony relates to the advent here of Tibetan Buddhism. It took a mid-century act of especially extreme violence to trigger the spread of this remarkably benign and benevolent form of the Dharma beyond its mountain-bound homeland.

In October 1950, Communist Chinese troops invaded Tibet. A great power in Asia seven hundred years ago, Tibet had fallen under the protection of its giant neighbor to the north and east by the nineteenth century. Then came the Chinese revolution of 1912, which effectively ended most contact between the two countries. Since then, Tibet had considered itself independent. The world took little notice one way or the other: Tibet was one of the most isolated, unknown, and ignored regions on the planet.

China, however, had never formally relinquished its claim on Tibet, and now Chinese troops were pressing that claim ruthlessly. In 1951 the

THE CANNIBAL MONK

In 1959, Chinese soldiers enforcing their country's occupation of Tibet destroyed the shrine of Padmapa Sangyay in the village of Tingri, near Mount Everest. Padmapa was an eleventh-century guru who came to that village from India and helped liberate Maching Labdron, the first Tibetan matriarch and founder of the Chod lineage. Before the soldiers had finished demolishing his shrine, an aged Tibetan monk managed to save a piece of the saint's embalmed body.

When the soldiers later heard of the crime, they captured the monk, brought him to a public interrogation in chains, and charged him with betraying the revolution. "Confess, old man," his accusers demanded, taunting him with the confiscated relic. "Did you hope to fool people into believing you could do magic with this dried-up piece of flesh?"

The monk replied, "Since I was a little boy, I have honored the holy saint, Padmapa Sangyay, the Buddha of Tingri. I was brought up to believe that people who are ready for liberation can gain it just by touching his relics or even by laying eyes on them. I wanted to preserve a piece for future generations. Must everything from our past be taken from us?"

Throwing the confiscated relic before the monk, his interrogators scornfully replied, "If a scrap of dead flesh is so holy, maybe you ought to eat it!" Much to their shock, he did!

The Chinese authorities were certain that the monk had now proved himself to be crazy as well as a criminal, guilty not only of counterrevolutionary activity but also of the heinous crime of cannibalism. Their propaganda sheets soon screamed from every post and tree, "Superstitious Monk Eats Corpse." Meanwhile, the Tibetans passing by these sheets murmured, "The holy monk has become a walking shrine."

sixteen-year-old Dalai Lama, the newly established religious and political leader of Tibet, was forced to sign a pact in China's favor, making his country an autonomous Chinese state. After nine years of uneasy truce, native Tibetans staged an uprising, and China responded with a massive military takeover. The Dalai Lama fled to Dharmsala, India, where, together with almost 100,000 refugees, he set up a Tibetan community, government-in-exile, and seat of Vajrayana (see page 219).

Since 1959, the Chinese forces occupying Tibet have killed over 1.3 million ethnic Tibetans (out of a total population of around 5 million) and destroyed over 6,000 temples and monasteries. Meanwhile, the peaceful perseverance of the Tibetan people, the vigorous spiritual and diplomatic mission of the Dalai Lama, and the scattering of Tibetan Buddhist teachers far and wide from their home base have attracted the attention of people all over the world to Vajrayana.

Actually the first major teacher of Tibetan Buddhism in the United States was a Mongolian—Geshe Wangyal of the Geluk lineage—who came to this country four years before the final Chinese takeover of Tibet. The Dalai Lama, head of the Geluk lineage and still living in the Potala Palace in the Tibetan capital of Lhasa, had perceived the need to spread Vajrayana outside the borders of beleaguered Tibet, and so he had sent Wangyal on a mission to establish a U.S. base.

Settling in New Jersey, Wangyal opened the Lamaist Buddhist Monastery of America and taught courses in Vajrayana at Columbia University. Among his students were Robert Thurman and Jeffrey Hopkins. Today, these two men are among the leading academic teachers of Buddhism in America: Thurman holds the Jey Tsong Khapa Chair of Indo-Tibetan Buddhist Studies at Columbia, and Hopkins is a professor of Indo-Tibetan studies at the University of Virginia.

The next important Vajrayana teacher to reach American shores was Deshung Rinpoche, coming directly from Lhasa to Seattle, Washington, in 1961. A former abbot in the Shakya lineage, he worked diligently for ten years conferring with American scholars and composing an English-Tibetan dictionary before taking on students of his own.

In 1969 Tarthang Tulku, representing the Nyingma lineage, arrived in Berkeley, California, and soon afterward founded the Tibetan Ny-ingma Meditation Center. Because teachers in the Nyingma lineage do not need to be celibate or monastic, they are accustomed to devel-oping lay Buddhist communities. The Tibetan Nyingma Meditation Center reflects this lay orientation and, therefore, has been particularly successful in attracting American members.

Tarthang Tulku went on to start Dharma Publishing and the Ny-ingma Institute in Berkeley, California. In 1975 he broke ground in Sonoma County, California, for Odiyan, a 144-acre retreat and study center scheduled to be finished in the near future.

Chogyam Trungpa Rinpoche of the Kagyu lineage came to the United States from England in 1970. His particular goal was to foster what he called an "enlightened society" in America, one that com-bined the values of Tibetan Buddhism with the Western ideals of lib-erty, democracy, self-reliance, and individual dignity.

To help build such a society, Trungpa created a secularized medita-tion program called "Shambhala Training," named for the utopic Shambhala (aka Shangri-La) in Tibetan legend. The program is also known as "Sacred Path of the Warrior." The martial image suggests the discipline and determination involved in practicing this program, which, although not religious in the strict sense of the term, is defi-nitely spiritual.

In 1971 Trungpa founded Naropa Institute in Boulder, Colorado, to function as an academic environment for studying not only Buddhism but also other religious, spiritual, philosophical, and artistic subjects. Naropa still thrives as one element of a larger enterprise, Nalanda, that promotes the use of Buddhist-related arts, healing practices, educa-tional principles, and ethics in everyday home, business, and commu-nity life. In the spirit of Nalanda, one of Trungpa's students started Shambhala Publications in Boston, currently among the country's leading Buddhist presses.

For the more traditional purpose of spreading Vajrayana, Trungpa founded the Dharma centers Karme-Choling in Vermont and, in Col-orado, the Rocky Mountain Shambhala Center and the Dorje Khyung

Dzong. They are now parts of an umbrella organization called Shambhala International that oversees more than one hundred other Vajrayana organizations throughout the world. Also among them is Gampo Abbey in Nova Scotia, founded in 1985 as the first Tibetan monastery for westerners in North America and headed by the U.S.-born nun Pema Chodron.

Another Kagyu institution, the Karma Triyana Dharmachakra Monastery and Retreat Center (KTD), was founded in 1978 outside Woodstock, New York, by the head of the Kagyu lineage, the sixteenth Gyalwa Karmapa. Serving as the Karmapa's official seat in North America, KTD has been expanding its facilities for the past twenty years and may soon become the largest Tibetan Buddhist monastery outside of Tibet (for more discussion of the Karmapa and KTD, see chapter 6).

In 1988, Brooklyn-born Catherine Burroughs became the first American to be recognized and enthroned as a *tulku*—that is, a reincarnation of a renowned lama or saint in Tibetan Buddhist history. Specifically, she was identified in India by Penor Rinpoche of the Nyingma school as the incarnation of a seventeenth-century yogini (female saint) named Genyenma Ahkon Lhamo. Now known as Jetsunma, she directs Kunzang Palyul Choling, a large, Western-flavored Vajrayana practice and study center in Poolesville, Maryland.

The following year, Geluk monks from the Tibetan monastery Drepung Loseling formed a performance-and-teaching ensemble, Sacred Music Sacred Dance Group, that toured the United States as well as other countries. In response to their appearances here, the North American branch monastery Losel Shedrup Ling was set up in Mineral Bluff, Georgia, to accommodate both Tibetans and Americans. It now has affiliates in Alabama, Tennessee, and Georgia.

In 1992 the Dalai Lama himself established his personal North American monastery, Namgyal, in Ithaca, New York. To date, it has housed only Tibetan monks of the Geluk lineage who have been relocated from Dharmsala, but the associated Namgyal Institute offers study programs geared toward lay westerners.

So far, most teachers of authentic Vajrayana in America—as well as everywhere else in the West—have been Tibetan lamas or *geshes* (senior monks). Meanwhile, most of their students have been Western-born Caucasians. In 1991 the Tibetan Resettlement Project began in the United States. It has since enabled over 1,500 ethnic Tibetans to relocate here, most of them settling in major cities. Only the future will tell how much of a role non-Tibetan Americans will have in the teaching of Vajrayana here, and how much presence ethnic Tibetan Americans will have in its practice.

In Europe, Vajrayana has not spread as rapidly or established itself as extensively as it has in the United States. However, lamas from all four traditions have been resident there since the late 1960s. The oldest and still largest Vajrayana institution in Europe is Samye-Ling Buddhist Centre at Eskadelemuire in Dumfriesshire, Scotland. Established by Akong Tulku and Chogyam Trungpa Rinpoche in 1967, it offers monastic and lay training and a three-year retreat program on Holy Island off Scotland's west coast.

Other major Vajrayana organizations in Britain are the Manjushri Institute at Ulcverstone, Cumbria, and the Madhyamika Centre near York. A number of smaller groups—either solely monastic or both monastic and lay—are scattered throughout Europe, mainly in Britain, France, Spain, and Switzerland.

Now, as the twenty-first century begins to unfold, it seems certain that Vajrayana—or Tibetan Buddhism—will become increasingly popular among westerners on both sides of the Atlantic, just as Mahayana in general and even Theravada will. What remains very unclear is how each of these forms of Buddhism will mutate within their new host cultures, and how these cultures themselves will be transformed in the process.

QUESTIONS AND ANSWERS

What personal reasons do westerners give for being drawn to Buddhism?
Among the hundreds of personal confessions and academic accounts in recent books and magazine articles discussing why westerners are attracted to Buddhism, several key patterns can be traced. One of the

most common ones involves an individual's desire to reclaim the kind of spiritual grounding he or she once had in the past.

Many Western converts to Buddhism experienced a strong, comforting connection to Christianity or Judaism when they were children that they lost—or renounced—as they matured. Quite a few had their religious upbringing interrupted or invalidated by their parents' divorce or remarriage, their family's moves from one community to another, or their own overindulgence in drugs, sex, the tribal teenage scene, or general rebelliousness.

Other converts didn't experience such disruptions but eventually came to regard their childhood religion as too judgmental or confining to follow as adults, either because of the overly harsh way it was imposed on them or because of their own, self-punishing interpretation of it. Some felt obliged to separate themselves from their family's faith in order to establish their own individual identity. Others simply couldn't maintain their belief in a creator God, papal infallibility, a Chosen People, a Judgment Day, a Book of Law, original sin, a men-only priesthood, or some other doctrine in their religion, and so they quit practicing it altogether.

Sooner or later, these people encountered something that made them want to regain a spiritual vision of the universe, or as Buddhists would say, to seek answers to the great questions of life and death. For some, the trigger was a negative event: a critical illness, a sudden loss of love, fortune, or security, or a final disgust with the greed, anger, ignorance, or plain old suffering that's pervasive in the Western world. For others, the catalyst was a positive occurrence: a new love, the birth of a child, a release from an onerous job or living situation. For a third group, the stimulus was a more general matter of reaching one of the two most appropriate stages in life for introspection and reassessment: adolescence or middle age.

Whatever their self-proclaimed motivation may have been at the time they turned to Buddhism—whether it was to end their suffering, to engage their freshly awakened spiritual impulses, or simply to get a better sense of how to go on with their lives—they chose this religion in large part because they'd already rejected Christianity or Judaism. Buddhism offered them a distinctly different context in which to extend their spirituality. It was a new religion for a new beginning.

The same positive, negative, and life-stage triggers have also led people to Buddhism who have never before harbored strong spiritual beliefs, at least to their conscious knowledge. For these people, Buddhism seemed somehow more accessible than other religions requiring a more extensive or encoded system of beliefs. In practice, it appears uniquely uncomplicated at first: Meditate, avoid extreme behaviors, and be kind to others.

Also, Buddhism has not yet accumulated as many problematic associations in Western culture as other, more well-trodden religious or spiritual paths have. For example, some people have trouble accepting Christianity because they can't get past the disturbing images they've encountered of televangelism, the commercialism surrounding Christmas, or war waged in the Christ's name. Others reject Judaism because they automatically link it with stereotypes of nagging mothers, guilt-ridden children, and obsessive concern with money. Still others discount nature-based, wiccan, or neoshamanic spiritualities because the media so often associates them with demonism or New Age kitschiness. Buddhism's reputation in the West has the benefit of being still comparatively untainted by familiarity, misappropriation, or prejudice.

In addition to its overall character, Buddhism has many specific qualities that attract specific students. Some are originally drawn to the religion for aesthetic reasons. In short, they like what they see. They may want to acquire the kind of awareness and sensibility that's reflected, for example, in the graceful composure of a meditating monk, the perceptive clarity of a Zen haiku, the elaborate cosmology of a Tibetan mandala, or the exquisite elegance of a Theravada sculpture. Others admire Buddhism because of its particular emphasis on nature, community, self-transcendence, nonmaterialism, or the mind-body connection.

Finally, there's the karmic explanation, most commonly advanced by Vajrayana Buddhists. For example, Bordor Tulku Rinpoche, a Tibetan master who teaches at the Karma Triyana Dharmachakra Center in Woodstock, New York, believes that Americans especially have "good karmic connections" developed through past lives. According to him, this karmic heritage inevitably pushes many of them toward Buddhism in this lifetime, even though they're not consciously aware of it. "What we strongly feel," he once said, speaking for himself and his colleagues, "is in the West many westerners have a very strong karma in the past, and the time has come to connect." They do this, he adds, by seeking a Buddhist teacher who can tap into that karmic past, "and whatever karma they have, naturally it comes up."

How does one choose a particular vehicle? Center? Teacher?
Buddhist teachers of all schools say that the key to this endeavor is also one of the fundamental tenets of Buddhism: Trust in yourself, and trust in the universe. Would-be students are generally advised to begin their search anywhere that seems promising, and as their practice leads them to become more attuned to their inner self, they will inevitably answer these questions quite naturally and effectively for themselves.

Generalities abound in print and conversation about which kind of vehicle is appropriate for which kind of person, situation, or quest. For example, the Buddhist-friendly art critic Regina Lasser declared on a recent TV talk show:

> You can tell the difference [among vehicles] by the look of their temples. Tibetan ones, with all their dazzling colors and designs, are like sensory overload. That's how they send you into another state of consciousness. Zen ones do it by sensory deprivation. Everything is very austere and regimented. In Theravada, there's a traditionally regal or courtly design, which works toward raising your consciousness in a more formal way.

The actor and Buddhist Richard Gere once explained to an interviewer that he first practiced Zen "for the mind" and then went on to Tibetan Buddhism "for the heart." The Buddhist scholar Jan Nattier, in a January 2000 article for *Civilization* magazine entitled "Why Buddhism, Why Now?" discussed a similar kind of typing involving comparisons to Christian sects: "Commenting on the differences between Tibetan Buddhists and her own Zen tradition, one longtime priest declared, 'They're Catholics, and we're Quakers.' Following this logic, [American] Vipassana practitioners are surely Unitarians" (69).

Such generalizations—and similar ones applying to specific centers or teachers—may or may not be useful as points of departure. It's important, however, to appreciate that they don't represent any sort of objective truth. They're strictly personal opinions. Above all, the only way to test vehicles, centers (in the generic sense of the word, which includes temples and monasteries as well), or teachers is through direct experience, so an individual search may involve trying out different ones over a period of time before making a commitment.

Listed below are guidelines commonly given by American Buddhists that relate to choosing centers and teachers. For many of the questions you're asked to pursue, there are no definitively positive or negative responses. Getting answers to them is simply a matter of becoming better informed.

1. Check into the background of the center. For example, read one of its newsletters, interview a staff member on the phone, and research it in a Buddhist directory. Find out the answers to these questions:
    *   How long has it been around?
    *   What kind of people go there? (Among the possibilities are ethnic and/or nonethnic Buddhists, drop-in visitors, retreatants, and/or formal students of the place.)
    *   Who are the teachers? (See page 198 for teacher-related questions.)
    *   Is it affiliated with other American centers, or with particular Buddhist schools or lineages in Asia?
    *   What range of services and programs does it offer, especially for first-time visitors and new students? (Among the possibilities are liturgical events, classes, workshops, retreats, residencies, and/or outreach campaigns.)

- Are there teachers, staff members, or experienced students you can easily consult to answer any questions you might have?

2. If possible, choose a center that's relatively close, so that you're more likely to visit it on a frequent, regular basis.

3. Take early advantage of opportunities to talk informally with other visitors or students at the center. If you find yourself talking with individuals you trust, ask them about their experiences there, and share any concerns or questions you have about your own participation. Otherwise, just get to know people better, and let them get to know you better.

4. Check into the background of the teacher. Find out the answers to these questions:
   - How is the teacher authorized to teach?
   - Has the teacher received formal transmission from another teacher?
   - What lineage(s) does the teacher represent?
   - How long has the teacher been teaching?
   - Does the teacher speak English or teach through an interpreter?
   - Is the teacher there on a permanent, temporary, part-time, full-time, or occasional basis?
   - In what various contexts are students able to interact with, or learn from, the teacher? Does the teacher have any books or tapes available?
   - Does the teacher work in conjunction with other teachers?

What can one expect to see or experience at a Western Buddhist center?
Most Buddhist centers, temples, or monasteries have certain scheduled times when they are open to the public and anyone is welcome to come. If you're not certain when these times are, it's best to call ahead and make sure.

Often visitors can attend a weekly service, similar in purpose and, in some cases, overall structure to weekly Christian or Jewish services. Regardless of which vehicle is involved, the service typically features chanting (often from books that are passed out), bowing, meditation (usually with cushions and sometimes benches or chairs provided), and a talk. There may also be incense lighting, various processions and recessions, a public question-and-answer period, a visitor-orientation session, or other kinds of ceremonial or instructional elements, depending on the occasion or institution.

During these services, visitors are usually free to participate in all that goes on, following along with whatever the other sangha members are doing. In fact, many places expect full participation from everyone present. The fact that you chant or bow with the rest of the sangha is not taken as a sign that you accept Buddhism as your religion but rather that you are there in good faith to be part of the assembly. If you don't bow or chant while others around you are doing so, it can distract their concentration and make you, too, feel self-conscious. For this reason, if you don't want to participate fully, it's better to sit or stand apart from the sangha, assuming that option is available.

Most places also expect you to dress conservatively—no wild-colored clothes, shorts, tank tops, bare midriffs, or high-impact accessories—and to take off your shoes and leave behind any outerwear, purses, or bags before you enter the space where the service are held. Other people there may be wearing various garments related to Buddhism, such as a robe (which usually indicates a monk but in some places could also indicate a lay student) and/or a *rakasu* (in Zen, a square, biblike garment representing the Buddha's robe, which is worn by monastic or lay students who have taken the precepts).

Most often, the person performing the main ceremonial functions during the service—such as making offerings at the altar—is a teacher, but he or she may instead be an experienced, nonteaching sangha member. In some cases, several teachers or members cooperate in handling different parts of the service. For example, one person may lead the chants, another may officiate at the altar, and yet another may give a talk. Usually no donation is requested *during* the service. In some places a greeter at the door asks for one. If not, there is almost always a box or other receptacle by the entrance where you can put one.

Sometimes the service is preceded or followed by a social period, which may or may not be officially designated as such, so you may want to go early or hang around afterward just in case. There may even be an open-to-the-public lunch, tea, dinner, or snack attached to the service.

The monastery, temple, or center may also or alternatively sponsor meditation-only periods, special events (like Buddhist ordinations or holiday celebrations), lectures, workshops, or retreat programs that are open to the public. In addition, it may offer residency programs, which allow you to stay at the facility and engage in its day-to-day life for an extended period of time—from a week to a year or more.

For contact information, see "Selected U.S. Buddhist Organizations" on page 230.

6 Buddhism and the New Millennium

Do not chase after the past
Or pin your hopes on the future.
What is past has gone behind,
And the future has yet to arrive. . . .
If you live with your whole heart
From morning to night
Then you have truly had an auspicious day.

—the Buddha

During the very week that the twentieth century turned into the twenty-first, one of the most dramatic events in modern Buddhist history occurred. It began at ten-thirty on the night of December 28, 1999. Exactly where it happened will be revealed later in this narrative.

While others in a large, residential building were watching TV, a fourteen-year-old boy wearing a down jacket and blue jeans climbed onto the roof outside his bedroom window and worked his away around it to the side facing the road. From there he dropped ten feet to the ground and sprinted to a waiting Mitsubishi SUV with three men inside. The boy joined them, and the car sped off into the night.

After twenty-four hours of steady driving, they neared a dangerous checkpoint, so the boy jumped out of the car to cross the forested mountainscape secretly on foot. Five hours later, his hands, legs, and cheeks all scratched and bruised, he rendezvoused with his companions. After three more hours of driving, they crossed the border, left the car with an accomplice, and rode on horseback through rough, roadless terrain for another two hours to the first resting place of their long, arduous trek.

Early the next morning, New Year's Eve, they mounted their horses again and continued riding southwest until well into New Year's Day. As night fell, they boarded a helicopter and flew to the next border, which they crossed in a taxi. Then, after another full day of traveling by rickshaw and train, they climbed into a taxi for the last leg of their journey. Moments later, death suddenly loomed before them. Their car spun off a fogbound mountain road. They braced to crash. Miraculously, they didn't.

At eleven-thirty the next morning, January 5, the exhausted boy, now with open sores on his feet, strode into the audience chamber of an astonished Dalai Lama. The two of them embraced. According to an eyewitness, it was "as if a father was meeting his dear son after a long separation."

The boy was—and is—the seventeenth Karmapa (in Sanskrit and Tibetan, "man of buddha-activity"), the leader of the Kagyu school, the oldest teaching lineage in Tibetan Buddhism. He undertook his harrowing, eight-day journey to escape escalating restrictions imposed by the Chinese government on his activities. It began at his home monastery in Tsurphu, Tibet, ranged across the Mustang region of Nepal, and ended in Dharmsala, India. The description above derives mainly from journalist Isabel Hilton's article, "Flight of the Lama," in the *New York Times Magazine* of March 12, 2000, but by that date countless stories about the event had been printed and broadcast in the United States and around the world.

Incredibly, many authoritative commentators predict that the Karmapa will ultimately settle in Woodstock, New York. In 1969 the village lent its name to the legendary music festival and, as a result, to the entire revolutionary generation of Americans it represented—one that was coming of age just as Tibetan Buddhism was first reaching the United States. In 1978, on a mountain just outside the village limits, the sixteenth Karmapa established Karma Triyana Dharmachakra (KTD), his North American seat. That founding occurred three years before his death, seven before the present Karmapa's birth, and fourteen before the young boy was identified by secret signs as the reincarnation of his predecessor.

Prior to escaping from Tibet, the seventeenth Karmapa wrote a prayer for the millennium that reads, "May auspicious excellence, prosperity, and goodness flourish, especially throughout the land of America. May the youthful lotus of teaching and practice bloom." According to Michael A. Doran, secretary of KTD, many of the Karmapa's followers interpret this poem to be further evidence that he intends to relocate there. They even think the "youthful lotus" in his poem may be a reference to himself as a transplant to America. Doran told reporters, "This [situation] is not an accident: the karma is right in America for his presence."

Given the possibility that the Karmapa may eventually make Woodstock his home, it seems as if Padmasambhava's mysterious, eighth-century prediction about the Dharma arriving in America ("land of the red man") during an era of planes and trains ("iron birds" and "horses run on wheels") is, indeed, coming true (see the full quote on page 155). It's even more amazing to consider that the Padmasambhava also prophesied the appearance of the original Karmapa, saying that this individual would be a man of great spiritual power who would be called an embodiment of Avalokiteshvara—an event that actually happened four centuries later.

Because the Karmapa is one of the most significant figures in Tibetan Buddhism, his presence in this country, one way or another, would definitely be an impetus to the spread of Vajrayana here. He's often designated as the third-highest lama, the first being the Dalai Lama and the second, the Panchen Lama (not the head of a teaching lineage but, rather, the abbot of one of the largest monasteries in Tibet).

In actual practice, the Karmapa may be even more important than that. According to professor Robert Thurman, "People always say that the Panchen Lama is the second-highest lama in Tibet, and that's true in the sense of perhaps the number of followers and the size of his monastery. But the Karmapas were widely beloved beyond the size of their order. They traditionally had very good relations with the Dalai Lama" (quoted in Barbara Crossette, "Buddhist Leader, 14, Flees Chinese Rule in Tibet for India," *New York Times,* January 7, 2000). This historical background has caused some authorities to believe that the present Karmapa might become the chief spokesperson and champion for Tibetan Buddhism after the Dalai Lama's death. Reflecting on the fate of this fourteen-year-old boy who talks, acts, and—at six feet tall—looks much more mature, Hilton notes,

> He is young and charismatic and could clearly provide a focus in the future for Tibetan loyalties. A respected spiritual leader and already a forceful character, the Karmapa could be well positioned to speak for his people in the absence of the Dalai Lama or during the infancy of the Dalai Lama's next reincarnation. . . . The Dalai Lama has tried to persuade his followers to discard sectarianism, and he insists that the new generation of spiritual leaders receive teachings from all four [Tibetan] schools of Buddhism. ("Flight of the Lama," 55)

On February 3, 2001, the Karmapa was formally granted asylum by the Indian government. His new status permits him to move freely inside—but not yet outside—India's borders. Whatever may happen in the years ahead, his story is meaningful now for what it symbolizes about the state of Buddhism at the start of the new millennium. It is no longer a stretch to imagine one of the most venerated leaders in this religion, so exotic to westerners a mere one hundred years ago, making a home for himself in small-town America. As a global culture has begun to emerge and sharp divisions between East and West have started to dissolve, the newest frontier for the Dharma—and perhaps the most promising one it has yet encountered—has become the West.

Indeed, Asian masters in all schools of Buddhism are turning their attention and, in many cases, their teaching careers toward the United States, the most powerful country not only in the West but also in the world. At no other time in history have all three Buddhist vehicles come together in one nation as they have here. The resulting synergy could well transform the religion itself as well as the lives of millions of Americans and perhaps even the future of humankind.

INVOCATION OF THE NEW MILLENNIUM

John Daido Loori Roshi, a Dharma heir of Hakuyu Taizan Maezumi Roshi, was raised a Roman Catholic Christian during the Great Depression and went on to become a successful research chemist in the food industry and a highly regarded photographer. He was first drawn to Zen in the early 1970s while studying photography with the well-known artist Minor White, a Zen practitioner who taught him meditation. Loori wound up training as a monk at Los Angeles Zen Center.

Loori is now the abbot of Zen Mountain Monastery in Mount Tremper, New York, one of the most prominent and authentic Zen training institutions in the United States, with affiliates in other states and abroad. He is also president of Dharma Communications and the author of numerous books, including *The Eight Gates of Zen: Spiritual Training in an American Zen Monastery* and *The Heart of Being: Moral and Ethical Teachings of Zen Buddhism*. Currently he is spearheading several projects designed to spread the Dharma by way of the Internet, which he considers a technological Indra's Net (see page 134). Among them is a CD-ROM that can facilitate introductory Zen training.

Here is Loori's "Invocation of a New Millennium."

Let us invoke our ancestors,
      both spiritual and genetic.
For we are the sole reason for their existence.
Let us invoke the children,
      and their children.
For they are the sole reason for our existence.
Let us invoke the mountains and rivers
          and this great earth,
          and acknowledge our intimacy
          and interdependence
with all things sentient and insentient.
Let us reflect that the gift of life
      is more fragile than the dewdrops
on the tips of the morning grasses.
Then, let us vow.
Let us vow to heal and nourish.
Let us vow to love and share.
Let us vow to alleviate suffering and bondage.
Let us vow to manifest peace and joy
          with wisdom and compassion.
May this century be known
          to future generations as the beginning of
The Great Millennium of the Endless Spring.

The noted historian Arnold Toynbee foresaw just such a development. In the 1930s, he wrote, "When historians look back at the twentieth century, they won't have much interest in things like communism or capitalism: Those will be ripples in the great historical picture. What will really be significant is the impact of Buddhism as it enters the West, because Buddhism has transformed every culture as it has entered, and Buddhism has been transformed by its entry into that culture" (quoted in "Looking Backward, Looking Forward," *Mountain Record,* 18, no. 3 [spring 2000], 20).

Now, at the beginning of the twenty-first century, Buddhism is by many accounts the fastest-growing religion in the United States. A 1997 study released by the *Journal of Buddhist Ethics* estimated the number of Buddhists and Buddhist centers in the United States and other major areas of the West as follows:

REGION	ALL BUDDHISTS	NONETHNIC	% OF POPULATION	ALL CENTERS
United States*	3–4 million	800,000	1.6	500–800
UK	180,000	50,000	.3	300
Russia	1 million	40,000	.7	100
rest of Europe	954,100	272,000	.3	780
Australia	140,000	14,000	.8	150

*NOTE: Among all U.S. Buddhists, the proportion of believers per vehicle was calculated to be 50 percent Mahayana, 30 percent Theravada, and 20 percent Vajrayana. Among nonethnic Buddhists, the percentage of Vajrayana Buddhists was estimated to be slightly higher; Theravada, slightly lower.

SOURCE: *Journal of Buddhist Ethics* 4 (1997): 198.

These figures are small in themselves, especially when compared to the numbers of Christian, Jewish, and Islamic people and centers in the same areas, or to the numbers of Buddhist people and centers in Asian countries. Nevertheless, they represent a dramatic shift toward Buddhism throughout the Western world and especially in America over a relatively short period of time.

Jan Nattier, who teaches Buddhist studies at Indiana University in Bloomington, Indiana, claims that the total number of Buddhists in the

United States (ethnic and nonethnic) reflects "at least a tenfold increase since 1960." Assuming the rate continues at only half that strength for a comparable period of time, our country will have 15 to 20 million Buddhists by 2035.

Another measure of Buddhism's remarkable recent growth in America has been the rapidly escalating media attention given to Buddhist topics over the past couple of decades. By the end of the 1990s, cover stories on the so-called Buddha boom had appeared in numerous periodicals, including *Time* and *Newsweek,* and Hollywood had released several big-budget motion pictures with Buddhist subjects, such as Bernardo Bertolucci's *Little Buddha* (1993), Martin Scorsese's *Kundun* (1997), and Jean-Jacques Annaud's *Seven Years in Tibet* (1997).

Popular books on Buddhist-related topics were also commonplace by the end of the twentieth century. They ranged from self-help best-sellers like *Wherever You Go, There You Are* by Jon Kabat-Zinn and *Thoughts without a Thinker* by Mark Epstein to works focusing more intently on the religion itself, like *Awakening the Buddha Within* by Lama Surya Das, *The Tibetan Book of Living and Dying* by Sogyal Rinpoche, *Freedom in Exile* by Tenzin Gyatso, the Dalai Lama, and *Being Peace* by Thich Nhat Hanh.

In 1999 the Internet bookstore Amazon.com listed over 1,200 titles under the keyword "Buddhism." Among them were numerous publications by presses (like Wisdom, Dharma, Parallax, Snow Lion, and Shambhala) or imprints (like Putnam's Riverhead and Bantam-Doubleday-Dell's Broadway) that focus on Buddhist works. Several high-profile magazines devoted to Buddhism also premiered during the final decade of the twentieth century, such as *Tricycle* (currently the biggest, with over 50,000 subscribers) and *Shambhala Sun.*

In keeping with the state of American popular culture, however, the lion's share of day-by-day interest in Buddhism has been fed by celebrities who have adopted, promoted, or otherwise represented the religion. For example, the actor Richard Gere, who practices Vajrayana, often shows up in photographs and videotapes escorting the Dalai Lama to public events. In fact, Gere does spend a considerable amount of time studying in Dharmsala and working to support Tibetan Buddhist institutions and causes in the United States.

Another outspoken American Vajrayana Buddhist is Adam Yauch, singer for the punk-rap group Beastie Boys and composer of its song "Bodhisattva Oath." Herbie Hancock, the jazz musician, and Tina Turner, the rock-and-roll star, are well-known Soka Gakkai adherents. The singer-songwriter Bonnie Raitt is a Zen student, and Phil Jackson, coach of the Chicago Bulls basketball team and author of the 1995 Buddhism-laced book on the game, *Sacred Hoops,* refers to himself as a Zen Christian. Other self-avowed Buddhists in the public eye include the politician Jerry Brown, the composer Philip Glass, the movie director Oliver Stone, and Mitch Kapor, developer of the Lotus 1–2–3 computer spreadsheet program.

Many earnest practitioners of the Dharma understandably wince at the Buddhism buzz that is currently being generated in Western popular culture. There's no denying that most of the would-be trendy talk-show references and marketing sound bites are superficial in themselves and often completely distort what Buddhism actually involves. How can one seriously expect to "find nirvana in a suede Banana Republic jacket" or recycle a bottle because "it deserves to be reborn too"?

Still, this kind of pop Dharma is a clear, inevitable signal that Buddhism has entered mainstream awareness. Certainly the pervasive if superficial hype prompts attention to the religion among many people who would otherwise never have thought or even known about it. And undoubtedly it stimulates some of them to look into the matter more deeply. The mystery is, what will ultimately come of all the interest?

In this final chapter, we'll look at major questions relating to the evolution of Buddhism in the United States. Most of them apply to Buddhism's growth in the rest of the West as well. And, given the steadily increasing interconnection of the world's nations and peoples, most of them also have a bearing on the future of Buddhism wherever it is practiced on Planet Earth.

How rapidly and strongly is Buddhism expected to grow in this country?
An essentially simple, highly experiential religion, Buddhism has a long
history of first coming into gentle contact with countries and then
slowly but surely being taken up by them. Compared to other religions, it is not a faith that has burst its way into new territory by
military conquest, aggressive proselytizing, or the sheer, seductive at-
tractiveness of its forms of worship.

Time after time, in China, Myanmar, Thailand, Korea, Vietnam,
Tibet, Japan, and so on, the Dharma itself has remained the same, but
the religion and the society have gone through a courtshiplike process
of mutual adaptation. As the host culture gradually assimilated Buddhism, every aspect of that culture was subtly imbued with a new Buddhist character. Simultaneously, a fresh, innovative variation of the
religion emerged bearing the host culture's likeness.

The same pattern is expected to occur in the United States and
throughout the West. Most students of Buddhism's history agree that
three to four hundred years will probably pass before Buddhism estab-
lishes itself here as a major religion, regardless of how many people are
calling themselves Buddhist by 2035 or 2135. Technology may accelerate the rates of change for many kinds of economic, political, social,
and educational developments, but the rate for spiritual conversion—
particularly on a culture-wide level—is not so manipulable.

This is especially true in regard to Buddhism, which is not at all
about doing things swiftly or superficially. As a person-to-person,
teacher-based religion, its survival and growth depend on a continu-
ous, increasingly abundant supply of skillful teachers who have undergone careful, intensive-and-extensive training.

So far, the only organizational structure that has been able to produce the kind of high-quality training required in Buddhism—as well
as to supervise, accredit, and refresh that training—has been the
monastery. Establishing a strong new monastic tradition in a country
takes a considerable amount of time. Whether or not the West can even
create such a tradition or replace it with something comparably effective remains to be seen.

For Buddhism to thrive in the United States, it must also attract an ever larger number of students who are committed practitioners, rather than merely casual or fair-weather believers. Centuries can go by before enough people in a given population are practicing a new religion with the requisite zeal to make it endure. Families need to acquire and pass down the tradition of such religious observance from generation to generation, and the culture as a whole has to reinforce this process with long-standing traditions, institutions, and attitudes.

The crux of the matter is whether the civilized Western world contains a sufficiently large stock of spiritually minded individuals who can devote themselves to a demanding practice like Buddhism. Buddhism may be simple, but it's not easy. Aside from engaging wholeheartedly in various day-to-day activities like meditating and chanting, students are required to invest years of time and energy in personal training with a teacher so that they can achieve stillness of mind and shed layers of behavioral conditioning that have built up over an entire lifetime.

In fact, one of Buddhism's great gifts to the West may be to deliver it from its obsession with speed, activity, entertainment, and immediate gratification. As Blaise Pascal, a seventeenth-century forerunner of the Western age of enlightenment, once maintained, "All the evil in the world issues from man's inability to sit quietly by himself for a while."

To what extent will Buddhism evolve as a philosophy rather than a religion?
So far in the West, Buddhism as a whole is just as often considered a philosophy as a religion. In fact, philosophy is only one aspect of the great spiritual path that evolved in Asia and that early Westerner observers dubbed "Buddhism." One can limit oneself to that perspective—and many in the West may choose to do so—but it's a partial, relatively shallow point of view that can yield little experience of what the religion is all about.

There are four basic reasons for the implicit downgrading that's involved when westerners think of Buddhism *in general* as a philosophy rather than a religion. First and foremost, despite all the Buddha-babble in the media, Buddhism as a religion is still not very familiar to the majority of people in the West. Chauvinistically but understandably, they tend to associate religion with something they *recognize* as a spiritual practice: Christianity, Judaism, Islam, and various Native American and African-derived spiritualities. A religion that is not as comprehensible to them as such, like Buddhism, tends to be minimized by the label "philosophy."

Second, Buddhism lacks two of the key attributes that westerners automatically associate with a religion: belief in a creator god and belief in the existence of a soul as an independent entity. Thus many Christians and Jews, for example, feel comfortable accepting Buddhism as a *philosophy* while still holding on to their original religion. They can do so because nothing in Buddhism overtly conflicts or competes with their own religious beliefs in God or soul.

Third, because of Buddhism's commonsense perspective on living and the systematic way its basic principles and symbolic cosmologies are organized, it can be perceived by westerners as appealing more directly or purely to the intellect than other religions do (a matter that is, of course, highly debatable). As indicated several times already in the book, some people even see it as a scientific vision of the universe filtered through a spiritual lens.

Fourth, Buddhism's core moral and ethical teachings are strong enough to stand on their own, apart from the more religious aspects of Buddhist doctrine and belief. This allows many atheists, agnostics, or nontheists to incorporate Buddhist principles into their way of life without feeling as if they've adopted a religion.

For all these reasons, some authorities assert that Buddhism will be acculturated into Western civilization mainly as a philosophy rather than a religion per se. They often support this claim by citing the fruitful dialogue already taking place between Buddhism and psychotherapy.

Without necessarily sharing this opinion about Buddhism's ultimate evolution in the West, Gil Fronsdal, a teacher of insight meditation at

Spirit Rock Center in California, acknowledges that psychotherapy is currently revitalizing itself by translating a great deal of Buddhist material into secular form. In the 1998 anthology *The Faces of New Buddhism,* edited by Charles S. Prebish and Kenneth K. Tanaka, Fronsdal writes, "Vipassana-derived mindfulness practices are taught in hospitals, clinics, prisons, and schools without any hint of their Buddhist source. Here the practice is primarily offered as an effective method of stress reduction, pain management, and self-understanding. The biggest influence vipassana practice will have on American society may eventually be in such non-Buddhist applications" (164–65). Fronsdal also refers to Daniel Goleman's 1995 best-seller *Emotional Intelligence* and to the numerous recent works of psychologist Jon Kabat-Zinn as "disguised" introductions of vipassana practice into Western culture.

Others more adamantly insist that Buddhism's destiny is to become a powerful, full-fledged religion in America and elsewhere in the West, not just some sort of stripped-down philosophy. They admit that Buddhism is capable of being secularized into a loose-knit set of philosophical or psychotherapeutic beliefs and practices that an individual can customize as he or she sees fit, but they feel that future westerners strongly attracted to Buddhism will far prefer to seek refuge in it as a religion. They point out that more and more people these days are yearning for spiritual renewal—not only on a personal level but also on a cultural one—and that Buddhism is uniquely poised to respond to this hunger and satisfy it.

Serious Buddhists agree. They say that while philosophy and psychotherapy may aim at strengthening the self and guiding it toward a normal, happy existence within society, the religion of Buddhism has a much greater goal: to help individuals become enlightened, to bring them together in wisdom and compassion, and to assist them in answering the great questions of life and death.

Many factors support the forecast that Buddhism will appeal to westerners in this century and beyond primarily as a religion rather than just a philosophy. For one thing, more and more westerners in recent decades have been exhibiting—in the ways they write, talk, paint, sculpt, sing, dance, love, or otherwise act—a desperate need to find meaning in their lives that goes beyond mere self-interest.

The latter half of the twentieth century brought with it a steady, broad-based erosion in the importance of family, community, and religion. From decade to decade, individuals experienced more and more isolation within society and, as a result, a growing obsession with self. This became evident, for example, in the increasing popularity of consumerism, hedonism, self-help movements, personal lawsuits, and talkshow confessionals. Unfortunately, things are not likely to change much in the near future.

For those westerners seeking an antidote to self-obsession as well as a reconnection with others, the religion of Buddhism, with its emphasis on selflessness, interdependence, and sangha, offers a compelling "new" alternative. Some experts are convinced that this dynamic alone will translate into ever more Western Buddhists in the years ahead.

In addition, Buddhism is a religion based firmly on the principle of nonviolence, and this characteristic also may attract more and more peace-seeking westerners as the next century progresses. Certainly the amount and degree of violence in the world has soared dramatically in the recent past and continues to escalate at a frightening rate, from individuals wounding themselves with drugs, stressful lifestyles, and reckless behaviors to schoolkids machine-gunning their classmates, terrorists bombing office buildings, and whole nations threatening the planet with nuclear holocaust.

Already large numbers of people concerned about such violence have been drawn to Buddhism as a spiritual path that addresses the problem directly. Besides offering them a means of committing themselves more actively to the cause of universal peace, it gives them a context for becoming more intimate with others who are likeminded. It therefore helps restore their hope that people can learn to live together in harmony. Many religious historians believe that this attraction is likely to continue into the foreseeable future.

A similar argument involves Buddhism's pronounced reverence for nature. Civilizations around the world are now wreaking ever more appalling havoc on Earth's physical environment as the years go by. In response to this atrocity, more and more alarmed individuals are being drawn to the religion of Buddhism at least partly because it's their way of honoring and helping to save all sentient beings, including humans, other animals, and plants. This trend also is widely expected to persist.

Then there's the elementary if somewhat mystical theory that the time has simply arrived for the religion of Buddhism to blossom in the West. The world is now witnessing the merger of East and West and, as a consequence, the dawning of a global form of consciousness in regard to political, economic, and social conditions. According to some commentators, many westerners with spiritual aspirations are certain to look on Buddhism, knowingly or not, as the "new" religion that best fits this new development in human affairs. In coming to Buddhism, they will see themselves as blending East with West—the best of both worlds—in their own spiritual lives.

Will the same three-vehicle structure of Buddhism persist, or will it change in some way?
Opinions vary widely about what will happen to Buddhism's three vehicles—Theravada, Mahayana, and Vajrayana—as they evolve side-by-side-by-side in the West. There is, however, one point on which most observers concur: Each vehicle has survived for centuries, inspiring and serving countless millions of people in all walks of life, so it is highly unlikely that any one of them will disappear in the near future. By all indications, they each have an intrinsic validity and drive that cannot be easily discounted.

Some experts maintain that the individuality of each vehicle will be reinvigorated and strengthened as it draws its particular crowd of Western believers. Referring to the multiple varieties of Christianity, Judaism, and Islam that have continued to flourish in the modern Western world, these authorities insist that people accustomed to freedom of choice will need, value, and support the existence of three different approaches to Buddhism.

Others believe that Buddhism in the West will evolve more ecumenically, with core elements from each of the three vehicles ultimately combining in practice to form one overall, nonsectarian form of Buddhism. They say that numerous smaller groups representing slightly different mixtures of ancient and new traditions may be contained within this framework, but there will be no sharp divisions among them.

People who believe in the advent of this new, more eclectic form of Buddhism assert that it would offer more appeal to democratic westerners. Each person would have a certain amount of freedom to develop his or her own personal practice of Buddhism within the context of a larger, "common-denominator" Buddhism that everyone could practice together. A single, interdenominational form of Buddhism would also help prevent the kinds of prejudices and animosities that can arise among people of different sects.

Don Morreale, a member of both the Insight Meditation Society in Barre, Massachusetts, and the Bhavana Society in High View, West Virginia, calls this hypothetical new form of Buddhism "Buddhayana" in his 1998 book *The Complete Guide to Buddhist America*. He sees signs of its emergence in movements like the Friends of the Western Buddhist Order (see page 177), the Unitarian Universalist Buddhist Fellowship based in Burlington, Vermont, and various nonsectarian events and projects like the annual "Change Your Mind Day" celebration of Buddhism in New York City's Central Park sponsored by *Tricycle* magazine.

The development of a nonsectarian form of Buddhism in both the United States and the Western world in general seems essential and even inevitable to many prominent Buddhists, including Lama Surya Das. Others don't believe that this kind of streamlined Buddhism could replace the three vehicles, nor that it would represent a evolutionary step ahead in the history of Buddhism.

In fact, they see ecumenical Buddhism as a great danger. They derogatively call it "designer Buddhism" or "cocktail Buddhism" and compare it to failed New Age attempts to create amalgams of tribal spiritualities. A strong religion works, they argue, because of the way it has grown up over the centuries. To assume that one can take it apart and reorganize it without weakening it is sheer hubris.

Finally, there's the contingent of observers who think that the future of American and Western Buddhism will involve four different forms of the religion coexisting along separate but cooperative lines: Theravada, Mahayana, Vajrayana, and Other. The "Other" form in this quartet, they believe, won't be any sort of unified approach or umbrella vehicle, but rather a patchwork panorama of different kinds of Buddhist practice, each existing with or without links to other groups.

What will happen regarding monasticism?

It appears certain that Buddhism will become a more lay-oriented religion in the West. The monastic tradition here is far weaker than it is in the East, and the culture here offers people much less, if any, encouragement to seek a monastic way of life.

This shift in focus for Buddhism will probably require the creation of more detailed ethical guidelines for lay living and a greater variety of liturgical activities that can be performed in a lay environment. It may also mean that subjects like family life and child-rearing will be more directly addressed in Buddhist teachings, and that more Buddhist ceremonies will be generated around personal rites of passage, public occasions, and religious and civic holidays.

To date, traditional Theravada has spread much more slowly among non-Asian Americans than the other vehicles precisely because it is so monastic in nature. The insight meditation movement (as represented by the Insight Meditation Society and Spirit Rock Center) is a popular, Western-bred alternative. Essentially, a core Theravada practice has been separated from its strict, doctrinal context and given a new, more eclectic Buddhist packaging that can more easily be taught and taken up by laypeople. In coming decades, this adaptation may be expanded into a lay-oriented form of Theravada as a whole, thereby making the need for Theravada monasteries less important.

Nevertheless, it's difficult to imagine that Buddhist monasticism will disappear altogether in the West. So far, monasticism has been the single most vital institution in all three vehicles of Buddhism. It has offered individuals seeking enlightenment the time-tested "best possible" lifestyle for the comprehensive kind of training they need, and it has provided laypeople with the highest-quality teachers and models of practice. There's no reason to think that Buddhists in the West can't gain the same benefits from having their own monasteries.

In fact, many people believe that Buddhism can't take hold in the West *without* monasteries. According to them, monasteries are necessary not only in the long run to train and provide teachers, but also in the short run to provide contexts in which Asian-trained teachers can transmit Buddhism to the West and in which Western-trained teachers can acquire accreditation from Asian sources.

Fortunately for the cause of Buddhist monasticism in the West, more and more successful monastic communities are appearing on the scene as the years go by. Among the most well-known today are Zen Mountain Monastery in Mount Tremper, New York, and Gampo Abbey (Vajrayana) on Cape Breton Island, Nova Scotia.

Some of these monastic communities come very close in structure and spirit to their Asian counterparts, with various adaptations made to suit either the Western temperament or the sociocultural surroundings. Others are hybrids, like residential establishments that include both laypeople and monks (the latter defined in nontraditional terms), centers where monks train but do not live, or places where laypeople learn to lead a monklike existence in the outside world.

The future of the Vajrayana monastic tradition in the West is an exceptionally pressing concern because it relates so closely to the survival of Vajrayana in general. Rodger Kamenetz, author of *The Jew in the Lotus,* believes that Tibetan Buddhism, now largely exiled from its homeland, may start taking the same path toward becoming a householder religion that Judaism did after the destruction of the First Temple in the sixth century B.C.E. No longer having this great institution to enshrine and perpetuate it during the subsequent Babylonian captivity, Judaism found its way via the rabbis into the home and the synagogue, which came to function as a combination study center and community gathering place.

THE DALAI LAMA

Born in 1935 to a peasant family in Tibet, Tenzin Gyatso was recognized by Vajrayana priests as the fourteenth Dalai Lama, the reincarnation of the bodhisattva Avalokiteshvara, at the age of two. He was enthroned as the spiritual leader of Tibet three years later. In 1951, after Chinese troops invaded Tibet and reasserted their claim to its territory, he also acquired temporal power over his native country as part of the truce.

The Dalai Lama finally felt compelled to flee Tibet in 1959, when China launched a massive repression, killing thousands of Tibetans and destroying many Buddhist monasteries. The twenty-four-year-old exile sought refuge in Dharmsala in northern India. There he established his seat and a community of displaced Tibetans and other disciples that today numbers over 100,000.

Since his escape, the Dalai Lama has traveled extensively throughout the world as a spokesperson on behalf of Tibetan Buddhism and world peace. In 1989 he was awarded the Nobel Peace Prize. His publications include *My Land and People; Kindness, Clarity, and Insight;* and *Ethics for the New Millennium.*

Perhaps the Dalai Lama's greatest contribution to humankind in the past half century has been his inspiring personal example of courage, compassion, and wisdom. Despite having lost his homeland to China, he argues against violent recrimination against, or hatred of, the Chinese people. He said in a 1998 interview, "As a Buddhist monk, when I pray for all sentient beings, that means a greater part of my prayer includes China, because it has the largest population."

In his *Ethics for the New Millennium,* the Dalai Lama writes,

The great movements of the last hundred years and more—democracy, liberalism, socialism—have all failed to deliver the universal benefits they were supposed to provide, despite many wonderful ideas. A revolution is called for, certainly. But not a political, an economic, or even a technical revolution. We have had enough experience of these during the past century to know that a purely external approach will not suffice. What I propose is a spiritual revolution. (16–17)

To keep alive, Tibetan Buddhism may also need to evolve beyond its present dependence on monasticism by creating lay environments for itself—places where it can be perpetuated as a common cause among everyone who believes in it. In "Partners in Exile," an article he wrote for the January 2000 issue of *Civilization* magazine, Kamenetz sums up the situation as follows:

In the face of systematic destruction of their religion and culture at home in Tibet and the seductions and allures of assimilation in exile, Tibetans living in diaspora need a strategy for preserving the memory of the lost homeland and its values. Sometimes to preserve a tradition it is also necessary to renew it. As Rabbi Irving "Yitz" Greenburg, president of the Jewish Life Network . . . explained to the Dalai Lama, the most important secret of Jewish survival was the reinvention of Judaism by the rabbis. They changed it from a temple-based cult to a religion of memory.

Kamenetz also states that Jews and Tibetan Buddhists can derive the same religious explanation from their historical predicaments:

The prophet Isaiah interpreted the Jewish exile as a calling for Jews to become "a light unto the nations"—to spread their teachings about God throughout the world. Similarly, some Tibetans have interpreted their exile as an opportunity to spread their religious teachings, or Dharma, throughout the world. (66–67)

What changes will be made in Buddhist institutions to ensure that women have the same opportunities that men do?
As a prelude to considering this question, it's helpful to review, however briefly, what little is known about the presence and impact of women in Buddhism. Regrettably, just as recorded history in general is overwhelmingly biased in favor of men, so is the recorded history of Buddhism.

Like all other major religions arising during this extended period of male dominance, Buddhism developed along patriarchal lines. Nevertheless, despite this built-in, prejudicial background, Buddhism was in the beginning much more open to women than other religions at the time, especially Hinduism. Dr. Lorna Devaraja, a professor of history in Sri Lanka, notes,

> When you read the teachings, you realize that the Buddha did not distinguish between men and women. There is no gender difference in many things that he said. For instance, in connection with the main tenets of Buddhism, when he says that salvation has to be achieved by one's effort, it presupposes the spiritual and intellectual equality of men and women. So there was no need to give a special address to women and when he spoke to his flock, he very often said bhikkhu, bhikkuni, upasaka, upasika, which means [in Pali] monks and nuns, male lay devotees and female lay devotees. So, he addressed all four sections of the gathering and whatever he said was meant for everyone. (Harris, *What Buddhists Believe,* 132)

Still, the Buddha had to be prodded by his aunt Prajapati and his disciple Ananda to establish an order of nuns (see page 19). When he did, he made it clear that the order of monks outranked it.

Initially, many Buddhist schools and teachers supported the idea that a woman needed to be reborn as a man before "she" could pass on to enlightenment. Also, early Buddhism in general perpetuated in its folk-lore and teaching tales the common myth that women, unlike men, are inherently predisposed to be irresponsible, seductive, and licentious, the same attitude one can discern, for example, in the Bible.

All of this sounds intolerably sexist to modern ears, but again, it must be remembered that religions emerge as products of their times, and they evolve to take on the cast of the societies that embrace them. As Buddhism matured, belief in the doctrine of enlightenment for men only became less and less prevalent, at least judging by the increasingly numerous accounts of women who experienced enlightenment *as women*.

In fact, two major Mahayana texts that were developed around the second century CE champion the notion that gender is irrelevant in terms of enlightenment. One is the Lotus Sutra, which refers to the es-sential asexuality or, at most, androgyny of all living beings in the con-text of enlightenment.

The other text is the Vimalakirti Sutra (or, to give its full Sanskrit title, *Vimalakirtinirdesha-sutra*), the name of which refers to the main character, Vimalakirti, a gifted lay disciple of the Buddha. Among other matters, it details the doctrine of "nondual dharma," which includes the belief that no living being can be definitely categorized or dis-criminated against by so-called false distinctions like male and female.

The Vimalakirti Sutra also features a lively, much-quoted debate be-tween a goddess and Shariputra, one of the Buddha's closest monastic students. As they banter, the goddess wins the point that she is entitled to become a bodhisattva without altering her gender. Using magic, she even changes Shariputra temporarily into a woman to demonstrate that gender is only a form.

Throughout Buddhist history, most schools have included orders of nuns. Many of these women have done outstanding work as teachers and leaders. The exception has been Asian-based Theravada. Its last lin-eage of nuns faded away during the twelfth century, and no new lin-eage has been started since then.

During the Buddha's lifetime, however, and for several generations afterward, nuns who were later considered part of the Theravada heritage contributed hauntingly beautiful religious poetry to the Buddhist oral tradition. Sometime in the second century C.E., seventy-three such poems were written into the Pali Canon as the Therigatha (in Pali, "Verses of Women Sages"), which has a good claim to being the earliest known collection of spiritual works composed by women. Many of the poems commemorate what appear to be enlightenment experiences, and some of the poets display a remarkably contemporary tone in describing their triumph as human beings over their hard, sociocultural lot as women.

Surveying Mahayana history, one encounters only rare, seemingly random allusions to specific women who were in one way or the other outstanding. Collectively these references show that it was at least possible for women to become prominent or to assume leadership roles from time to time in various Mahayana schools.

Among the most celebrated woman in Mahayana Buddhist history is Ling Chao P'ang, daughter of the eighth-century Ch'an layman Yun P'ang (more commonly called "Layman P'ang," who, although never a monk, became a great Ch'an master). Ling Chao's grasp of the Dharma is said to have exceeded that of her more famous father, whom she accompanied and assisted during his homeless career as a wandering teacher.

A century later, the nun "Iron Grindstone" Liu became a Ch'an teaching master. Her noteworthy name derived from her reputation of being so forceful and dynamic that she would wear down the deluded challenges of the students she encountered and sharpen their minds for enlightenment.

Several generations after Liu, a nun named Dieu-nhan (d. 1115) was designated as the seventeenth patriarch in her Vietnamese Zen lineage, perhaps the sole woman to achieve such a high rank in Ch'an/Zen history. Later in Japanese Zen history, the nun Myozen is said to have enlightened seventeen monks.

At the end of the eighteenth and beginning of the nineteenth centuries, Otagaki Rengetsu, a Japanese Pure Land nun, achieved great fame as a religious artist. To raise money for the relief of disaster victims, she made pottery pieces inscribed with her own paintings and drawings, which are now priceless collector's items.

Except for the occasional scholar-nun, the recorded history of Vajrayana makes singularly few references to women. However, the vehicle itself pays a great deal of attention to the female principle in its imagery and symbolism.

Tara, the archetypal female buddha dubbed "Great Protector," is one of its primary objects of veneration. As such, she bears comparison to Kuan-yin in Ch'an (Kannon or Kanzeon in Zen), the female transmutation of the bodhisattva Avalokiteshvara, whom Theravada and Vajrayana Buddhists characterize as male.

Also in Vajrayana, wisdom (*prajna*) and compassion (*karuna*) are associated with male and female respectively. The two elements are believed to be paired metaphorically within every enlightened being.

Now it's the West's turn to grapple with gender issues in Buddhism. The big hope—and a highly likely one to come true—is that Buddhism in a Western setting will promote men and women as equals in every respect and give them the same opportunities to practice, engage in training, teach, and hold positions of authority. Referring to the patriarchy that still persists in Asian Buddhism, Martine Batchelor, a Son (Korean Zen) nun living in England, says, "There is no doubt that this can't be continued in the West. After a while it does not feel right. If you are told that you are a lesser birth, at first you might say, 'Who cares!' but after a while you say, 'No, I'm not a lesser birth. I'm of an equal birth' " (Harris, *What Buddhists Believe,* 151).

Rick Fields, Jack Kornfield, Lama Surya Das, and other prominent male spokespeople on the future of Buddhism in the West also agree that it must—and will—feature gender equality. Surya Das recently pointed out that already half the teachers of Buddhism in the West are women, and this factor alone should help guarantee that women get fair representation and treatment in Western sanghas.

Joanna Macy, professor of philosophy and religion at the California Institute of Integral Studies and a frequent writer on Buddhist-related topics, offered the following, still timely summation on the viewpoint of American Buddhist women in her 1986 essay "The Balancing of American Buddhism": "As American women opening up to the Dharma, we are participating in something beyond our own little scenarios. We find ourselves reclaiming the equality of the sexes in the Buddha–Dharma. We are participating in a balancing of Buddhism that has great historic significance" (*Primary Point* 3, no. 1 [February 1986]: 6).

THICH NHAT HANH

Thich Nhat Hanh was born in Vietnam in 1926 and became a Buddhist monk during his youth. He captured world attention during the 1960s as a leader of the Vietnamese peace movement. In 1966 he traveled to the United States, then deeply embroiled in the Vietnam War, and spoke with Secretary of Defense Robert McNamara. He also met Martin Luther King Jr., who nominated him for the next year's Nobel Peace Prize.

Early in the Vietnam War, Nhat Hanh created the Tiep Hien order, known in the West as the Order of Interbeing, to help victims of the conflict. It continues to function as an international organization supporting social justice, peace, and ecological conservation.

Nhat Hanh himself makes frequent visits to America and Europe to give workshops and talks on Buddhism and to promote the interests of the Order of Interbeing. He also teaches and leads retreats at his home community in France, Plum Village. Among his many highly popular books are *Being Peace; The Miracle of Mindfulness; Old Path, White Clouds;* and *Peace Is Every Step.*

Nhat Hanh's concept of interbeing is based on the Buddhist doctrine of interdependence, which teaches that all things are intimately interrelated with each other, and therefore, that we can't separate our selves from the world around us. He offers the following explanation:

"In one sheet of paper, you can see the sun, clouds, the forest, even the logger. The paper is made of non-paper elements. The entire world conspired to create it, and exists within it. We, ourselves, are made of non-self elements, the sun, the plants, the bacteria, the water and the atmosphere. Breathing out, we realize the atmosphere is made of all of us. I am, therefore you are. You are, therefore I am. We inter-are."

How will Buddhism address the many social, economical, and environmental problems in the world?
So far, Buddhism in the West has been characterized by a pronounced and distinctive tendency toward what is called "social engagement." The phrase itself, in the context of "socially engaged Buddhism," was coined in 1966 by Thich Nhat Hanh, who then applied it mainly to the peace and civil rights movements in the United States. His purpose at the time was to encourage Western Buddhists to take an active, compassionate role in assisting both of these efforts toward ending wide-scale suffering.

The message was immediately well-received. Kenneth Kraft theorizes why in his 1992 essay, "Prospects of a Socially Engaged Buddhism": "Because Buddhism is not perceived to have been socially active in Asia (at least in comparison to Christianity's role in the West), Western Buddhists have had to reassure themselves that their adopted tradition really sanctions the sociopolitical engagement to which they are drawn" (Kenneth Kraft, ed., *Inner Peace, World Peace,* 12).

In 1978 Robert Aitken and several other Buddhists founded the Buddhist Peace Fellowship (BPF), the most well known and extensive socially engaged Buddhist organization, now based in Berkeley,

California. Over the past three decades the BPF has supported hundreds of domestic and international projects aimed at promoting human rights and assisting human survival, including many outreach programs to Buddhist countries in Asia like Tibet, Myanmar, Sir Lanka, Thailand, and Cambodia.

Meanwhile, many other kinds of socially engaged ventures have arisen in America. For example, Bernard Tetsugen Glassman, one of Hakuyu Taizan Maezumi's Dharma heirs, created Greyston Bakery in New York City to provide jobs for the homeless and to raise revenue for the purchase of buildings that can be converted by the homeless into low-cost housing. He has also set up "Street Retreats," in which Buddhist students, who collect donations for the cause ahead of time, live as homeless people for a week.

In addition, more and more Buddhist teachers and students in America have been publically promoting a lifestyle of what has come to be called "voluntary simplicity," which involves cutting down on unnecessary material possessions, consuming less energy, recycling more resources, and adopting smaller-scale ways of living that are less destructive to personal, family, and social well-being. Also, self-proclaimed Green Buddhists have led campaigns throughout the United States to restore wetlands and forests, establish wilderness protectorates, and advocate clean air and water legislation; and many Buddhist sanghas have developed hospices or relief programs for people with AIDS-related illnesses.

Overall, Western Buddhism's emphasis on social engagement appears to be making a very valuable contribution to the West, to other areas of the world, and to Buddhism in general. However, its rapidly escalating popularity, especially among young people, has caused a certain amount of concern on the part of some Buddhist teachers. They point out that would-be or actual students may run into problems if they confuse social engagement in itself with the practice of Buddhism.

According to these cautionary Buddhist observers, many of whom are deeply and responsibly involved in their own socially engaged projects, Buddhism isn't about *intentionally* doing good—that is, behaving as what the press has dubbed a "Red Cross Buddhist." To do so, they claim, is to risk inflating one's sense of self as a charitable person, stir-ring up feelings of indebtedness and inferiority among the people one helps, losing one's bearings at crucial moments, and burning out early. Instead, Buddhism is about becoming the type of person who *instinctively* does good. To achieve this state of focus, clarity, and selfless com-passion—with no gaps between thought and deed—requires serious practice; and if that practice is forsaken or overlooked in favor of social engagement, all sentient beings suffer in the long run.

What these concerned teachers underscore is that individual Bud-dhists need to put the horse before the cart: to become sincere and committed practitioners of Buddhism first, so that they can then enter into the most constructive kind of Buddhist-related social engage-ment. In other words, it isn't really socially engaged *Buddhism* unless there's a genuine Buddhist doing it.

THE NOBLE TRANSPLANT

Now, at the beginning of the new millennium, no one doubts that Buddhism is growing in American soil. The question is, will it mature into a strong, enduring, expression of the true Dharma? As we consider this matter, we need to keep in mind Buddhism's emphasis on the fleeting brevity of life, for no one reading these pages now will live to learn the answer.

In his book *Opening the Hand of Thought,* the Japanese Zen master Kosho Uchiyama uses the image of a persimmon tree to describe the long, slow process involved in transplanting Buddhism from one soci-ety to another. There are two types of persimmon trees, he explains: One kind produces sweet fruit, and the other, a very astringent, inedi-ble fruit. If you plant the seeds from either type of fruit, you get a tree that produces astringent fruit. The only way you can get sweet persim-mons from such a tree is to graft onto it a branch from a sweet persim-mon tree. Given time and a lot of skillful handling, the grafted tree will eventually produce sweet fruit. The nagging question is, how do you grow a sweet persimmon tree in the first place?

Uchiyama often pondered this mystery in the back of his mind, until finally he asked a botanist about it. He was told that a persimmon tree takes at least one hundred years to produce a sweet fruit. Such very old specimens are relatively few in number, but sweet persimmon branches for grafting onto younger trees can only come from them. Drawing the analogy to Buddhism, Uchiyama writes,

> If you leave humanity as it is, it has an astringent quality no matter what country or what part of the world you look at. It just so happened, however, that several thousand years ago in India, in the culture of that day, a sweet persimmon tree was born; that was Buddhism. . . . After a time, a branch was cut off and transplanted in the astringent ground of China. From there a branch bearing sweet fruit was brought to Japan. . . . Now the sweet persimmon is being nurtured in America, and it needs to be tended and cultivated so it can flower and ripen here. It doesn't happen automatically.

Indeed, as discussed above, it's almost certain to take several centuries of care and feeding.

As far as individuals are concerned, however, the process can occur within a single lifetime. We can graft onto our day by day existence the sweetness of the Dharma, learned from a teacher whose roots go all the way back to Shakyamuni. In the words of Uchiyama:

> I would like for as many of you as possible to become sweet persimmon branches bearing the sweet fruit of Buddhism, finding a true way to live as you settle on your astringent tree—which is, after all, your own life, and your family, co-workers, and society. (15–16)

SELECTED U.S. BUDDHIST ORGANIZATIONS

The following list represents only a small sampling of some of the more prominent Buddhist institutions in the United States that offer services and programs open to the public. Other sources for contact information are the magazines *Tricycle* and *Shambhala Sun*, both of which offer directories in each monthly issue, and *The Complete Guide to Buddhist America* by Don Morreale, a book that provides ample descriptions with each entry.

THERAVADA OR VIPASSANA
Bhavana Society. Rt. 1, Box 218–3, High View, WV 26808; (304) 856–2241
Insight Mediation Society. 1230 Pleasant Street, Barre, MA 01005; (508) 355–4378
Spirit Rock Center. P.O. Box 909, 5000 Sir Francis Drake Blvd., Woodacre, CA 94973; (415) 488–0164
Wat Thai. 13440 Layhill Road, Silver Spring, MD 20906; (301) 251–6101

MAHAYANA
Hsi-Lai Temple. 3456 South Glenmark Drive, Hacienda Heights, CA 91745; (818) 961–9697
Minnesota Zen Meditation Center. 3343 East Calhoun Parkway, Minneapolis, MN 55408; (612) 822–5313
Nichiren Buddhist International Center. 3570 Mona Way, San Jose, CA; (408) 557–0111
Providence Zen Center. 99 Pound Road, Cumberland, RI 02864; (401) 658–1464
Rochester Zen Center. 7 Arnold Park, Rochester, NY 14607; (716) 473–9180
San Francisco Zen Center (affiliated with Green Gulch Farm/Center and Tassajara Zen Mountain Center). 300 Page Street, San Francisco, CA 94102; (415) 863–3136
Shasta Abbey. P.O. Box 199, 3612 Summit Drive, Mount Shasta, CA 96067; (916) 926–4208
Zen Center of Los Angeles. 923 South Normandie Avenue, Los Angeles, CA 90006; (213) 387–2351

Zen Center of New York City. 500 State Street, Brooklyn, NY 11217; (212) 642–1591

Zen Community of New York. 14 Ashburton Place, Yonkers, NY 10703, (914) 376–3900

Zen Mountain Monastery. P.O. Box 197, South Plank Road, Mount Tremper, NY 12457; (914) 688–2228

VAJRAYANA

Karma Triyana Dharmachakra. 352 Meads Mountain Road, Woodstock, NY 12498; (914) 679–5906

Karme Choling Buddhist Meditation Center. 369 Patenaude Lane, Barnet, VT 05821; (802) 633–2384

Kunzang Palyul Choling. 18400 River Road, Poolesville, MD 20837; (301) 428–8116

Los Angeles Shambhala Meditation Center. 8218 West 3rd Street, Los Angeles, CA 90048; (213) 653–9342

Losel Shedrup Ling/Tibetan Buddhist Center. Woodlake Office Park, 2531 Briarcliff Road, Northeast, Suite 100, Atlanta, GA; (770) 908–3358

New York Shambhala Meditation Center. 118 West 22nd Street, New York, NY 10011; (212) 675–6544

Nyingma Institute. 1815 Highland Place, Berkeley, CA 94709; (510) 843–6812

Glossary

Unless otherwise indicated in parentheses, all non-English words and expressions in the glossary are in the Sanskrit language. In selected cases, the Pali language version, if different, is given in brackets immediately after the Sanskrit one.

ahimsa. The concept of nonharming, applied to living beings. It's the underlying principle of the vegetarianism practiced by many Buddhists.

Amitabha (also in Sanskrit, Amita; in Japanese, Amida). In Mahayana, the transcendent or archetypal buddha of boundless light; the ruler of the western paradise Sukhavati and a primary object of veneration in the Pure Land school.

anatman. The concept of no-self or no-soul. In Buddhism, it refers to the doctrine that a person has no fixed entity called a self or soul, as opposed to the doctrine based on the concept of *atman* (self or soul) in Hinduism.

Ango (Japanese). Literally, "peaceful dwelling"; in Zen, a seasonal period of intensified spiritual training each year.

arhat [arahant]. In Theravada, one who has attained the highest level of training and may or may not be a teacher. He or she is considered enlightened and will enter nirvana at death rather than be reborn into samsara.

Ashoka. The Mauryan dynasty king who reigned over much of northern India from 272 B.C.E. until 236 B.C.E. The most powerful early convert to Buddhism, he instituted policies based on Buddhist principles of nonviolence and erected pillars proclaiming the Dharma throughout his kingdom.

Avalokiteshvara. In Mahayana and Vajrayana, the transcendent or archetypal bodhisattva of compassion, viewed in some schools as male and in others as female; also known as Kuan-yin (China), Kannon or Kanzeon (Japan), and Chenrezig (Tibet)

bardo (Tibetan). Any of six transitional states between death and rebirth (described most notably in the Tibetan Book of the Dead, or *Bardo thodol*).

bhavana. Literally, "meditation"; the two major kinds were early distinguished as *shamatha* (tranquillity) and *vipashyana* (in Pali, *vipassana;* insight). Among the subtypes under shamatha meditation are *dhyana* (absorption) and *samadhi* (concentration).

bhikshu [bhikku]. A fully ordained monk (male).

bhikshuni [bhikkuni]. A fully ordained nun (or female monk).

Bodh Gaya. Name given to the town in India where the Buddha experienced his enlightenment; now a place of Buddhist teaching and pilgrimage.

bodhi. Literally, "awakened"; the bodhi tree is the name given to the pipal (fig) tree under which Shakyamuni attained enlightenment.

bodhicitta. In Mahayana and Vajrayana, the attitude of enlightenment or of the desire to attain enlightenment, which includes loving-kindness and compassion to all beings.

Bodhidharma (c. 470–540 C.E.). The first patriarch in the Ch'an tradition of China and Zen tradition of Japan (known in Japanese as Bodaidaruma or Daruma).

bodhisattva [bodhisatta]. Literally, "enlightenment being;" in Theravada, the term applies to Shakyamuni before his enlightenment, at which time he became a buddha. It also applies to him in all his previous lives leading up to the life of Shakyamuni. In Mahayana and Vajrayana, it can additionally refer to Shakyamuni after his enlightenment (because he postpones entering nirvana until all sentient beings are saved) and to transcendent or archetypal buddhas (see *Trikaya*).

buddha. Literally, "awakened one"; a term that can be applied to anyone who attains full enlightenment, it is most widely known as Shakyamuni's title ("the Buddha"). In Theravada, it can also be applied to the buddhas of previous and future eras. In Mahayana and Vajrayana, it can additionally be applied to transcendent or archetypal buddhas (see *Trikaya*).

buddha-dharma. The religion of the awakened one; the expression used in Asia for what westerners call Buddhism.

buddha nature. In Mahayana and Vajrayana, the eternal principle in each sentient being that makes him or her inherently capable of becoming enlightened (or in other words, of being a buddha).

Buddhaghosa (end of the fourth century C.E.—beginning of the third century C.E.). The most influential Theravada translator of, and commentator on, Buddhist texts, his most well known work being the Visuddhimagga (in Pali, "Path of Purity").

buji-zen (Japanese). In Zen, a frivolous or misconceived attitude toward training whereby, for example, a person decides that "everything is Zen" or that he or she doesn't need to practice in any formal sense.

Ch'an (Chinese; in Japanese, Zen; in Korean, Son). Literally, "meditation"; the name of the Mahayana school that emphasizes the practice of meditation.

daiosho (Japanese). Literally, "great priest"; a title given to Zen masters.

daka/dakini (respectively, male/female). In Vajrayana, a power of higher consciousness, often depicted iconically as a spirit or archetypal bodhisattva; also, a highly realized practitioner.

Dalai Lama (Tibetan). Literally, "Ocean [or Great] Teacher"; honorary title for the head of the Geluk lineage in Tibetan Buddhism. Tenzin Gyatso, the current Dalai Lama, is the fourteenth in succession.

deva. A godlike being who dwells in the highest of the six realms of existence.

Dharma [dhamma]. The word *dharma* can be generally applied to mean the law or way of the universe or, in Mahayana, all phenomenon in the universe. In a more specific sense, when capitalized, it refers to the teachings of Shakyamuni, the second of the the Three Jewels in Buddhism, the other two being (in order) Buddha and Sangha.

dharmakaya. In Mahayana and Vajrayana, the eternal or truth body of a buddha (see *Trikaya*).

dhyana (in Chinese, ch'an; in Japanese, zen). A form of meditation originally referred to as "absorption" meditation (see *bhavana*).

Diamond Sutra. One of the major Mahayana/Vajrayana scriptures.

Dogen (also Eihei Dogen, Dogen Zenji, or Master Dogen; 1200–1253). One of the most prominent Japanese Zen masters and the founder of the Soto school in Japan. His compilation of Dharma discourses, the *Shobogenzo,* is regarded as a masterpiece in Buddhist literature.

dojo (Japanese). A room or hall in which one of the trainings related to Zen is practiced, for example, *kendo* (the way of the sword) or *kyudo* (the way of the bow).

dokusan (Japanese). Formal, face-to-face encounter between a Zen teacher and student; a context for koan study as well as other forms of individual instruction.

dorje (Tibetan). In Vajrayana, the masculine aspect of enlightenment, associated with skillful means (see *upaya*); the counterpart of the feminine aspect, associated with wisdom (see *prajna*).

duhkha [dukkha]. Suffering, unsatisfactoriness.

dzogchen (Tibetan). Literally, "great perfection"; a type of Vajrayana meditation that focuses on the realization of pure awareness.

Eightfold Path, Noble. As stated in the Fourth Noble Truth, the path to enlightenment, consisting of eight parts: right ideas, right resolution, right speech, right behavior, right livelihood, right effort, right mindfulness, and right meditation.

empowerment. In Vajrayana, a ceremony during which a teacher transmits to students a special teaching or authorization to do a special practice.

emptiness. See *shunyata.*

Enlightenment. Also called "awakening," the mind's heightened awareness of the self as an empty illusion, bringing with it a realization of oneness with the universe. The teachings of Buddhism are based on Shakyamuni's enlightenment and are designed to facilitate the student's own enlightenment.

five aggregates. See *skandha.*

Five Precepts. Principles of conduct that Buddhists agree to apply to their lives, often taken as vows (perhaps along with other precepts) on becoming a Buddhist and always taken along with other precepts on being ordained as a monastic. Specific language varies from school to school, but a common formulation is as follows: (1) avoid causing harm to other sentient beings; (2) avoid taking anything that is not freely given; (3) avoid sexual misconduct; (4) avoid untruthfulness; and (5) avoid clouding the mind with drugs.

five realms. See *six realms.*

Four Noble Truths. As revealed to Shakyamuni during his enlightenment, these are: (1) all life is suffering; (2) the cause of suffering is desire; (3) suffering can be ended; and (4) the way to end suffering is the Noble Eightfold Path.

gassho (Japanese). The Zen term for an ancient expression of greeting, gratitude, and reverence throughout Asia: a slight bow made with palms placed together.

Gautama [Gotama]. The Buddha's surname or family name.

Geluk (Tibetan; also Geluk-pa). One of the major teaching lineages of Tibetan Buddhism, founded in the fourteenth century. The Dalai Lama is its current head.

geshe (Tibetan). Literally, "spiritual friend"; title given to advanced monastics in the Geluk tradition.

guru. Literally, "teacher"; Hindu term for spiritual teacher occasionally used in Buddhism, especially in Vajrayana.

hara (Japanese). The spot approximately two inches below the navel that represents an individual's physical and spiritual center; in Zen, a source of energy for meditation and other forms of practice.

Heart Sutra (in Sanskrit, Mahaprajnaparamita-hridaya-sutra). The most widely chanted sutra in Mahayana and Vajrayana, so named because it concisely articulates the core doctrine of emptiness conveyed in the larger sutra compilation called the Prajnaparamita-sutra.

Hinayana. Literally, "lesser vehicle"; pejorative term used by early proponents of Mahayana (literally, "great vehicle") to distinguish their branch of Buddhism from the more conservative schools, including Theravada (literally, "school of elders").

inka (Japanese). In Zen, a teacher's official confirmation that a student has completed his or her training with that teacher, which entitles the student to become a teacher on his or her own.

interdependence. Important Buddhist doctrine referring to several aspects of life, including (a) the sequence of causes and effects that binds individuals to the wheel of life; and (b) the notion that everything is interrelated with everything else, so that nothing exists on its own (the concept of emptiness).

jataka. Literally, "birth story"; one of the tales of the previous lives of Shakyamuni Buddha; 547 are included in the Sutra-pitaka, part of the Pali Canon.

Jodo-shin-shu (Japanese). Literally, "True School of the Pure Land"; a reformed school of Pure Land Buddhism in Japan, founded in the thirteenth century.

Jodo-shu (Japanese). Literally, "School of the Pure Land"; first school of Pure Land Buddhism in Japan, transferred from China in the ninth century.

joriki (Japanese). Literally, "mind power"; the mental, physical, and spiritual energy built up by zazen.

jukai (Japanese). Literally, "receiving the precepts"; in Zen, the ceremony of taking vows and receiving the precepts that represents a monk's or layperson's formal entry into Buddhism.

Kagyu (Tibetan). One of the major teaching lineages of Tibetan Buddhism, founded in the eleventh century by Marpa.

kalpa. A vast amount of time, variously used as a unit to measure the time between the earthly appearances of a buddha or, on an even larger scale, whole world cycles.

karma [kamma]. The law of cause and effect, i.e., that every thought or deed has a consequence that leads to another thought or deed, and so on; a key concept in all schools of Buddhism. The karma of one life sets up the next life, but doesn't determine the unfolding of that life.

karuna. Compassion, one of the major Buddhist virtues; in Mahayana and Vajrayana, embodied in the archetypal bodhisattva Avalokiteshvara.

Kashyapa [Kassapa] (also Mahakashyapa [Mahakassapa]). One of Shakyamuni's foremost disciples and the convoker of the first Buddhist Council after Shakyamuni's death; according to Zen, the only disciple who received transmission from Shakyamuni and, therefore, the first (Indian) patriarch of Zen.

kensho (Japanese). Literally, "seeing one's nature"; in Zen, a sudden awakening or enlightenment experience.

kinhin (Japanese). In Zen, walking meditation, usually practiced between periods of zazen (sitting meditation).

koan (Japanese). In Zen, a paradoxical teaching question or story designed to confound linear, rational thought and, therefore, to help condition the mind for enlightenment. Typically, a Zen student sits with a koan in zazen (sitting meditation).

Kuan-yin (Chinese; in Sanskrit, Avalokiteshvara). The archetypal bodhisattva of compassion.

kyudo (Japanese). The art of archery, one of the Zen ways of practice.

lama (Tibetan). In Vajrayana, a religious master, teacher, or guru. When westerners first encountered Tibetan Buddhism, they often called it "Lamanism" because of the importance of the lama (see *Dalai Lama*).

Lin-chi (d. 867[?]). In China, founder of the Ch'an school named after him, which in Zen is called the Rinzai school and features koan study.

Lotus Sutra (in Sanskrit, Saddharmapundarika-sutra). One of the major Mahayana sutras and a primary focus of the Japanese Nichiren school of Buddhism.

Mahakashyapa. See *Kashyapa.*

Mahayana. Literally, "great vehicle"; a major branch of Buddhism that arose during the first century C.E. in opposition to the more conservative Theravada ("way of the elders") branch. While the Theravada ideal is the scholarly, monastic, self-perfected *arhat,* the ideal in Mahayana, which aims at broader appeal to laypeople, is the *bodhisattva,* the one who postpones his or her own liberation in order to save all other sentient beings.

Maitreya. Literally, "friend"; the next historical buddha—or *nirmanakaya*—to appear in the distant future, after the Dharma as taught by Shakyamuni has been forgotten.

maitri [metta]. Kindness or loving-kindness; one of the major Buddhist virtues. A frequent object of meditative practice in the Theravada tradition.

mandala. Literally, "circle"; in Vajrayana, a symbolic depiction of the Buddhist cosmos, used as a basis of meditation, visualization, ceremony, and art practice.

Manjushri. The archetypal bodhisattva of wisdom.

mantra. An especially powerful syllable, word, or series of syllables or words used as a basis for chanting or meditation.

Mara. In the story of Shakyamuni's enlightenment, the embodiment of evil, who tries to distract Shakyamuni by inflaming his passions and challenging his authority.

Marpa (1012–1097). In Tibetan Buddhism, a major figure in the early history of the Kagyu lineage and the master of Milarepa.

Maya. Two different, unrelated meanings: (1) the phenomenal world of appearances, which has only a deceptive reality; and (2) the mother of Siddhartha, who became the Buddha.

merit. In Tibetan Buddhism, the positivity one develops by performing virtuous actions, which can contribute to future happiness.

Middle Way. The avoidance of extremes, a primary doctrine of Buddhism. Relating specifically to the life of Shakyamuni as a model, it refers to the avoidance of either a life devoted to sensual pleasure or a life devoted to asceticism.

Milarepa (1025–1135). Literally, "the cloth-wearer"; the most famous saint of Tibet and a prominent early figure in the Kagyu lineage.

Milinda (also Milindo; in Greek, Menander). Greek king over much of northwestern India during the first century C.E.; engaged in a famous dialogue with the Buddhist monk Nagasena, which is recorded in the Pali Canon as the Milindapanha ("Questions of Milinda"); may have converted to Buddhism.

mu (Japanese). Literally, "nothing"; in Rinzai Zen, the name of one of the most well known beginning koans, which students sit with in zazen (sitting meditation) to condition their minds for awakening. A fuller version of the koan is: "A monk asked Master Joshu, 'Does a dog have buddha nature?' Joshu replied, 'Mu.' What is *mu*?"

mudra. Literally, "sign"; a certain posture of the hands that has a symbolic meaning. For example, in the meditation mudra, maintained during meditation, the fingers of the left hand rest on top of the fingers of the right hand (palm-sides-up), and the two thumbs lightly touch each other, forming an oval.

Nalanda. A large, internationally famous Buddhist university in northern India, operating from the third century until the Mongol invasions of the 1200s.

Naropa (1016–1100). One of the best-known teachers at Nalanda, the Buddhist university. His student Marpa carried his teachings into Tibet.

nembutsu (Japanese). Literally, "naming buddha"; the recitation performed by practitioners of the Jodo-shu (School of the Pure Land) or Jodo-shin-shu (True School of the Pure Land) in Japan: *namu-Amida-Butsu* ("Glory to Amida Buddha").

Nichiren (1222–82): Founder of the Nichiren school of Buddhism in Japan, which has the core practice of chanting the phrase *namu-myoho-renge-kyo* ("Glory to the Lotus Sutra").

nirmanakaya. In Mahayana and Vajrayana, the "form body" of a buddha (see *Trikaya*).

nirvana. Literally, "extinguished"; the state of freedom from the cycle of birth-death-rebirth *(samsara),* which is a goal of enlightenment; oneness with the universe; sometimes used very broadly as a synonym for *shunyata* (emptiness).

No (Japanese). Very refined, dramatic dance originated by Ze-ami (1363–1443) and infused with the spirit of Zen; considered a Zen art or way by many authorities.

Nyingma (Tibetan; also Nyingma-pa). The oldest among the major teaching lineages of Tibetan Buddhism, founded in the eighth century by Padmasambhava and others.

om-mani-padme-hum. Literally, "OM, jewel in the lotus, HUM"; one of the oldest and most important mantras in Tibetan Buddhism.

oryoki (Japanese). Literally, "just enough"; ceremonial eating with special bowls, practiced in Zen monasteries and centers and conidered a Zen art or way by many authorities.

Padmasambhava (c. 755–797). Literally, "lotus-born"; one of the founders of Tibetan Buddhism in general and of the Nyingma school in particular; known by his followers as "the second Buddha."

pagoda. In China, Japan, and Korea, the typical, multistoried, towerlike form of the stupa, which is a Buddhist reliquary, memorial, or monument.

Pali. Dialect of Sanskrit; liturgical language of Theravada.

Pali Canon. The body of Theravada scriptures derived from oral tradition, most of which is believed to reflect the Buddha's own words; composed in Sri Lanka in the first century B.C.E. and first century C.E.; oldest surviving scriptures in Buddhism (see *Tripitaka*).

patriarchs. In Ch'an and Zen, succeeding masters in a teaching lineage.

prajna. Wisdom, one of the major Buddhist virtues; in Mahayana and Vajrayana, embodied in the archetypal bodhisattva Manjushri.

precepts. See *Five Precepts.*

Pure Land. A form of Mahayana Buddhism, offering hope of escaping the cycle of birth–death–rebirth to dwell in the "pure land" of an archetypal bodhisattva, the most significant being the western paradise of Amitabha (in Japanese, Amida).

Pu'tai (Chinese; in Japanese, Hotei). In Ch'an and Zen, a legendary tenth-century Chinese Buddhist monk who appeared to be a carefree, somewhat peculiar beggar but was in fact a very enlightened master capable of performing wonders. As a character commonly portrayed in Ch'an and Zen art, he has become among westerners the popular, misconceived image of the fat, jolly buddha.

Rahula. Literally, "fetter"; the Buddha's son, whom the Buddha left behind when he went on his spiritual quest but later accepted as a monk in his sangha.

rakasu (Japanese). In Zen, a rectangular, biblike piece of clothing made of patches that symbolizes Shakyamuni's robe and is worn by monks and laypeople after taking Buddhist vows.

rinpoche (Tibetan). Honorific title bestowed upon a lama (master or teacher) of Tibetan Buddhism.

Rinzai. See *Lin-chi.*

roshi (Japanese). Literally, "old (or revered) master"; in Zen, a monk who has received transmission and functions as a teacher. The title is properly conferred to honor only an elder or very distinguished teacher, such as an abbot or head of a school.

Sakya (Tibetan; also Sakyapa). One of the major schools of Tibetan Buddhism, founded in the eleventh century.

samadhi. Mental firmness, clarity, or "one-pointedness" (as opposed to distraction or dualistic thinking).

sambhogakaya. In Mahayana and Vajrayana, the bliss body—or archetype—of a buddha or bodhisattva (see *Trikaya*).

samsara. The cycle of birth–death–rebirth, characterized by suffering; the world of phenomenal things.

sangha. Community; capitalized: the third of the Three Jewels of Buddhism (along with Buddha and Dharma); lower case: strictly, the local community of monastics, and more generally, the local community of monastics and laypeople, or all Buddhists, or all sentient beings.

satori (Japanese). Literally, "to know"; in Zen, enlightenment, often of a sudden nature; sometimes used as a synonym for *kensho,* although satori more properly applies to a more profound kind of awakening or to the awakening of a buddha or bodhisattva.

sesshin (Japanese). Literally, "collecting the mind"; in Zen, a period of time (typically a week or ten days, but sometimes shorter or longer) when a monastery or center devotes more hours than normal per day to meditation. Often it is a regular event in the monthly calendar and features special talks as well as increased opportunities for face-to-face teaching.

Shakyamuni [Sakyamuni]. Literally, "Sage of the Shakya Clan"; title given to the historical Buddha, Siddhartha Gautama, after he left his father's court and went on his search for enlightenment.

Shambhala (aka Shangri-la). In Buddhist lore, name of a mythical kingdom variously associated with human perfection, the origin of special teachings, or a utopic land within—but apart from—the everyday world; especially prominent in Tibetan Buddhism, where it is also identified with a past or future golden age or with the homeland of a future savior of humankind.

Shariputra [Sariputta]. One of the principal disciples of the Buddha; directly addressed in the Heart Sutra.

shikantaza (Japanese). Literally, "nothing but sitting"; in Zen, meditation without any added techniques such as counting the breath or koan study.

shunyata [sunnata]. Emptiness; key concept in Buddhism, referring to the impermanent, nonessential, interdependent nature of all things, so that no one thing exists in itself; often contrasted with form, the apparent existence of things. In many schools of Mahayana and Vajrayana, *shunyata* is synonymous with nirvana or the nondual absolute.

Siddhartha [Siddhatta]. Literally, "all is fulfilled"; name given to the historical Buddha at birth.

six realms. In many schools of Mahayana and Vajrayana, the various forms of life into which one can be reborn; in ascending order based on comfort, the realms inhabited by (1) demons, (2) hungry ghosts, (3) animals, (4) humans, (5) demigods, and (6) gods. Other schools, which do not recognize a separate realm of demigods, teach five realms rather than six.

skandha [khanda]. The five aggregates that collectively make up a person's identity or personality, even though no such thing as a separate "self" exists: (1) matter, (2) sensations, (3) perception, (4) mental formation, and (5) consciousness.

Soto (Japanese). One of the main schools of Zen, imported from China by Dogen in the thirteenth century and centering around the practice of *shikantaza,* or meditation without any added technique such as koan study.

stupa. Buddhist architectural style used mainly for reliquaries, memorials, or monuments; in India, Southeast Asia, and Tibet, typically dome- or pedestal-shaped with a central spire; in China, Korea, and Japan, typically pagoda-shaped with multiple stories.

Sukhavati. In Pure Land, the western paradise ruled by the archetypal bodhisattva Amitabha (in Japanese, Amida).

sutra [sutta]. Buddhist scripture that is presumed to represent the Buddha's teachings in his own words.

Suzuki, D(aisetsu) T(eitaro) (1870–1966). Zen scholar, writer, and academic teacher; first came to the United States for the 1893 World's Parliament of Religions when he was a student of Shaku Soen; afterward one of the earliest and most influential transporters of Zen from Japan to the United States.

Suzuki, Shunryu (1905–1971). Soto Zen master who founded Zen Center of San Francisco and the first Soto Zen monastery in the West, Zen Mountain Center in Tassajara, California.

swastika. Ancient sign used in Buddhism as a symbol of the teachings or of the transmission of the teachings.

tantra. Strictly speaking, various advanced or specialized practices in Tibetan Buddhism and, to a lesser degree, other Mahayana schools that are based on so-called magical Buddhist texts, combining ancient yogic elements with Buddhist ones; more generally speaking, the distinctive practices of Vajrayana as a whole.

Tao (Chinese; in Japanese, Do). Literally, "the way"; refers to the universal principle, truth, or nature of things; central concept in Taoism, as first articulated by the scholar Lao-Tse, a near contemporary of the Buddha. When Mahayana entered China early in the first millennium, one strain absorbed much of Taoist philosophy, resulting in Ch'an (Zen) Buddhism.

Tara (in Tibetan, Dolma). An emanation of the archetypal bodhisattva Avalokiteshvara; particularly important in Tibetan Buddhism, where it is associated with the feminine aspect of compassion and divided into twenty-one forms that are distinguished iconographically by color (the most popular being Green Tara and White Tara).

Tathagata. Literally, "thus-perfected one"; one of the Buddha's titles.

tathata. Literally, "thusness" or "suchness"; key concept of Mahayana and Vajrayana, referring to the absolute nature of all things and, accordingly, each thing.

thangka. In Tibetan Buddhism especially, a scroll depicting religious iconography.

Theravada. Literally, "teachings of the elders"; the oldest of the three major vehicles of Buddhism, dating to the period immediately after the Buddha's death. Its ideal figure is the *arhat,* or enlightened monastic scholar, as opposed to the ideal figure of Mahayana and Vajrayana, the *bodhisattva.*

Three Jewels (in Sanskrit, *triratna*). The core elements in all schools of Buddhism: Buddha, Dharma, and Sangha; also known as the Three Treasures.

three vehicles (in Sanskrit, *triyana*). Different embodiments of doctrine that can bring one to enlightenment; in the Lotus Sutra, identified as (1) Theravada; (2) Mahayana; and (3) Pratyeka or "middle vehicle," which teaches a route to buddhahood without going through the *arhat* or *bodhisattva* stage; in more recent times identified as (1) Theravada; (2) Mahayana; and (3) Vajrayana, which, according to different perspectives, is a variation or evolution of Mahayana and differs altogether from Pratyeka.

Tibetan Buddhism. The Tibetan form of Vajrayana, also prevalent in other Himalayan mountain regions and in Mongolia. Vajrayana is used as a synonym for Tibetan Buddhism, although technically speaking there are elements of Vajrayana—known as tantra or tantric practices—in other Mahayana schools as well.

Trikaya. Literally, "three bodies"; key concept in Mahayana and Vajrayana, referring to the various manifestations of a buddha/bodhisattva: (1) *dharmakaya,* the truth or essence body, which is the absolute nature of a buddha; (2) *sambhogakaya,* the bliss or archetypal body, which is an emanation of certain aspect of a buddha/bodhisattva; and (3) *nirmanakaya,* the form body, which is the physical incarnation of a buddha/bodhisattva—the most recent one being Shakyamuni.

Tripitaka. Literally, "three baskets"; the core body of Buddhist scriptures, especially important in Theravada, consisting of three parts: (1) Vinaya-pitaka, the monastic codes; (2) Sutra-pitaka, the discourses of the Buddha; (3) Abhidharma-pitaka, assorted other texts. The oldest surviving version is the Pali Canon of the first century B.C.E.–first century C.E.

Trungpa, Chogyam (1940–1987). Tibetan master who came to the United States via Europe after the Chinese invasion of Tibet and became one of the primary teachers and promoters of Tibetan Buddhism here.

tulku (Tibetan). A person who is a reincarnation of another enlightened person and/or of a bodhisattva. The heads of many teaching lineages in Tibet, including the four major ones, are considered to be tulkus. Each head is sought out by priests and verified as a reincarnation of his predecessor to ensure spiritual continuity in that particular lineage.

upaya. Literally, "skillful means"; the most effective way, given the situation, to express the Dharma or enact the precepts. Every Buddhist aspires to use skillful means at all times, but it's especially a characteristic of a bodhisattva.

vajra. Literally, "diamond"; in Tibetan Buddhism, a scepter representing the indestructability of the Dharma.

Vajrayana. Literally, "diamond vehicle"; one of the three major vehicles of Buddhism and the prevailing one in Tibet, other regions of the Himalayas, and Mongolia; often used as a synonym for Tibetan Buddhism. It evolved out of Mahayana and retains the same body of scriptures and belief in the bodhisattva ideal. However, it also incorporates many of the magical and visionary elements of ancient Indian spirituality. It is thus perceived by its adherents as the final evolutionary stage of Buddhism, combining and extending each of the other two vehicles.

vihara. In Theravada, residence for monks or, more loosely, monastery.

vipassana (Pali; in Sanskrit, *vipashyana*). Literally, "insight"; commonly associated with a form of meditation, most prominent in Theravada, that is aimed at seeing a particular phenomenon or concept with full clarity.

yab-yum (Tibetan). Literally, "father-mother"; in Vajrayana, term applied to the iconic image of male and female deities united sexually, a recurring theme in Tibetan art meant to symbolize the healthy integration of male and female energies within a person.

yogi/yogini. In Tibetan Buddhism, a practitioner of Vajrayana, often used to refer to a saint or solitary practitioner of exceptional virtue or capability.

zabuton (Japanese). In Zen, the square mat on which a *zafu* (or meditation cushion) is placed.

zafu (Japanese). In Zen, the cushion on which one meditates.

zazen (Japanese). Literally, "just-sitting meditation"; the Zen form of meditation, in which one simply sits and frees the mind from thoughts.

Zen (Japanese; in Chinese, Ch'an). Literally, "meditation"; the main school of Buddhism in Japan, carried over from the Chinese Ch'an school beginning in the thirteenth century. It emphasizes meditation over all other practices as a means of achieving enlightenment within one's lifetime.

zendo (Japanese). Large hall or room in which *zazen* is practiced.

Bibliography

Aitken, Robert. *The Path of Zen.* San Francisco: North Point Press, 1982.

Arvon, Henri. *Buddhism.* New York: Walker and Company, 1962.

Badiner, Allan Hunt. *Dharma Gaia.* Berkeley, Calif.: Parallax Press, 1990.

Bancroft, Ann. *Zen: Direct Pointing to Reality.* London: Thames and Hudson, 1979.

Bechert, Heinz, and Richard Gombrich. *The World of Buddhism.* London: Thames and Hudson, 1984.

Beck, Charlotte Joko. *Everyday Zen.* San Francisco: Harper and Row, 1989.

Boisselier, Jean. *The Wisdom of the Buddha.* New York: Henry N. Abrams, 1994.

Burtt, E. A., ed. *The Teachings of the Compassionate Buddha.* New York: Mentor Books, 1955.

Buswell, Robert E. Jr. *The Zen Monastic Experience.* Princeton, N.J.: Princeton University Press, 1992.

Byrom, Thomas. *Dhammapada.* Boston: Shambhala, 1991.

Cabezon, Jose Ignacio. *Buddhism, Sexuality, and Gender.* Albany: State University of New York Press, 1992.

Capra, Frithjof. *The Tao of Physics.* Boston: Shambhala, 1976.

Chodron, Pema. *Start Where You Are.* Boston: Shambhala, 1994.

Chodzin, Sherab, and Alexandra Kohn. *The Wisdom of the Crows and Other Buddhist Tales.* Berkeley, Calif.: Tricycle Press, 1997.

Cleary, Thomas. *Zen Antics.* Boston: Shambhala, 1993.

Conze, Edward. *Buddhist Scriptures.* New York: Penguin, 1959.

Das, Surya. *The Snow Lion's Turquoise Mane: Wisdom Tales from Tibet.* San Francisco: HarperSanFrancisco, 1992.

Davids, Caroline A. F. Rhys. *Stories of the Buddha.* New York: Dover, 1989.

de Bary, Wm. Theodore, ed. *The Buddhist Tradition.* New York: Modern Library, 1969.

Delay, Nelly. *The Art and Culture of Japan.* New York: Henry N. Abrams, 1999.

Deshimaru, Taisen. *The Ring of the Way.* New York: E. P. Dutton, 1983.

Dowman, Keith. *Buddhist Masters of Enchantment.* Rochester, Vt.: Inner Traditions, 1988.

Dumoulin, Heinrich. *Zen Buddhism: A History.* Vol. 1, *India and China.* New York: Macmillan, 1988.

———. *Zen Buddhism: A History.* Vol. 2. *Japan.* New York: Macmillan, 1990.

Erricker, Clive. *Buddhism.* Lincolnwood, Ill.: NTC/Contemporary, 1995.

Feldman, Christina, and Jack Kornfield, eds. *Stories of the Spirit, Stories of the Heart.* San Francisco: HarperSanFrancisco, 1991.

Fields, Rick. *How the Swans Came to the Lake: A Narrative History of Buddhism in America.* Boston: Shambhala, 1992.

Freke, Timothy. *The Wisdom of the Tibetan Lamas.* Boston: Tuttle Publishing, 1998.

Glassman, Bernard, and Rick Fields. *Instructions to the Cook.* New York: Bell Tower, 1996.

Goldberg, Natalie. *Long Quiet Highway: Waking Up in America.* New York: Bantam, 1993.

Goldstein, Joseph. *Insight Meditation.* Boston: Shambhala, 1993.

Gross, Rita M. *Buddhism after Patriarchy.* Albany: State University of New York Press, 1993.

Gyatso, Tenzin (Dalai Lama). *The Good Heart.* Somerville, Mass: Wisdom Publications, 1996.

———. *Ethics for the New Millennium.* New York: Penguin Putnam, 1999.

Hagen, Steve. *Buddhism Plain and Simple.* New York: Charles E. Tuttle, 1997.

Halifax, Joan. *The Fruitful Darkness.* San Francisco: HarperSanFrancisco, 1993.

Harrer, Heinrich. *Seven Years in Tibet.* London: Rupert Hart-Davies, 1953.

Harris, Elizabeth J. *What Buddhists Believe.* Oxford: Oneworld Publications, 1998.

Harrison, Gavin. *In the Lap of the Buddha.* Boston: Shambhala, 1994.

Herold, A. Ferdinand. *The Life of the Buddha.* Rutland, Vt.: Charles E. Tuttle, 1954.

Kamenetz, Rodger. *The Jew in the Lotus.* San Francisco: HarperSanFrancisco, 1994.

Kapleau, Philip. *The Three Pillars of Zen.* New York: Doubleday, 1989.

———. *The Wheel of Life and Death.* New York: Doubleday, 1989.

———. *Zen: Dawn in the West.* Garden City, N.Y.: Doubleday, 1979.

Karthar, Khenpo, Rinpoche. *Dharma Paths.* Ithaca, N.Y.: Snow Lion, 1992.

Kaza, Stephanie, and Kenneth Kraft. *Dharma Rain.* Boston: Shambhala, 2000.

Kerouac, Jack. *The Scripture of the Golden Eternity.* San Francisco: City Lights, 1994.

Khan, Noor Inayat. *Twenty Jataka Tales.* Rochester, Vt.: Inner Traditions, 1985.

Kornfield, Jack. *A Path with Heart.* New York: Bantam Books, 1993.

Kraft, Kevin, ed. *Inner Peace, World Peace.* Albany: State University of New York Press, 1992.

Leggett, Trevor. *Zen and the Ways.* Rutland, Vt.: Charles E. Tuttle, 1987.

Loori, John Daido. *The Eight Gates of Zen.* Mount Tremper, N.Y.: Dharma Communications, 1992.

———. *The Heart of Being.* Rutland, Vt.: Charles E. Tuttle, 1996.

———. *Mountain Record of Zen Talks.* Mount Tremper, N.Y.: Dharma Communications, 1992.

———. *Two Arrows Meeting in Mid-Air.* Rutland, Vt.: Charles E. Tuttle, 1994.

———, ed. *Zen Mountain Monastery Liturgy Manual.* Mount Tremper, N.Y.: Dharma Communications, 1998.

Lowenstein, Tom. *The Vision of the Buddha.* Boston: Little, Brown and Company, 1996.

Maezumi, Hakuyu Taizan, and Bernard Tetsugen Glassman. *The Hazy Moon of Enlightenment.* Los Angeles: Center Publications, 1978.

———, eds. *On Zen Practice.* Los Angeles: Zen Center of Los Angeles, 1976.

Maguire, Jack. *Waking Up: A Week inside a Zen Monastery.* Woodstock, Vt.: Sky-Light Paths, 2000.

Martin, Rafe. *The Hungry Tigress: Buddhist Myths, Legends, and Jataka Tales.* Cambridge, Mass.: Yellow Moon Press, 1999.

———. *One Hand Clapping.* New York: Rizzoli, 1995.

Matthiessen, Peter. *Nine-Headed Dragon River.* Boston: Shambhala, 1987.

McLean, Richard. *Zen Fables for Today.* New York: Avon, 1998.

Merton, Thomas. *Mystics and Zen Masters.* New York: Farrar, Straus and Giroux, 1967.

———. *Zen and the Birds of Appetite.* New York: New Directions, 1968.

Mertz, Henriette. *Pale Ink: Two Ancient Records of Chinese Exploration in America.* Chicago: Swallow Press, 1972.

Mitchell, Robert Allen. *Buddha: His Life Retold.* New York: Paragon House, 1989.

Miura, Isshu, and Ruth Fuller Sasaki. *The Zen Koan.* New York: Harcourt Brace Janovich, 1965.

Moore, Dinty W. *The Accidental Buddhist.* Chapel Hill, N.C.: Algonquin Books, 1997.

Morreale, Don. *The Complete Guide to Buddhist America.* Boston: Shambhala, 1998.

Muller, F. Max, ed. *The Sacred Books of the East.* Oxford: Clarendon Press, 1900.

Nhat Hanh, Thich. *Old Path, White Clouds: Walking in the Footsteps of the Buddha.* Berkeley, Calif.: Parallax Press, 1991.

———. *Peace Is Every Step: The Path of Mindfulness in Everyday Life.* New York: Bantam, 1991.

Pauling, Chris. *Introducing Buddhism.* Birmingham, England: Windhorse, 1990.

Prebish, Charles S. *Luminous Passage: The Practice and Study of Buddhism in America.* Berkeley and Los Angeles: University of California Press, 1999.

Prebish, Charles, S. and Kenneth K. Tanaka, eds. *The Faces of Buddhism in America*. Berkeley and Los Angeles: University of California Press, 1998.

Price, A. F., and Wong Mou-lam. *The Diamond Sutra and the Sutra of Hui-Neng*. Boston: Shambhala, 1990.

Rahula, Walpola. *What the Buddha Taught*. New York: Grove Weidenfeld, 1974.

Renard, John. *Responses to 101 Questions on Buddhism*. New York: Paulist Press, 1999.

Reps, Paul. *Zen Flesh, Zen Bones*. New York: Doubleday, 1970.

Ross, Nancy Wilson. *The World of Zen*. New York: Random House, 1960.

Saddhatissa, Hammalawa. *Before He Was Buddha*. Berkeley, Calif.: Seastone, 1998.

Salzberg, Sharon. *A Heart as Wide as the World*. Boston, Mass.: Shambhala, 1997.

Schulberg, Lucille. *Historic India*. New York: Time-Life, 1967.

Schumann, Hans Wolfgang. *Buddhism*. London: Quest, 1973.

Shainberg, Lawrence. *Ambivalent Zen*. New York: Pantheon, 1995.

Shearer, Alistair. *Buddha: The Intelligent Heart*. London: Thames and Hudson, 1992.

Simpkins, C. Alexander, and Anneleen Simpkins. *Simple Zen*. Boston, Mass.: Tuttle Publishing, 1999.

Smith, Huston. *Essays on World Religion*. New York: Paragon House, 1995.

———. *The Religions of Man*. New York: Harper and Brothers, 1958.

Snelling, John. *The Elements of Buddhism*. Longmead, England: Element Books, 1990.

Sogyal Rinpoche. *The Tibetan Book of Living and Dying*. San Francisco: Harper-San Francisco, 1992.

St. Ruth, Diana, and Richard St. Ruth. *The Simple Guide to Zen Buddhism*. Folkestone, England: Global Books, 1998.

Storlie, Erik Fraser. *Nothing on My Mind*. Boston: Shambhala, 1986.

Sunim, Mu Soeng. *Heart Sutra: Ancient Buddhist Wisdom in the Light of Quantum Reality*. Cumberland, R.I.: Primary Point Press, 1991.

Suzuki, Daisetz T. *Zen and Japanese Culture*. Princeton, N.J.: Princeton University Press, 1959.

Suzuki, Shunryu. *Zen Mind, Beginner's Mind*. New York: John Weatherhill, 1970.

Thomas, E. J., ed. *Buddhist Scriptures*. London: John Murray, 1913.

Thurman, Robert A. F. *Essential Tibetan Buddhism*. San Francisco: HarperSan Francisco, 1995.

———, trans. *The Holy Teaching of Vimalakirti*. University Park: Pennsylvania State University Press, 1976.

———. *Inner Revolution*. New York: Penguin Putnam, 1998.

Toms, Michael. *Buddhism in the West*. Carlsbad, Calif.: Hays House, 1998.

Tonkinson, Carole, ed. *Big Sky Mind: Buddhism and the Beat Generation*. New York: Riverhead, 1995.

Trungpa, Chogyam, Rinpoche. *Cutting through Spiritual Materialism.* Boston: Shambhala, 1987.

———. *The Myth of Freedom.* Boston: Shambhala, 1988.

———. *The Sacred Path of the Warrior.* Boston: Shambhala, 1985.

Tworkov, Helen. *Zen in America.* New York: Kodansha International, 1994.

Uchiyama, Kosho. *Opening the Hand of Thought: Approach to Zen.* New York: Penguin, 1993.

Whitmyer, Claude. *Mindfulness and Meaningful Work.* Berkeley, Calif.: Parallax Press, 1994.

Winokur, Jon. *Zen to Go.* New York: Penguin, 1990.

Index